# A Short History of Ethics

"Alasdair MacIntyre is one of the most learned, as well as one of the most original, of contemporary philosophers. In this book, he condenses three thousand years of reflection on moral questions into a narrative that can be read by someone with no previous background in philosophy. *A Short History of Ethics* not only provides a perspicuous historical overview, but introduces its readers to MacIntyre's own controversial account of the present situation of moral philosophy, and to the views he went on to develop in his *After Virtue*."

*Richard Rorty*

"MacIntyre is always provocative, and this book will continue to excite engagement with fundamental moral issues."

*Choice*

"Professor MacIntyre subtitles his book 'a history of moral philosophy from the Homeric ages to the twentieth century'. He has bravely taken on an extraordinarily difficult task, and the result is a book of great interest, for the most part easy to read, and full of insights."

*Mary Warnock*

Routledge Classics contains the very best of Routledge publishing over the past century or so, books that have, by popular consent, become established as classics in their field. Drawing on a fantastic heritage of innovative writing published by Routledge and its associated imprints, this series makes available in attractive, affordable form some of the most important works of modern times.

For a complete list of titles visit
www.routledgeclassics.com

Alasdair
# MacIntyre

## A Short History of Ethics

A history of moral philosophy from the Homeric
Age to the twentieth century

 London and New York

First published 1967
by Routledge & Kegan Paul

Second edition published 1998 by Routledge

First published in Routledge Classics 2002
by Routledge
2 Park Square, Milton Park, Abingdon, Oxon, OX14 4RN

Reprinted 2004, 2005, 2006, 2007 (twice)

*Routledge is an imprint of the Taylor & Francis Group, an informa business*

© 1966, 1998 Alasdair MacIntyre

Typeset in Joanna by RefineCatch Limited, Bungay, Suffolk
Printed and bound in Great Britain by
TJ International Ltd, Padstow, Cornwall

*British Library Cataloguing in Publication Data*
A catalogue record for this book is available from the British Library

ISBN10: 0–415–28749–9 (pbk)
ISBN10: 0–415–28748–0 (hbk)

ISBN13: 978–0–415–28749–4 (pbk)
ISBN13: 978–0–415–28748–7 (hbk)

# Contents

# PREFACE

*A Short History of Ethics* was first published in the United States by Collier Books, a division of Macmillan Publishing Company, in 1966 and then in Britain by what was then Routledge & Kegan Paul. It has since been translated into Spanish, Dutch, Norwegian, German, Slovenian, and, most recently in 1995, into Polish. The translator of the Polish edition, Professor Adam Chmielewski, invited me to write a preface for Polish readers and I gratefully used this opportunity to consider some of the respects in which the original text needs to be corrected or modified and some of the ways in which my perspectives on the history of ethics have changed. First of all I need to note that the title is misleading: this is a short history of *Western* ethics, not of ethics. And I now have an opportunity to take account of the pertinent criticisms on particular issues made by others, to whom I am most grateful, and at least to recognize the fact that Western moral philosophy has continued to have a history since 1966. But I have not attempted to bring the story up to date.

My own most fundamental dissatisfactions with this book derive from changes in my own philosophical and moral standpoint. I do of course still endorse a great deal of what I then asserted. But, when I now read the story that I told then, I see it as a story in need of revision, one in a succession of genuinely instructive stories about the history of moral philosophy which have been told by philosophers—for example, Hegel's, Marx's, and Sidgwick's (although I am well aware that my work does not rank with theirs)—each of which could later be improved upon. And in my own later writings—especially *After Virtue* (Notre Dame: University of Notre Dame Press, second edition, 1982), *Whose Justice? Which Rationality?* (Notre Dame: University of Notre Dame Press, 1988), and *Three Rival Versions of Moral Enquiry* (Notre Dame: University of Notre Dame Press, 1990)—I have tried on various topics to improve upon *A Short History of Ethics*.

I am, however, conscious both of how much there is in the *Short History* with which I still agree and that it was only by first writing that book and then reflecting upon it that I learned how to do better. And since many contemporary readers may well find themselves more at home with the standpoint which was mine in 1966 rather than that which is now mine, it seems important still to invite readers to make the story told in the *Short History* their own starting-point for learning about and then reflecting upon the history of ethics. What I hope to do in this preface is to explain why I think this story needs nonetheless to be challenged. But, before I subject myself and the story that I then told to some radical questioning, I need to attend not to my own view of the overall narrative, but to the more important of the criticisms that have been leveled at the book by others.

Those criticisms have mostly concerned inadequacies in my treatments of particular authors, a type of criticism which I predicted and welcomed in advance in my original Preface. I too have become highly critical of such inadequacies, quite as much as other critics have been, in those areas where what I wrote plainly needs to be corrected or supplemented. Let me therefore try to supply something of what is needed by way of correction and supplement, nothing however that just as it was an attempt to summarize large and complex theses and arguments all too briefly, which was a major source of defects and omissions in the original text, so what I have to say now will necessarily once again be compressed and perhaps too compressed. This is a difficulty that I shall be able to overcome only when I finally do write that as yet nonexistent book that I think of as "*A Very Long History of Ethics*."

Four of the chapters where particular corrections are needed are chapter 9 on Christianity, chapter 12 on the British Eighteenth-Century Argument, chapter 14 on Kant, and chapter 18 on Modern Moral Philosophy. Let me deal with these in turn:

*Chapter 9: Christianity.* This chapter is the most striking example in the book of a kind of defect which I pointed out in the Preface when I wrote that "This book is inevitably the victim of the author's overnumerous intentions." Between 105 pages on Greek ethics and 136 pages on Western European ethics from the Renaissance to 1964 I sandwiched ten pages within which I attempted to identify the distinctive moral outlook of the Christian religion *and* to bridge the historical gap of 1300 years between Marcus Aurelius and Machiavelli *and* to give some account of the importance of medieval moral philosophy. What an absurdity! But it was not only my absurdity. This error of mine reflected a widespread, even if far from universal, practice in the then English-speaking world—which still unfortunately persists in numerous colleges and universities—of ignoring the place both of the earlier Christian eras and of the high middle ages in the history of philosophy. So, for example, in the then Oxford undergraduate curriculum there had been for a very long time a large place assigned to the study of ancient philosophy, and also to that of modern philosophy, but almost no place at all to medieval philosophy.

What is needed to repair my own errors and omissions is of two different kinds. First the account of Christianity which I then gave needs not only to be expanded, but to be radically revised. The core of that account imputes to distinctively Christian ethics an, as I then thought, unresolvable paradox, that it "tried to devise a code for society as a whole from pronouncements" originally addressed to individuals or small communities who were to separate themselves off from the rest of society in expectation of a Second Coming of Christ, which did not in fact occur (pp. 111–112). What I failed to recognize was that this paradox had already been resolved within the New Testament itself through the Pauline doctrines of the church and of the mission of the church to the world. Those doctrines successfully define a life for Christians informed *both* by the hope of the Second Coming *and* by a commitment to this-worldly activity in and through which human beings rediscover the true nature of their natural ends and of those natural virtues required to achieve those ends, as a result of coming to understand them in the light of the theological virtues identified in the New Testament. Those virtues are, on a Christian view, the qualities necessary for obedience to God's law, that obedience which constitutes community, whether it is that obedience to God's law apprehended by reason which constitutes natural community or that obedience to revelation which constitutes the church. (My earlier failure to recognize this was due to my having been overimpressed by biblical critics who falsely thought that they had discovered a large and incoherent eclecticism in the New Testament. What corrected my earlier view was in part a larger knowledge of that same criticism. I learned especially from the work of Heinrich Schlier.)

What Christianity therefore presented to those who encountered it was a conception of law and the virtues which stood in a problematic relationship to the various philosophical conceptions of human good and virtue encountered in the ancient world. Because I had not understood this adequately, I was unable to pose the right questions about that relationship. I noticed, for example, how New Testament conceptions differed from Platonic, Aristotelian, and Stoic conceptions. But I failed to enquire systematically whether or not it was possible to integrate one or more of these philosophical views with Christianity so as to present at once a more adequate moral philosophy and a philosophically defensible account of Christian moral views. Hence what I had to say about Augustine and Aquinas was misleading, because I had failed to ask the right questions. But my failure was not only about Christianity.

A second set of omissions concerns Judaic and Islamic ethics. Judaism's ethics of divine law raised philosophical questions which anticipate and generally parallel those of Christianity, but Jewish contributions to the answering of those questions have an independent importance for the history of ethics. When in chapter 10 I discussed Spinoza as one of those who inaugurated distinctively modern ethical debate, I characterized him only as an atheist, failing to recognize that he was one heir, even if a deviant one, of the traditions of medieval Jewish moral philosophy and especially of the greatest of medieval Jewish philosophers, Moses Maimonides. There is no name whose absence from the index of *A Short History of Ethics* is more regretted by me now than that of Maimonides (see for a first account and a bibliography Colette Sirat, *A History of Jewish Philosophy in the Middle Ages*, Cambridge: Cambridge University Press, 1985).

It was as great a mistake to have made no mention of such Islamic philosophers as ibn Sina (Avicenna), al-Ghazali, and above all ibn Rushd (Averroes). And these absences were responsible for a further inadequacy in my treatment of Aquinas' moral thought, since Aquinas' synthesis of theology with Aristotle was deeply and importantly indebted to Maimonides, Avicenna, and Averroes (for a first account of Islamic philosophy see Oliver Leaman, *An Introduction to Medieval Islamic Philosophy*, Cambridge: Cambridge University Press, 1985).

*Chapter 12: The British Eighteenth-Century Argument.* There are two English philosophers whose views are discussed in this chapter where on central matters something more or different needs to be said. With Bishop Butler (pp. 159–161) it is in part a matter of an unjust treatment of the theological element in his thought, one stemming from the inadequacy of my treatment of Christianity in general. But also, and as importantly, I failed to emphasize Butler's seminal importance for subsequent debate as the first philosopher to state compellingly the thesis that there are two distinct and independent sets of principles governing human conduct, on the one hand, those of reasonable self-love and, on the other, those of conscience. Henry Sidgwick in his *Outlines of the History of Ethics* (London: Macmillan, fifth edition, 1902) takes this recognition to be the source of a major, perhaps the major contrast between ancient Greek ethics, for which generally there is only one set of principles governing human conduct, those of reason variously conceived, and modern ethics. And certainly from the eighteenth century onwards the question of what the relationship is between the principles of reasonable self-love and the impersonal requirements of morality becomes a central one for moral philosophers.

One philosopher whom Sidgwick names as having to some degree anticipated Butler in recognizing this dualism is William Wollaston. My treatment of Wollaston (p. 165) failed to distinguish sufficiently between what Wollaston actually held and Hume's presentation of Wollaston's views for the purpose of criticism. Wollaston did indeed assert "that the distinction between vice and virtue which reason apprehends is simply the distinction between the true and the false" (p. 165). The actions of a wrongdoer always, on his view, give expression to a judgment which is false and which thus misrepresents some reality. And Wollaston asks whether we may not say of someone who lives and acts as what he is not "that he *lives a lie?*" (*The Religion of Nature Delineated* I, iii). I followed Hume in imputing to Wollaston the view that every wrong action is a lie. It might perhaps be argued that Hume is right in judging that this does follow from what Wollaston says. But I have been persuaded by Joel Feinberg ("Wollaston and His Critics" in *Rights, Justice and the Bounds of Liberty*, Princeton: Princeton University Press, 1980) that I, like Hume, had misread Wollaston. And that Wollaston's view, as he himself stated it, may be open to criticism, but not to that particular criticism by Hume.

*Chapter 14: Kant.* In a review of *A Short History of Ethics* in *The Journal of Philosophy* (LXVI, 9, May 8, 1969) Hans Oberdiek declared that "What is worst about this book may be found in the incredibly brief chapter on Kant." Oberdiek then lists a number of topics which it would have been desirable to discuss or to discuss at greater length and in particular accuses me of being misleading in asserting that "Kant takes the existence of an ordinary moral consciousness for granted" (p. 184).

I have a good deal of sympathy for Oberdiek's accusations. Short accounts are likely to do least justice to the greatest and most complex philosophers and, while Kant receives more attention than any other modern philosopher except for Hobbes and Hegel, the space allocated to his ethics is less than half of that allocated to Aristotle. So what needs most to be emended or added?

Oberdiek was right in pointing out that, although Kant thinks that the ordinary moral agent, innocent of philosophy, is well able to grasp the requirements of the categorical moral imperative, the actual moral consciousness of such ordinary persons may always have become infected by error and confusion and must be evaluated by the standards of practical reason. Insofar as what I said suggested otherwise I was at fault. Even more importantly however I omitted to remark upon Kant's identification of one of the distinguishing marks of any morality that has a claim upon the attention of rational persons.

I did of course discuss Kant's conception of the categorical imperative as enjoining that we act only on maxims which we are able to treat as universalizable laws. But I omitted to notice his second formulation of the categorical imperative: "Act so that you treat humanity, whether in your own person or that of another, always at the same time as an end and never just as a means." What this formulation brings out is that in appealing to any authentically moral standard as providing a sufficient reason for some person to act in one way rather than another, I invite that person to evaluate the rational justification for accepting the authority of that standard for her or himself. I treat that person— whether someone else or myself—as a rational person, not as someone whom I am attempting to manipulate by some type of nonrational persuasion, some appeal to their inclinations. What Kant has captured here is a feature of rational moral discourse as such, one evident in the practice of Socrates and in all his philosophical heirs.

My doubts about Kant therefore were not and are not about his injunction to treat persons as in this sense autonomous. And I should have made this clear. My doubts were and are about Kant's account of how moral standards are to be justified. If in fact Kant's universalizabil- ity arguments fail, as I held and hold that they do—although I willingly grant that there is a great deal more to be said on that issue than I was able to say in chapter 14—then central Kantian concepts, such as that of duty, conceived as Kant conceived it, do not deserve the respect that Kant and Kantians have accorded to them. And any widespread belief that such concepts are in fact rationally defensible may permit them to play a part in social life that gives a false and harmful authority to certain types of claim.

Chapter 18: Modern Moral Philosophy. There is one serious mistake in my treatment of the views of R. M. Hare. I wrote that "on Hare's view . . . what I hold I ought to do depends upon my choice of fundamental evaluations, and that there is no logical limit to what evaluations I may choose" (p. 253). Here I had mixed together a criticism of Hare advanced both by others and by myself and the statement of Hare's own views and I did so in a way that resulted in a misrepresentation, for which I owe Hare an apology. It was and is Hare's view, if I now understand it correctly, that anyone who uses the idiom of morality, and more particularly the word "ought" in its primary moral sense, is constrained in her or his judgments by the meaning of the key moral words and by logic in such a way that genuinely universalizable judgments must embody a summing of the preferences of everyone relevantly affected by the proposed course of action about which she or he is judging. The content of one's moral judgments is therefore fully determined by the requirements of universality and prescriptivity, if these are rightly understood. And what I wrote does not convey this.

What I had intended by way of criticism however still stands. First, what Hare understands as the language of morals still seems to me only one moral idiom among several. Underlying any use of moral language which conforms to Hare's account of the meaning of moral terms there therefore has to be a choice—characteristically an unacknowledged choice—to understand morality in one way rather than in a number of other rival ways. And this choice because it is prior to the moral reasoning which issues from it is, in this sense, arbitrary. Second, Hare himself allows that it is possible without irrationality to be an amoralist (*Moral Thinking*, Oxford: Oxford University Press, 1981). But this entails that under-lying all moral judgments there is a non-rational, prerational choice of morality rather than of amoralism. What at first sight therefore seemed to be a position with a strong claim to have reformulated more adequately Kant's identification of the requirements of morality with the categorical requirements of practical reason turns out to be—quite contrary to Hare's intentions and claims—much closer in its unintended implications to Kierkegaard's *Either-Or*. I should add however that Kierkegaardians have usually been as dissatisfied with my account of Kierkegaard as Kantians have been with my account of Kant (for an excellent recent statement of their case see Edward Mooney, *Selves in Discord and Resolve: Kierkegaard's moral-religious psychology from* Either-Or *to* Sickness unto Death, London: Routledge, 1996).

It is in the same last chapter that there emerge most strongly some of the presuppositions of a point of view which underlies the narrative structure of the whole book. Throughout the book I had stressed both how rival moral philosophies articulate the rational claims of different types of moral concept and judgment and how those different types of moral concept and judgment are themselves rooted in and give expression to different actual and possible forms of social order. And I had correspondingly denied from the outset that there is only one "language of morals" (p. 1). Some of my critics, including Hans Oberdiek in the review from which I have already quoted, supposed that this committed me to what Oberdiek described as "MacIntyre's social-historical relativism" (op. cit., p. 268). It seemed to Oberdiek that on my account there could be no way in which the claims of any one set of moral beliefs, articulating the norms and values of one particular mode of social life, could be evaluated as rationally superior to those of another. Each would have to be judged in its own terms. And I may unintentionally have lent support to Oberdiek's interpretation of my views by what I wrote in chapter 18 about the individual's choice between different and incompatible moral vocabularies and moral judgments. For I may well have appeared to have ruled out the possibility of an appeal to any standards beyond those of the forms of life of particular cultures, when, for example, I wrote that it is not possible to "look to human nature as a neutral standard, asking which form of social and moral life will give to it the most adequate expression. For each form of life carries with it its own picture of human nature" (p. 259).

Nonetheless I was very far from being any sort of consistent relativist, as Peter Winch acutely noted in a critical discussion of *A Short History of Ethics* in which he accused me not of relativism, but, and more justly, of incoherence ("Human Nature" in *Ethics and Action*, London: Routledge & Kegan Paul, 1972). Winch said of me, quite rightly, that "He follows his argument for the illegitimacy of saying that any particular form constitutes the logical form of moral argument with a discussion designed to show the 'superiority' of the Aristotelian view of human nature and of its relation to morality" (op. cit., p. 81). Had I then simply contradicted myself?

What I had certainly been unable to do was to reconcile two positions, to each of which I was committed. The first was that which gave the appearance of relativism. Each fundamental standpoint in moral philosophy not only has its own mode of conceptualizing and understanding the moral life, which gives expression to the claims of some actual or possible type of social order, but each also has its own set of first principles, to which its adherents appeal to vindicate the claims of their own stand-point to universality and to rational superiority over its rivals. What I had failed to stress adequately was that it was indeed a claim to universality and to rational superiority—indeed a claim to possess the truth about the nature of morality—that had been advanced from the standpoint of each particular culture and each major moral philosophy. And what I had not therefore taken account of was that these philosophical attempts to present rationally justifiable universal claims to moral allegiance, claims upon human beings as such, claims about human nature as such, in the local and particular terms which each culture provides for its moral philosophers as their starting-point, had generated for each major moral philosophy its own particular difficulties and problems, difficulties and problems sometimes acknowledged and sometimes not. The subsequent history of each such moral philosophy revealed the extent to which each possessed or lacked the resources necessary to become aware of and to resolve those difficulties and problems—each by its own particular standards. And by this standard the major claimants in modern moral philosophy seemed to me then and seem to me now to fail.

The conception of choice between standpoints that I presented in chapter 18 was therefore misleading, and this in two ways. First, the alternatives between which I then believed that we had to choose—the emotivist or prescriptivist or existentialist theories expressive of an individualist social order or those particular local versions of Catholic theology or of Marxist dialectics by which these had been opposed in post-1945 French debates—had all failed and continued to fail to deal adequately with their own difficulties and problems. So that none of them could in fact have been chosen as a standpoint by a rational person. And indeed my own account of choice, as Winch perceived, exhibited some of these difficulties. For I spoke of the choice of fundamental moral standards as at once prior to the adoption of any particular moral standpoint and yet as itself expressive of one particular type of moral standpoint, that of moral individualism.

Should the story then have ended merely as an account of the failure of the projects of moral philosophy? Both I and most of my contemporary critics would answer this question with an unhesitating "No," but for two very different kinds of reason. They from their various standpoints would each claim that their own particular ongoing project in modern moral philosophy has so far vindicated itself in rational terms. And since 1966 there has been a body of highly distinguished philosophical work from a variety of differing and rival modern standpoints in moral philosophy: contractarian, utilitarian, post-Lockean, post-Kantian, prescriptivist, and emotivist. The problem from my point of view is that the adherents of every one of these standpoints find in the unresolved difficulties and unsolved problems of their opponents' positions sufficient reason to reject those rival positions. And so do I. It is by attending to the debates between the adherents of rival positions within modern moral philosophy that we find sufficient reason for rejecting each of the positions defended in those debates.

So why are my own present conclusions not merely negative? Winch had the insight to recognize a strong, if inadequately formulated, Aristotelian allegiance coexisting uneasily in the *Short History* with other allegiances. I had been justifiably anxious in my discussion of Aristotle to criticize that which had tied his ethics too closely to the structures of the fourth-century Greek *polis* and more especially to reject his ill-founded exclusion of women, slaves, and ordinary productive working people from the possibility of the virtues of rule and self-rule and of the achievement of the human good. What I had not at that time recognized was how much had already been achieved within later Aristotelian tradition by way of purging Aristotle's ethics of these inessential and objectionable elements and how Aristotle's central theses and arguments are in no way harmed by their complete excision. This recognition, when I finally achieved it, was accompanied by another.

Aristotle's ethics, in its central account of the virtues, of goods as the ends of human practices, of the human good as that end to which all other goods are ordered, and of the rules of justice required for a community of ordered practices, captures essential features not only of human practice within Greek city-states but of human practice as such. And because this is so, whenever such practices as those of the arts and sciences, of such productive and practical activities as those of farming, fishing, and architecture, of physics laboratories and string quartets and chess clubs, types of activity whose practitioners cannot but recognize the goods internal to them and the virtues and rules necessary to achieve those goods, are in a flourishing state, then Aristotelian conceptions of goods, virtues, and rules are regenerated and reembodied in practice. This is not to say that those who practice them are aware that they have become to some significant degree, in their practice, although commonly not in their theory, Aristotelians. It is to say that

Aristotelianism always has possibilities of revival in new forms in different cultures.

This, even if true, would not be sufficient to vindicate the claims to rational superiority of Aristotle's ethics against its rivals, whether ancient, medieval, or modern. How those claims are to be evaluated depends, as I have already suggested, on the answers to such questions as: Does Aristotelian ethics possess the resources to resolve the difficulties and problems internal to it? How far have its adherents been successful in making use of those resources? Is Aristotelianism superior to its major rivals in this respect? Is it able to provide explanations of why those rivals should confront the particular sets of difficulties and problems which arise for each of them? Is it able to show that the resources of those rivals for so doing are inadequate and to explain why?

These are the key tests to which contemporary protagonists of Aristotle's ethics must subject both their own and Aristotle's theses and arguments. Whether they can do so in such a way as to vindicate Aristotle's ethics or not is a matter of contention. In my later books I have tried to argue that there are sufficient grounds for reasserting central Aristotelian positions. If I and those who agree with me in this conclusion are in the right, then the story told in *A Short History of Ethics* ought to be rewritten so as to end in a way that shows this. If those who disagree—the large majority of contemporary moral philosophers— are in the right, then the story should be rewritten so as to end in quite another way. The story in fact ends therefore by posing to the reader a set of further questions. It is up to the reader her- or himself to carry this enquiry further.

Every philosopher is indebted to her or his critics, and I more perhaps than most. Let me conclude therefore by emphasizing how very grateful I am to all the critics of the *Short History*, whether named or unnamed.

*Alasdair MacIntyre*
*Duke University, 1997*

# PREFACE TO THE FIRST EDITION

This book is inevitably the victim of the author's over-numerous intentions. The most workaday of these is simply to provide some historical background and perspective for the reading of those selected texts which form the core of the study of moral philosophy in most British and American universities. In particular I wanted to give some account of Greek thought for those undergraduate students restricted to the treadmill of Hume, Kant, Mill, and Moore. But this apparently simple intention is complicated by my views of the nature of moral philosophy. A discussion limited to an account of philosophical themes, omitting all reference to the moral concepts for the elucidation and reconstruction of which the theories were elaborated, would be absurd; a history not only of moral philosophies but also of moral concepts and of the moralities embodying and defined by these concepts would fill thirty volumes and thirty years. I have therefore continually compromised, and nobody will be satisfied with the result. I certainly am not.

No one could write in English on the history of moral philosophy and not feel awed by the example of Henry Sidgwick's *Outlines of the History of Ethics*, published in 1886 as a revision of his *Encyclopaedia Britannica* article, and intended primarily for the benefit of ordinands of the Church of Scotland. The perspective of my book is necessarily very different from that of Sidgwick, but the experience of writing has increased my admiration for him. In his journal he wrote, "Went up to London yesterday to see Macmillan about a stupid blunder in my outlines. I have represented a man whom I ought to have known all about—Sir James Mackintosh—as publishing a book in 1836, *four years after he was dead!* The cause of the blunder is simple carelessness—of a kind that now seems incredible." Somewhere in this book I am sure that there must be more than one example of an equally simple carelessness. It will not, however, be about Sir James Mackintosh—who does not appear. For, like Sidgwick, I have had not only to compress but also to select. I am unhappily aware, too, that on very many points of disputed interpretation, I have had to take a point of view without being able to justify it. I could not be more certain that students of particular authors and periods will be able to find many faults.

My debts are many: in general, to philosophical colleagues and pupils at Leeds, Oxford, Princeton, and elsewhere; in particular, to Mr. P. F. Strawson, Mrs. Amélie Rorty, and Professor H. L. A. Hart, who read either the whole or parts of the manuscript and made of this a better book than it would otherwise have been. To them I am profoundly grateful. I am especially conscious of how much in general I owe to Princeton University and to the members of its Department of Philosophy, where I was Senior Fellow to the Council of the Humanities in 1962–63 and Visiting Professor in 1965–66. This book is in no way adequate to any of these debts. I must also thank Miss M. P. Thomas for all her secretarial help.

*Alasdair MacIntyre*

# 1

---

# THE PHILOSOPHICAL POINT
# OF THE HISTORY OF ETHICS

Moral philosophy is often written as though the history of the subject were only of secondary and incidental importance. This attitude seems to be the outcome of a belief that moral concepts can be examined and understood apart from their history. Some philosophers have even written as if moral concepts were a timeless, limited, unchanging, determinate species of concept, necessarily having the same features throughout their history, so that there is a part of language waiting to be philosophically investigated which deserves the title "the language of morals" (with a definite article and a singular noun). In a less sophisticated way, historians of morals are all too apt to allow that moral practices and the content of moral judgments may vary from society to society and from person to person, but at the same time these historians have subtly assimilated different moral concepts—and so they end up by suggesting that although what is held to be right or good is not always the same, roughly the same concepts of right and good are universal.

In fact, of course, moral concepts change as social life changes. I deliberately do not write "because social life changes," for this might suggest that social life is one thing, morality another, and that there is merely an external, contingent causal relationship between them. This is obviously false. Moral concepts are embodied in and are partially constitutive of forms of social life. One key way in which we may identify one form of social life as distinct from another is by identifying differences in moral concepts. So it is an elementary commonplace to point out that there is no precise English equivalent for the Greek word δικαιοσύνη, usually translated *justice*. And this is not a mere linguistic defect, so that what Greek achieves by a single word English needs a periphrasis to achieve. It is rather that the occurrence of certain concepts in ancient Greek discourse and of others in modern English marks a difference between two forms of social life. To understand a concept, to grasp the meaning of the words which express it, is always at least to learn what the rules are which govern the use of such words and so to grasp the role of the concept in language and social life. This in itself would suggest strongly that different forms of social life will provide different roles for concepts to play. Or at least for some concepts this seems likely to be the case. There certainly are concepts which are unchanging over long periods, and which must be unchanging for one of two reasons. Either they are highly specialized concepts belonging within stable and continuing disciplines, such as geometry; or else they are highly general concepts necessary to any language of any complexity. I have in mind here the family of concepts expressed by such words as *and*, *or*, and *if*. But moral concepts do not fall into either of these two classes.

So it would be a fatal mistake to write as if, in the history of moral philosophy, there had been one single task of analyzing the concept of, for example, justice, to the performance of which Plato, Hobbes, and Bentham all set themselves, and for their achievement at which they can be awarded higher or lower marks. It does not of course follow, and it is in fact untrue, that what Plato says about δικαιοσύνη and what Hobbes or Bentham says about *justice* are totally irrelevant to one another. There are continuities as well as breaks in the history of moral concepts. Just here lies the complexity of the history.

The complexity is increased because philosophical inquiry itself plays a part in changing moral concepts. It is not that we have first a straightforward history of moral concepts and then a separate and secondary history of philosophical comment. For to analyze a concept

philosophically may often be to assist in its transformation by suggesting that it needs revision, or that it is discredited in some way, or that it
has a certain kind of prestige. Philosophy leaves everything as it is—
except concepts. And since to possess a concept involves behaving or
being able to behave in certain ways in certain circumstances, to alter
concepts, whether by modifying existing concepts or by making new
concepts available or by destroying old ones, is to alter behavior. So the
Athenians who condemned Socrates to death, the English parliament
which condemned Hobbes' Leviathan in 1666, and the Nazis who
burned philosophical books were correct at least in their apprehension
that philosophy can be subversive of established ways of behaving.
Understanding the world of morality and changing it are far from
incompatible tasks. The moral concepts which are objects for analysis
to the philosophers of one age may sometimes be what they are partly
because of the discussions by philosophers of a previous age.

A history which takes this point seriously, which is concerned with
the role of philosophy in relation to actual conduct, cannot be philosophically neutral. For it cannot but be at odds with the view of all
those recent philosophers who have wanted sharply to distinguish
philosophical ethics as a second-order activity of comment from the
first-order discourse which is part of the conduct of life, where moral
utterances themselves are in place. In drawing this distinction such
philosophers have tried so to define the realm of philosophy that it
would be a conceptual truth that philosophy could not impinge upon
practice. A. J. Ayer, for instance, has written about one particular ethical
theory that it " . . . is entirely on the level of analysis; it is an attempt to
show what people are doing when they make moral judgments; it is
not a set of suggestions as to what moral judgments they are to make.
And this is true of all moral philosophy as I understand it. All moral
theories . . . in so far as they are philosophical theories, are neutral as
regards actual conduct."[1]

My quarrel with this view will emerge from time to time in these
essays. But what I hope will emerge even more clearly is the function of
history in relation to conceptual analysis, for it is here that Santayana's
epigram that he who is ignorant of the history of philosophy is
doomed to repeat it finds its point. It is all too easy for philosophical
analysis, divorced from historical inquiry, to insulate itself from

correction. In ethics it can happen in the following way. A certain unsystematically selected class of moral concepts and judgments is made the subject of attention. From the study of these it is concluded that specifically moral discourse possesses certain characteristics. When counterexamples are adduced to show that this is not always so, these counterexamples are dismissed as irrelevant, because not examples of moral discourse; and they are shown to be nonmoral by exhibiting their lack of the necessary characteristics. From this kind of circularity we can be saved only by an adequate historical view of the varieties of moral and evaluative discourse. This is why it would be dangerous, and not just pointless, to begin these studies with a definition which would carefully delimit the field of inquiry. We cannot, of course, completely avoid viewing past moralists and past philosophers in terms of present distinctions. To set out to write the history of moral philosophy at all involves us in selecting from the past what falls under the heading of moral philosophy as we now conceive it. But it is important that we should, as far as it is possible, allow the history of philosophy to break down our present-day preconceptions, so that our too narrow views of what can and cannot be thought, said, and done are discarded in face of the record of what has been thought, said, and done. We have to steer between the danger of a dead antiquarianism, which enjoys the illusion that we can approach the past without preconceptions, and that other danger, so apparent in such philosophical historians as Aristotle and Hegel, of believing that the whole point of the past was that it should culminate with us. History is neither a prison nor a museum, nor is it a set of materials for self-congratulation.

# 2

## THE PREPHILOSOPHICAL HISTORY OF "GOOD" AND THE TRANSITION TO PHILOSOPHY

The suggestion that asking and answering moral questions is one thing, and asking and answering philosophical questions about morality quite another thing, may conceal from us the fact that in asking moral questions of a certain kind with sufficient persistence we may discover that we cannot answer them until we have asked and answered certain philosophical questions. A discovery of this kind provided the initial impulse for philosophical ethics in Greek society. For at a certain period, when moral questions were asked, it became clear that the meaning of some of the key words involved in the framing of those questions was no longer clear and unambiguous. Social changes had not only made certain types of conduct, once socially accepted, problematic, but had also rendered problematic the concepts which had defined the moral framework of an earlier world. The social changes in question are those reflected in Greek literature in the transition from the Homeric writers through the Theognid corpus to the sophists.

The society reflected in the Homeric poems is one in which the most important judgments that can be passed upon a man concern the way in which he discharges his allotted social function. It is because certain qualities are necessary to discharge the function of a king or a warrior, a judge or a shepherd, that there is a use for such expressions as *authoritative* and *courageous* and *just*. The word ἀγαθός, ancestor of our *good*, is originally a predicate specifically attached to the role of a Homeric nobleman. "To be *agathos*," says W. H. Adkins, "one must be brave, skilful and successful in war and in peace; and one must possess the wealth and (in peace) the leisure which are at once the necessary conditions for the development of these skills and the natural reward of their successful employment."[2] Aγαθός is not like our word *good* in many of its Homeric contexts, for it is not used to say that it is "good" to be kingly, courageous, and clever—that is, it is not used to commend these qualities in a man, as our word *good* might be used by a contemporary admirer of the Homeric ideal. It is rather that ἀγαθός is a commendatory word because it is interchangeable with the words which characterize the qualities of the Homeric ideal. So in our ordinary English use of *good*, "good, but not kingly, courageous, or cunning" makes perfectly good sense; but in Homer, "ἀγαθός, but not kingly, courageous, or clever" would not even be a morally eccentric form of judgment, but as it stands simply an unintelligible contradiction.

How do adjectives of appraisal, such as ἀγαθός and others, function in Homer? First of all, to ascribe the qualities for which they stand to someone is to make a factual statement, in the sense that whether what you have said is true or false is settled by the man's performances and settled simply and solely by his performances. The question, Is he ἀγαθός? is the same as the question, Is he courageous, clever, and kingly? And this is answered by answering the question, Does he, and has he, fought, plotted, and ruled with success? The point of such ascriptions is in part predictive. To call a man ἀγαθός is to tell your hearers what sort of conduct they can expect from him. We ascribe dispositions to the agent in the light of his behavior in past episodes.

From this alone it is strikingly plain that the Homeric use of ἀγαθός does not square at all with what many recent philosophers have thought to be the characteristic properties of moral, and indeed of evaluative, predicates. For it has often been held[3] to be an essential feature of such predicates that any judgments in which one is ascribed to a subject cannot follow logically as a conclusion from premises which are merely factual. No matter what factual conditions are satisfied, these by themselves can never provide sufficient conditions for asserting that an evaluative predicate holds of a subject. But in the Homeric poems, that a man has behaved in certain ways is sufficient to entitle him to be called ἀγαθός. Now, assertions as to how a man has behaved are certainly in the ordinary sense factual; and the Homeric use of ἀγαθός is certainly in the ordinary sense evaluative. The alleged logical gulf between fact and appraisal is not so much one that has been bridged in Homer. It has never been dug. Nor is it clear that there is any ground in which to dig.

Moreover, I fail to be ἀγαθός if and only if I fail to bring off the requisite performances; and the function of expressions of praise and blame is to invoke and to justify the rewards of success and the penalties of failure. You cannot avoid blame and penalty by pointing out that you could not help doing what you did, that failure was unavoidable. You may, of course, certainly point this out; but if your performance failed to satisfy the appropriate criteria, then you simply cannot prevent the withdrawal of the ascription of kingliness, courage, and cleverness or cunning. And this is to say that Homeric moral predicates are not applied, as moral predicates have been applied in our society, only where the agent could have done other than he did. Excuses, praise, and blame must all play different parts. We cannot even inquire whether (in the Kantian sense) *ought* implies *can* for Homer, for in Homer we cannot find *ought* (in the Kantian sense). So Odysseus blames the suitors, when he returns to Ithaca, for having had a false belief: "Dogs, you did not think that I would return home from Troy; for you have consumed my possessions, lain with my maidservants by force, and wooed my wife while I was yet alive, fearing neither the gods who inhabit the broad heaven, nor yet that there would be any retaliation from men hereafter; but now the doom of death is upon you all."[4] The suitors are blamed precisely for having a false belief; but this is what in a modern sense we would feel we could not blame people for. For to believe is not to perform an avoidable action. And it is not that Homer thinks that beliefs are voluntary; he is engaged in an assessment to which what the agent could or could not have done otherwise is irrelevant.

It will be useful now to look at a cognate of ἀγαθός in Homer, the noun ἀρετή, usually and perhaps misleadingly translated *virtue*. A man who performs his socially allotted function possesses ἀρετή. The ἀρετή

of one function or role is quite different from that of another. The
ἀρετή of a king lies in ability to command, of a warrior in courage, of a
wife in fidelity, and so on. A man is ἀγαθός if he has the ἀρετή of his
particular and specific function. And this brings out the divorce of
ἀγαθός in the Homeric poems from later uses of *good* (including later
uses of ἀγαθός). When Agamemnon intends to steal the slave girl
Briseis from Achilles, Nestor says to him, "Do not, ἀγαθός though you
be, take the girl from him."[5] It is not that, being ἀγαθός, Agamemnon
can be expected not to take the girl, nor that he will cease to be ἀγαθός
if he does take her. He will be ἀγαθός whether he takes her or not. The
way in which "ἀγαθός" is tied so completely to fulfillment of function
is also brought out in its links with other concepts. Shame, αἰδώς, is
what is felt by a man who fails to perform his allotted role. To feel
shame is simply to be aware that you have entitled people to accuse you
of having fallen short of that which the socially established description
both you and others had applied to yourself had led them to expect. It
is to be aware that one is liable to reproach.

This whole family of concepts, then, presupposes a certain sort of
social order, characterized by a recognized hierarchy of functions. It is
noteworthy that the value predicates can only be applied to those men
who fall under the descriptions which taken together constitute the
social vocabulary of the system. Those who fall outside the system fall
outside the moral order. And this is indeed the fate of slaves; the slave
becomes a chattel, a thing, rather than a person. It would miss the point
to comment upon this that the Homeric poems are not a historically
accurate picture of early Greek society or that no society as rigorously
functional in fact existed. What we get in Homer is rather an idealization of one form of social life; we are presented with a social order and
its concepts in a fairly pure form, rather than in the kind of admixture
of several forms which a total society often presents. But for our conceptual purposes this is none the worse. For we have other literary
documents in which we can see how the breakdown of a social hierarchy and of a system of recognized functions deprives the traditional
moral terms and concepts of their social anchorage. In the body of
poems which pass under the name of Theognis of Megara,[6] and which
were written in post-Homeric and preclassical Greece, we find startling
changes in the uses of ἀγαθος and ἀρετή. They can no longer be

defined in terms of the fulfillment in a recognized way of a recognized function; for there is no longer a single and unified society in which evaluation can depend on established criteria of this kind. Words like ἀγαθός and κακός (bad) become sometimes merely neutrally descriptive of social position. Or they may acquire an even more radical extension of meaning. Both processes are seen at once in a passage which runs: "Many κακοι are rich and many ἀγαθοί are poor, but we will not take the wealth in exchange for our ἀρετή; for the one remains with a man always, but possessions pass from one man to another." Here ἀγαθός and κακός seem to mean *noble-born* and *baseborn* or some such equivalents. They have lost their old meaning and been transformed into one of the key identifying descriptions under which those to whom the terms applied in their old sense now fall. But they are no longer evaluative in the same way. Whereas in Homer one would have said of a chieftain that he was ἀγαθός if and only if he exercised his true function, now ἀγαθός describes someone who comes of a chieftain's line, whatever function he may exercise or fail to exercise or whatever his personal qualities may be. But the transformation of ἀρετή in the same passage is quite different. For ἀρετή now denotes not those qualities by means of which a particular function may be discharged, but certain human qualities which may be divorced from function altogether. A man's ἀρετή is now personal to himself; it has become far more like what modern writers think of as a moral quality.

Thus evaluative predicates come to refer to dispositions to behave in certain ways relatively independent of social function. With this change comes another. In Homeric society the dominant hierarchy of functional roles determines which are the dominant qualities; skill, cunning, and courage of various sorts. When this hierarchy collapses, the question can be opened in a far more general way of what the qualities are which we would wish to see in a man. "The whole of ἀρετή is summed up in δικαιοσύνη," writes one Theognid author. "Every man, Cyrnus, is ἀγαθός if he has δικαιοσύνη." Here anybody can be ἀγαθός exercising the quality of justice, δικαιοσύνη. But what does this consist in? The pressures of the time not only make ἀγαθός unstable in meaning, they also raise doubts about the nature of δικαιοσύνη. For the idea of a single moral order has broken down.

It has broken down partly because of the breakdown of formerly unified social forms. These were reinforced by a mythology with the status of a sacred writing, including the Homeric poems, which suggested a single cosmic order. In Homer the order of necessity reigns over gods as well as over men. *"Υβρις*, willful pride, is the sin of overstepping the moral order of the universe. *Νέμεσις* awaits whoever commits it. The moral order and the natural order are not sharply distinguished. "The sun will not go beyond his measures; otherwise the *'Εριν ́υες*, the handmaids of justice, will find him out," said Heraclitus. But this mythological assertion of order changes its function too, as Greek society changes. Anthropologists very commonly assert that myths express social structure. And myths can do this in more than one way. Between Homer and writers five centuries later there is a great change in Greek myths about the order in the universe. The Homeric myth does reflect, though with much distortion, the workings of an actual society in which a close form of functional organization is presupposed by the moral and evaluative forms of appraisal which are in use. The later assertions of order in the universe reflect not a structure that is, but one that was, or one that is struggling to survive. They are conservative protests against the disintegration of the older forms and the transition to the city-state. The myths themselves cannot but open up the question of the difference between the order of the universe and the order of society. But above all, this question is sharpened by a widening awareness of radically different social orders.

The impact of the Persian invasions, of colonization, of increase in trade and therefore in travel, all these bring home the fact of different cultures. The result is that the distinction between what holds good in Egypt but not in Persia, or in Athens but not in Megara, on the one hand, and what is the case universally as part of the order of things becomes overwhelmingly important. The question asked about any moral rule or social practice is, Is it part of the essentially local realm of *νόμος* (convention, custom) or of the essentially universal realm of *φύσις* (nature)? Linked to this is of course the question, Is it open to me to choose what rules I shall make my own or what restraints I shall observe (as it may be open to me to choose which city I shall live in and what therefore shall be the *νόμος* by which I live)? or does the nature of the universe set limits upon what I may legitimately choose?

To the task of answering these questions there came in the fifth century BC a new class of teachers and a new class of pupils. Books on moral philosophy commonly concentrated on the teachers, the sophists, whom we see mainly through the antagonistic eyes of Plato. But the activities of the sophists as suppliers are unintelligible apart from the demand which they met. So let us try to specify this demand still more precisely.

We have seen how the word ἀγαθός had become unstable in its attachments and so had its cognate words, especially ἀρετή. "Virtue" is what the good man possesses and exercises. It is his skill. But what virtue is and what constitutes a good man, these have become matters of conflicting opinion in which the Homeric concept of the ἀγαθός has been divided up between rival inheritances. There is, on the one hand, the good man conceived as the good citizen. The values of the conservative Athenian whom Aristophanes portrays are loyalty to the city and more especially to the older forms of social order. In this there is certainly an element of the Homeric ἀγαθός. But equally, the Homeric chieftain's personal values, the values of the courageous, cunning, and aggressive king, are now, if exercised by the individual in the city-state, antisocial. Self-aggrandizement, the use of the state as something to be preyed upon, these are the only courses open to the individual who wants in the fifth century to behave like a Homeric hero. The social order in which his qualities were an essential part of a stable society has given way to one in which the same qualities are necessarily disruptive. So the relationship of the ἀγαθός to the social values and especially to justice has become a crucial issue. But δικαιοσύνη (which though very inadequately translated as justice, is as inadequately translated by any other word, for it has a flavor all its own and combines the notion of fairness in externals with that of personal integrity in a way that no English word does) is of all notions the one that appears most to be put in question by the discovery of rival social orders. Different cities observe different customs and different laws. Does and should justice differ from city to city? Does justice hold only within a given community between citizens? or should it hold also between cities? The Athenians condemn the character of Alcibiades because he did not observe the restraints of δικαιοσύνη in his behavior within the Athenian state. But their own envoys behave just like Alcibiades in their attitude to other states. That is, they equate what is morally permissible with what the agent has the power to do. Their envoys can say to the representative of Melos, an island which wished to remain neutral in the Peloponnesian War, "For of the gods we believe, and of men we know, that by a law of their nature whenever they can rule they will. This law was not made by us, and we are not the first who have acted upon it; we did but inherit it, and shall bequeath it to all time, and we know that you and all mankind, if you were as strong as we are, would do as we do."[7]

Thus the redefinition of evaluative predicates creates a problem for those who wish to use them, even in formulating their own intentions. The terms ἀγαθός and ἀρετή have become genuinely problematic, as has their relation to καλός, the predicate characterizing what is well thought of, and as has their relationship to δικαιοσύνη. The moral and political conservative still feels able to give the words a fixed connotation. He uses texts and tags from Homer or Simonides to provide him with definitions. But, in general, slides in the meanings of words become appallingly easy and frequent. It is often impossible to distinguish two separate phenomena, moral uncertainty and uncertainty as to the meaning of evaluative predicates. In the moments of greatest perplexity in fifth-century Greece these two uncertainties are one. Thucydides has recorded the corruption of language in describing the revolution at Corfu: "The meaning of words no longer had the same relation to things, but was changed by them as they thought fit. Reckless doing was held to be loyal courage; prudent delay was the excuse of a coward; moderation was the disguise of unmanly weakness; to know everything was to do nothing."[8]

How does Ayer's conception of the distinction between moral philosophy and moral judgment or practice apply in this situation? Can we distinguish two separate activities, "the activity of a moralist, who sets out to elaborate a moral code, or to encourage its observance, and that of a moral philosopher, whose concern is not primarily to make moral judgments but to analyse their nature?"[9] It must at once be conceded to Ayer that there are some questions involved in moral philosophy which are purely philosophical and others which are entirely independent of philosophy. There are many cases where what is important is to emphasize that to commit oneself to a particular philosophical analysis of moral judgments does not entail committing oneself to making a particular specified set of moral judgments. In a contemporary context two utilitarian philosophers might agree in their analysis of the expression *wrong* and without a shadow of inconsistency disagree as to whether it is the case that all wars are wrong or that only some wars are wrong. Equally, two pacifists might agree on this latter issue, but one might be a philosophical intuitionist, the other an emotivist. When Ayer argues that philosophical theories of moral concepts and judgments are neutral as regards conduct this is clearly the type of case he has in mind. But the point at which Greek moral philosophy begins suggests that there is also a quite different type of case.

In Ayer's type of case the moral vocabulary is taken as given and determinate. There are then two problems, How shall I use it? (morals) and, How shall I understand it? (philosophy). Philosophy, it should be noted, becomes an essentially after-the-event activity. But in the cases where the meaning of the moral vocabulary is itself in doubt, the answer to the question, How shall I use the moral vocabulary? will consist in formulating rules, no doubt partly already implicit in the previous uses of the word, but partly perhaps also designed to avoid incoherences and ambiguities in previous uses. These rules will set the limits upon the possible uses of the moral predicates, and so philosophical elaboration of the concept will partly determine the moral uses of those predicates. Thus the question of the criteria which are to be employed in moral evaluation cannot be clearly demarcated as moral but not philosophical, or as philosophical but not moral. Of course, to clear up the conceptual problems is not of itself to determine completely how we ought to act or to judge, but it does determine the limits of moral possibility in part. The task of the moralist and the task of the philosopher are not identical; but they are not entirely distinct either.

# 3

## THE SOPHISTS AND SOCRATES

The peculiar cultural relativism of the sophists is an attempt to meet the simultaneous demands of two tasks: that of assigning a coherent set of meanings to the evaluative vocabulary, and that of explaining how to live well—that is, effectively—in a city-state. They begin from a situation in which the prerequisite of a successful social career is success in the public forums of the city, the assembly, and the law courts. To succeed in that milieu it was necessary to convince and to please. But what would convince and please in one place might fail to convince and please in another. Individual sophists, men such as Protagoras and Gorgias and their disciples, all had their own doctrines and theories in the face of this problem. But we can pick out a general amalgam of sophistic theory, which is what Plato objected to and Socrates earlier criticized and rivaled. This amalgam would run as follows:

The ἀρετή of a man is his functioning well as a man. To function well as a man in the city-state is to be a successful citizen. To be a successful citizen is to impress in the assembly and the law courts. To succeed there it is necessary to conform to the prevailing conventions as to what is just, right, and fitting. Each state has its conventions on these matters. What one must do therefore is to study prevailing usages and learn to adapt oneself to them, so as to mold one's hearers success-fully. This is the τέχνη, the craft, the skill, which it is at once the business and the virtue of a sophist to teach. It is a presupposition of this teaching that there is no criterion of virtue as such, apart from success, and no criterion of justice as such, apart from the dominant practice of each particular city. In the *Theatetus* Plato outlines a doctrine which he puts into the mouth of the sophist Protagoras. This links moral relativism with a general relativism in the theory of knowledge. Protagoras' most famous saying was that "Man is the measure of all things; of the things which are, that they are, and of the things which are not, that they are not." Plato interprets this as referring to sense perception, and as meaning that as things seem to be to an individual percipient, so they are (to him). There is no "being hot" or "being cold" as such; there is simply "seeming hot to this man" or "seeming cold to that man." So it makes no sense to ask of a wind which feels warm to one man but chilly to another, Is it *really* hot or cold? The wind is nothing *really*; it is to each whatever it appears to each.

Is it the same with moral values? Protagoras is in difficulty here over his own standing as a teacher. For if Protagoras concedes that everything is as it seems to be to the individual subject, then he seems to allow that no one can ever judge falsely, and Plato does in fact put this admission into the mouth of Protagoras. But if no one judges falsely, then all are equal in respect of the truth, and nobody can be in the superior position of a teacher or in the inferior position of a pupil. So it seems to follow that if Protagoras' doctrine is true, then he has no right to teach it. For nobody's doctrine is or can be truer than anyone else's. Protagoras attempts to avoid this difficulty by arguing that although nobody's judgment can be false, some men by their judgments produce better effects than others do. This of course only involves him in the same paradox in a different way; for the assertion that Protagoras' judgments produce better effects than those of others is now treated as a truth such that, if a man denied it, he would judge falsely. But on the original premises nobody ever judges falsely. So the paradox would be unresolved. Protagoras however is allowed by Plato to ignore this and consequently to argue that "the wise and good orators make good things seem just to their cities instead of pernicious ones. Whatever in any city is regarded as just and admirable is just and admirable in that city for so long as it is thought to be so."[10] Thus the criteria of justice are held to differ from state to state. It does not of course follow that the criteria either must or can be entirely different in different states, and in another dialogue, the *Protagoras*, Plato appears to credit Protagoras with the view that there are some qualities necessary for the continuing social life of any city. But this is quite consistent with maintaining that there are no sufficient criteria for determining what is just or unjust, independent of the particular conventions of each particular city.

So what the sophist has to teach is what is held to be just in each different state. You cannot ask or answer the question, What is justice? but only the questions, What is justice-at-Athens? and, What is justice-at-Corinth? From this there seems to follow an important consequence, which both reinforces and is reinforced by a new twist that was lent to the distinction between nature and convention. For an individual is offered no criteria by which to guide his own actions if he is merely asked to note that the prevailing criteria vary from state to state. From this he can draw nothing to answer the questions, What am I to do? How am I to live? For he has to choose for himself between the differing criteria of different states (Where and how shall I choose to live?) and also whether to regard with any serious respect the standards which prevail where he does happen to live. But since the whole moral vocabulary is defined by the sophists in terms of the prevailing usage in different states, and since this usage *ex hypothesi* cannot provide an answer to these crucial questions, both the questions and the possible answers to the questions, What am I to do? How shall I live? have to be treated as nonmoral and premoral. It is at this point that a new use is found for the distinction between nature (φύσις) and convention (νόμος).

A man who lives in a given state and conforms to its required standards is a creature of convention; a man who is equally at home in any state or none, depending upon his own personal and private purposes, is a creature of nature. Within every conventional man there hides a natural man. This doctrine rests squarely on a separation of the standpoint of the individual agent from that of the socially established conventions which it is up to him to accept or reject. When to that is added an identification of the moral with the conventional, the identification of the premoral and nonmoral agent with the natural man is complete. The natural man has no moral standards of his own. He is therefore free from all constraints upon him by others. All men are by nature either wolves or sheep; they prey or are preyed upon.

The natural man, conceived thus by the sophist, has a long history in European ethics in front of him. The details of his psychology will vary from writer to writer, but he is almost always—though not always— going to be aggressive and lustful. Morality is then explicable as a necessary compromise between the desire of natural men to aggress upon others and the fear of natural men that others will aggress upon them with fatal consequences. Mutual self-interest leads men to combine in setting up constraining rules to forbid aggression and lust, and powerful agencies to inflict sanctions on those who break the rules. Some of these rules constitute morality; others law. A good deal of variation is possible in the way that this intellectual fairy tale is told, but its central themes, like those of all good fairy tales, are remarkably constant. And above all, at the heart of the account there remains the idea that social life is perhaps chronologically and certainly logically secondary to a form of unconstrained nonsocial human life in which what men do is a matter of their individual natural psychology. Can we make sense of this notion of the natural, presocial man?

At this early stage in the argument it is worth making one factual and one conceptual point about this particular Greek version of the doctrine of natural man. The factual point is that the character who appears in the guise of man devoid of social conventions (in, for example, the account which Plato puts into the mouth of Thrasymachus) is not a child of nature at all. Nor is he in fact devoid of social conventions. What he is devoid of is any genuine adherence to the conventions of the fifth-century city-state. What he expresses is not nature, but the social attitudes of the Homeric hero. He is a man transposed from a social order where his attitudes and actions are accepted forms of move in the social game, and have accepted forms of response, into a quite different social order where he can appear only as an aggressive outsider. But this does not mean that he is a social impossibility. "Scratch Thrasymachus," writes Adkins, "and you find Agamemnon." Give him more of a veneer, we may add, and you find Alcibiades.

The factual point is, then, that the so-called natural man is merely a man from another and earlier culture. The conceptual point is that this is no accident. For the character of the natural presocial man is described in terms of certain traits which he possesses: selfishness, aggressiveness, and the like. But these traits, or rather the words which name and characterize them and enabled them to be socially recognized traits, belong to a vocabulary which presupposes an established web of social and moral relationships. Words like *selfish*, *unselfish*, *aggressive*, *mild*, and the like are defined in terms of established norms of behavior and established expectations about behavior. Where there are no normal standards there is no possibility of failing to come up to them, of doing more or less than is expected of one, or of elaborating and using names and descriptions of the traits and dispositions of those who so behave. Thus the description of the so-called natural man is formed in a vocabulary drawn from social life; what was alleged to be presocial turns out to presuppose the existence of some social order. Thus the concept of the natural man suffers from a fatal internal incoherence.

What the sophists, and the long tradition which was later to follow them, failed to distinguish was the difference between the concept of a man who stands outside and is able to question the conventions of some one given social order and the concept of a man who stands outside social life as such. And this error sprang from their attempt to bring the distinction between the natural and the conventional into play at points at which it necessarily lacked application. What follows from this error? Natural man portrayed in Thrasymachean guise has two main characteristics. His psychological make-up is simple: he is out to get what he wants, and what he wants is narrowly circumscribed. Power and pleasure are his exclusive interests. But to get what he wants this wolf has to wear the sheep's clothing of the conventional moral values. His masquerade can only be carried through by putting the conventional moral vocabulary to the service of his private purposes. He must say in the law courts and the assembly what people want to hear, so that they will put power into his hands. Thus the ἀρετή of such a man is to learn the craft, the τέχνη, of molding people by rhetoric. He must take them by the ear before he takes them by the throat. It is to this doctrine that Socrates seeks to present an alternative.

Socrates found himself confronted both by moral conservatives using an incoherent moral vocabulary as if they were sure of its meaning and by sophists whose innovations he found equally suspect. It is therefore scarcely surprising that he appears different from different points of view. It has been said that in Xenophon's writings he appears as merely a fifth-century Dr. Johnson; in Aristophanes' he can appear as a particularly distressing sophist; in Plato he is many things, and above all, Plato's mouthpiece. It is clear, then, that the task of delineating the historical Socrates is inherently controversial. But one may perhaps not solve, but avoid the problem by trying to paint a composite portrait from two palettes. The first is Aristotle's account of Socrates in the *Metaphysics*,[11] where Aristotle, unlike Plato, Xenophon, or Aristophanes, seems to have no ax of personal interest to grind. The second is the set of dialogues by Plato which are accepted as chronologically early and in which Plato's own metaphysical doctrines of the soul and of the forms are not yet elaborated. For we learn from Aristotle that Socrates "did not make the universals or the definitions exist apart" as Plato does in the dialogues of the middle period. Aristotle ascribes to Socrates what he calls universal definitions and what he calls inductive arguments, and he makes two statements about Socrates' intentions which are of peculiar interest in the light of Plato's portrait. He says that "Socrates was occupying himself with the excellences of character, and in connection with them became the first to raise the problem of universal definition"; a few lines farther on Aristotle remarks that it was natural that Socrates should be seeking the essence, for he was seeking to syllogize, and " 'what a thing is' is the starting point of syllogisms." What I wish to fasten upon here is Aristotle's remark that Socrates was preoccupied with the search for definitions because he wished to syllogize when we might have expected him to say that he syllogized in the interest of discovering definitions. What Aristotle is pointing to can be clearly seen in the early Platonic dialogues.

Socrates repeatedly puts such questions as, What is piety? What is courage? What is justice? We see him use what Aristotle calls inductive arguments (arguments which invoke examples and generalize from them), and we see him syllogizing (that is, drawing conclusions deductively from various premises). But he does this with the apparent intention of convicting his interlocutors of inability to answer the question rather than with the intention of supplying an answer. In scarcely one of the dialogues up to and including Book I of the *Republic* (if, as some scholars assert, this was originally composed separately) does Socrates answer his own original question; he always leaves the interlocutor in a fury. How are we to understand this procedure? When the Delphic oracle described Socrates as the wisest of the Athenians he concluded that he deserved this title because only he, among them all, knew that he knew nothing. So it would not be surprising if Socrates envisaged his duty as a teacher as that of making his pupils wiser by making them discover their own ignorance. To this it may be objected that Socrates is too often pictured by Plato as driving his interlocutors into an exasperated fury, and that this is scarcely a convincing method of moral education. But infuriating someone may indeed be the only method of disturbing him sufficiently to force him into philosophical reflection upon moral matters. Of course, for the majority of those so assaulted there will be no admirable consequences of this kind. But there is no evidence that Socrates expected the activity of an intellectual gadfly to benefit more than a tiny minority. Moreover Socrates' method is both more intelligible and more justifiable if it is understood as aimed at securing a particular sort of change in the hearers rather than arriving at a particular conclusion. It is not just that he does not arrive at conclusions; it is rather that his arguments are *ad hominem* in this sense, that they derive contradictory or otherwise absurd consequences from admissions secured from his interlocutor, and induce the interlocutor to retract. This desire to secure conviction in the interlocutor is underlined in the *Gorgias*, where Plato makes Socrates say to Polus that he will have achieved nothing unless he can convince him. It is therefore a mistake to complain[12] of the particularity of the Socratic method. The whole point lies in its particularity. But why does Socrates have the aims which he has?

His dissatisfaction with someone such as Euthyphro, who wrongly believes that he has a clear concept of piety, is complex; he thinks and shows that Euthyphro does not know what piety is, although Euthyphro invokes established usage. But he does this not because he has a more radical moral judgment to make than Euthyphro, but indeed to produce scepticism in Euthyphro about his own dissent from an older and more conservative order of things. Euthyphro is engaged in prosecuting his own father for the murder of a family dependent, a slave. Both Euthyphro's relatives and Socrates are more shocked at a man's prosecuting his father than they are at allowing a slave to be murdered. Likewise, Socrates is very gentle with Cephalus at the beginning of *Republic* I. He honors moral conservatism, and mocks moral innovation. (This is one of the points at which Xenophon's Boswellian portrait fits well with what Plato says.) And this is in part because he cannot get clear from the sophists and the innovators any more than he can from established usage what sense moral expressions can have. So the discovery of one's own ignorance survives as the one well-founded moral aim.

Socrates' positive doctrines are at first sight perhaps not easy to square with this. His great point of agreement with sophists is his acceptance of the thesis that ἀρετή is teachable. But paradoxically he denies that there are teachers. The resolution of the paradox is found only later in Plato, in the thesis that the knowledge is already present in us and has only to be brought to birth by a philosophical midwife. Its statement depends on the Socratic thesis that virtue is knowledge (ἐπιστήμη). The examples with which Socrates elucidates this thesis leave it obscurer rather than clearer. Socrates breaks with the sophists in not allowing that rhetoric can have the status of a τέχνη, but his closely allied use of ἐπιστήμη and τέχνη make it clear that to acquire virtue is to acquire some τέχνη, even if not rhetoric. Rhetoric is nonrational—a matter of knacks, hints, and dodges. The knowledge that constitutes virtue involves not only beliefs that such and such is the case but also a capacity for recognizing relevant distinctions and an ability to act. These are all bound together by the Socratic uses of ἐπιστήμη and τέχνη, and any attempt to separate them out inevitably leads at once to a simplification and to a falsification of the Socratic view.

Aristotle says of Socrates that "he believed that all the moral virtues were forms of knowledge; in such a way that when we knew what justice was, it followed that we would be just," and Aristotle's own comment on this clarifies its meaning: "Yet where moral virtue is concerned," he says, "the most important thing is not to know what it is, but how it arises; we do not wish to know what courage is, we wish to be courageous."[13] That Socrates is all of the intellectualist that Aristotle makes him out to be is clear from the parallel Socratic saying to "Virtue is knowledge"; namely, "No one errs willingly." No one willingly goes wrong, for no one voluntarily chooses other than what would be good for himself. There are two assumptions behind this doctrine. One is that what is good for a man and what is good *simpliciter* cannot be divorced. The sophists see no good that is not the simple getting by some man of what he wants. In the *Lysis*, however, Socrates points out that giving a child what is good for him is quite different from giving him what he wants. So that "what is good for X" and "what X wants" do not mean the same. At the same time how could a man want what would be bad for himself? Very simply, we are tempted to reply, in the way that a drug addict wants drugs, or an alcoholic wants alcohol, or a sadist wants victims. But the Socratic answer would surely be that for these men the object of desire apparently falls under the concept of some genuine good—pleasure, the diminution of a craving, or whatever it is. Their mistake is the intellectual one of mis-identifying an object, supposing it to be of some kind other than it is, or of not noticing some of its properties, not remembering perhaps. On the Socratic view an alcoholic does not say, "The whisky will rot my liver, and I don't care"; he says, "One more drink will steady my hand enough to call up Alcoholics Anonymous." To this we are strongly disposed to reply that sometimes the alcoholic does just say, "The whisky will rot my liver, but I want a drink, and I don't care." How does Socrates come to ignore this kind of rejoinder? The answer is perhaps to be understood by looking back to Aristotle's accusation against Socrates.

When Aristotle says in criticism of Socrates that "where moral virtue is concerned, the most important thing is not to know what it is, but how it arises" he makes a distinction which Socrates, on his own premises, cannot be expected to make. Precisely why Socrates was prepared to equate virtue and knowledge so roundly is not entirely clear. For he is quite explicit about the consequences: "No one errs willingly"; that is, if men do what is wrong, it is intellectual error not moral weakness that is the cause. And this, as Aristotle points out, is contrary to what ordinary men take to be an obvious fact of moral experience. We can put the best possible face upon the Socratic view by considering the plausibility of the thesis that a man's moral beliefs are evidenced in his actions. If a man says that he believes that he ought to do something, and when occasion arises neither performs the action in question nor exhibits regret or remorse, we shall certainly conclude that he did not really believe what he said. He was only talking. (Or he may of course have changed his mind.) But there is still a striking difference between the case where a man never does what he says he believes he ought to do (when we should need the strongest reasons for not supposing that his behaviour gives the lie to his avowals) and the case where a man occasionally does not do what he says he believes he ought to do (which is what constitutes a moral lapse, in most circles a commonplace occurrence). And this difference Socrates just does not recognize: if a man *really* knows what he ought to do, what power could be greater than knowledge and so prevent him from doing what he ought? So Socrates is represented as arguing in the *Protagoras*.

One might try to argue again that since Socrates almost never answers his own question, What is X? where X is the name of some moral quality—piety, justice, or the like—the whole and only point of the Socratic inquiry is to engender self-knowledge in the form of a knowledge of one's own ignorance. So that virtue is an aim rather than an achievement. But the spirit of the *Apology* of Socrates at his trial is inconsistent with this, in the light of his claim that he was inspired by a daemon. Moreover, in the *Laches* the inquiry into the nature of courage yields a partial answer in terms of knowledge of a certain kind, and although the inquiry runs into difficulties which lead to its suspension, the impression is not at all of an inquiry which is necessarily bound to fail.

What remains unambiguously clear is that the Socratic position combined the assertion of several bold and apparently paradoxical theses with a good deal of ambiguity and uncertainty in his presentation of them. In Plato's *Gorgias*, for example, it is not at all clear whether Socrates is advancing the view that pleasure is the good in order to discuss but finally dismiss it or in order to defend it as at least a possible view, and scholars have notoriously differed in their interpretations on this point. But what is plainer than the contentions of either party is that rival interpretations are in a way beside the point; what Socrates is presented as saying simply is ambiguous. And it is in no way out of character that Socrates should be concerned to puzzle his interlocutors rather than to present them with a clear position of his own.

This ambiguity is perhaps more than a personal quirk of Socrates. Socrates had raised the key philosophical questions in ethics. How do we understand the concepts which we use in decision and appraisal? What is the criterion for their correct application? Is established usage consistent? and if not, how do we escape inconsistency? But to have asked the philosophical questions about how we are to understand concepts will only take Socrates part of the way. Clearly, if our moral concepts are concepts at all, if our moral words are words, then there must be criteria for their use. They could not be part of our language unless there were rules for their use, rules which could be taught and learned, rules which are socially established and socially shared. It follows from this that the kind of sophist who thought that moral words could simply be *given* a meaning, either by the philosopher or the ruler, at will, is talking nonsense. For in order for the *meaning* to be a *meaning* it would have to be teachable in terms of the existing criteria which govern the use of the relevant expressions. So that Socrates is right to present conceptual inquiry as a task which can yield correct and incorrect results, as an activity in which there are objective standards of success and failure. But it does not follow that the investigation of how a concept is in fact employed will yield one clear and consistent answer. Socrates' questioning of his pupils relies upon the examples of contemporary Greek moral usage which they produce. If I am right, the problematic moral character of Greek life at the time of Socrates arises from and partially consists in the fact that moral usage has ceased to be clear and consistent. And so to discover unambiguous and practically useful moral concepts, one will have to undertake a different sort of inquiry.

Just this is what Socrates' successors undertake, and they move in two main directions. Plato accepts the fact that moral concepts are only intelligible against the background of a certain sort of social order; he then tries to delineate it, providing or attempting to provide at the same time a justification in terms of the order of the universe. The Cynics and Cyrenaics by contrast seek to provide a moral code independent of society, tied only to the individual's choices and decisions, and attempting to make the individual moral life self-sufficient. To them I shall return briefly later on, but the next stage of the argument belongs to Plato. Yet it is worth remarking that those philosophers, like Socrates, whose analyses of moral concepts suggest defects in contemporary morality are not unlikely to be unwelcome to authority, even if the lack of prestige of philosophers usually makes it a waste of time to inflict the death penalty. It is a mark of Socrates' greatness that he was not surprised at his own fate.

# 4

## PLATO: THE *GORGIAS*

I have already said that it is impossible to produce more than a plausible account of the historical Socrates; and the most obvious reason for this is that it is impossible to say at what point in Plato's dialogues the character called Socrates became merely a mouthpiece for the mature Plato. But so far as the philosophical import of what is said in the dialogues is concerned, this need not trouble us. For a clear pattern of argument can be discerned. In the *Gorgias*, which is certainly a fairly early dialogue, we see Plato set most of his central problems in ethics. In the *Meno* and the *Phaedo* a metaphysical background is being constructed, which in the *Republic* provides an essential part of a proposed solution to problems which are a restatement of those in the *Gorgias*. In the dialogues after the *Republic* there is a sustained critique of the metaphysics, but there are also two substantial afterthoughts on the problems of ethics, the *Philebus*, on pleasure, and the *Laws*.

The *Gorgias* falls into three sections, in each of which Socrates has a different interlocutor, and each of which establishes certain positions once and for all before passing on. The function of the first part is to dispose of the claims of rhetoric to be the τέχνη whereby virtue is taught and also to establish a distinction between two senses of *persuasion*. Gorgias himself is the upholder of the view that rhetoric, as the art of persuasion, is the means to man's supreme good. For the supreme good is freedom ($\grave{\varepsilon}\lambda\varepsilon\upsilon\theta\varepsilon\rho\acute{\iota}\alpha$), and by freedom is meant the freedom to have one's own way in everything. In order to have one's own way in the city-state, one must be able to sway one's fellow citizens. Socrates introduces a distinction between the kind of persuasion which produces knowledge in the man who is persuaded and the kind that does not. In the first case persuasion consists in offering *reasons* for holding a belief, and if the belief is accepted, an account can be given to back it up in terms of those reasons; in the second case persuasion consists in subjecting the audience to a psychological pressure which produces an ungrounded conviction. Now Gorgias makes it plain that rhetoric is persuasion not of the former, but of the latter kind. One of the praises of the orator is that he can persuade audiences upon topics on which he himself is unskilled; Gorgias' example is the success of Themistocles and Pericles in persuading the Athenians to build the docks, harbors, and defense works necessary for Athenian imperialism, although they themselves were politicians and neither naval nor military engineers. Socrates inquires whether the orator needs a knowledge of right and wrong, any more than he needs a knowledge of engineering. Gorgias is not entirely consistent on this point; he appears to suggest that an orator will on occasion need to be a just man, but is vague as to how he may become just. Rhetoric itself he presents as a morally neutral technique which can be used for either right or wrong purposes: to blame a teacher of rhetoric for its misuse by his pupils would be as silly as to blame a teacher of boxing for the uses to which pupils may put their craft afterwards.

The idea that techniques of persuasion are morally neutral is a recurrent one in human society. But in order to hold that such techniques are neutral, it is necessary also to hold that it is morally irrelevant whether a man comes to a given belief by reasoning or in some non-rational way. And in order to hold that this is morally irrelevant, one would have to hold also that a man's exercise of his rationality is irrelevant to his standing as a moral agent, irrelevant, that is, to deciding whether he is entitled to be called "responsible" and his actions "voluntary." Thus different elucidations of the concepts of responsibility and voluntary actions are presupposed by different moral attitudes to the standing of the techniques of persuasion. The philosophical task of elucidation cannot therefore be morally irrelevant. And one of the more obscurantist features of a sophist like Gorgias—and indeed of his later successors among the electioneering politicians of liberal democracy, the advertising executives, and other open and hidden persuaders—is the willingness to assume a whole philosophical psychology. It is this which leads Socrates to develop an argument to show that rhetoric is not a genuine art at all but a mere spurious imitation of an art.

By this time Gorgias has been replaced in the argument by his pupil Polus. Polus reiterates that the moral point of the use of rhetoric is the acquisition of power. The successful orator can do whatever he wants. Socrates' retort to this is that a man may do whatever he thinks it good to do, and nonetheless not be doing what he desires. Here Socrates' point is that where a man does one thing for the sake of another, if he is intellectually mistaken as to the character of the connection between what he does and that for the sake of which he does it, he may in fact be defeating his own ends. The despot who inflicts injury and death upon others may be doing what appears to him to minister to his own good, but he is mistaken. For, says Socrates, it is worse for a man to inflict wrong than to suffer it.

Polus' counterexample is the tyrant Archelaus of Macedon, who had acquired power by successive episodes of treachery and assassination; everybody, says Polus, would like to be Archelaus if he could. Socrates' point is, however, that whether that is what people wish or not is irrelevant. For if that is what they wish, it can only be because of a mistake on their part as to what is for their own good. He now proceeds to convict Polus of such a mistake, but he is able to do so only because of the state of the moral vocabulary which has already been described. Polus is not prepared to admit that it is worse (κακιόν) to inflict injury without due cause than to suffer it, but he is prepared to concede that it is more disgraceful (αἰσχιόν). In order to understand this we must recall the contrast between the pairs of adjectives, good-bad (ἀγαθός-κακός) and honorable-disgraceful (καλός-αἰσχρός). What is καλός is what is well thought of. To be the Athenian ideal of a gentleman (καλὸς κἀγαθός) one had both to be and to be thought good. The reference of καλός and of αἰσχρός is to how a man appears. Polus is prepared to redefine ἀγαθός because the customary sense has become unclear. But because precisely of his commitment to winning popular favor, he is committed to popular estimations of reputation. He cannot commend his own valuations to his hearers unless at some point at least he appears to accept theirs. (This is why Plato is able to observe later in the dialogue that the man who seeks to master the people by persuading them is forced in order to do this to accept their standards and so is mastered by them.)

Polus therefore accepts the view that it is more disgraceful to inflict injury undeservedly than it is to suffer it. But Socrates forces upon him the recognition that the predicates καλός and αἰσχρός are not criterionless. Socrates takes examples of these predicates applied elsewhere (note that once again there is a translation difficulty; καλός means both "beautiful" and "honorable," αἰσχρός both "ugly" and "disgraceful")—namely, to sounds and colors, to ways of life, and to sciences. From these examples he draws the conclusion that we are entitled to call something καλός if it is useful or pleasant, or both, in the eyes of a disinterested spectator. Thus if Polus agrees that to suffer injury undeservedly is more honorable, it must be because it is pleasanter and more beneficial. But for Polus these define the content of "what a man wants," so he can no longer consistently dissent from Socrates' view.

A further very simple conceptual point is at issue here which Plato does not bring out explicitly. Anyone who tries to explain good as meaning "what X thinks to be good" is involved in a vicious—because both vacuous and interminable—regress. For in order to understand this elucidation, we must already understand good in some other way; if not, we are involved in writing out our definition as "what X thinks to be 'what X thinks to be "what X thinks to. . . ."' " Now, to attempt to define moral terms by reference to how people in general define them presupposes likewise that if one is not to be involved in such a regress, one already grasps the moral concepts possessed by people in general. And it is this that traps Polus.

His successor in the dialogue, Callicles, is not prepared to be trapped. He grasps that what betrayed both Polus and Gorgias was their insufficiently systematic redefinition of moral terms. For Callicles the supreme good is power to satisfy all desires. Callicles' position is indeed a complex one. He is contemptuous of the life of theorizing and contemptuous therefore of Socrates. He is involved at once in two disagreements with Socrates. The first is over the concept of desire. Socrates argues that the man of boundless desires is like a leaky sieve, never filled, never satisfied; therefore, to have great and violent desires is to make it certain that you will not get what you want. Unless our desires are delimited, they are not satisfiable. Callicles refuses to accept this. All that we need to do at this point is to underline the fact that the concepts of desire and of satisfaction present problems which Callicles' analysis passes by.

Secondly, when Callicles at an earlier stage in the dialogue proclaimed the right of the strong man to rule, he clearly intended by this to glorify the despot. Socrates, however, points out that the populace are in an obvious sense stronger than the tyrant, and therefore on Callicles' view ought to rule. Callicles has therefore to redefine the concept of the "stronger" as meaning the "more intelligent." And this at once raises for him the problem of what intelligence in a ruler consists in. Before Socrates can compare his answer on this point to that of Callicles, he clarifies certain key philosophical differences between them. The first of Socrates' points is that the pair of concepts "good-bad" differs from the concepts "pleasure-pain" in that the former are contradictories, the latter not. If I assert that something is in some respect good, then it follows that I am committed to the view that the same thing is not bad in the same respect; but according to Socrates if I assert that something is pleasant in some respect, it does not follow that it is not painful or unpleasant in the same respect. This unfortunate argument depends upon a thoroughly misleading example. If I am taking pleasure in eating because I am not yet satisfied, my discomfort at not yet being satisfied and my pleasure coexist. So I enjoy pleasure and pain simultaneously. But of course the pleasure is and derives from one thing, the pain is and derives from another.

The opposite point that Socrates makes is that *good* and *bad* cannot be synonymous with *pleasant* and *painful*, for we use *good* and *bad* in evaluating pleasures and pains. Callicles thinks the good man to be intelligent and courageous. But a coward may feel more relief than a courageous man when danger is avoided, and so more pleasure. Callicles is therefore persuaded to concede a distinction between kinds of pleasure, and this is just what the Platonic Socrates needs. Socrates then develops his own positive view, and in so doing, gains certain permanent ground in moral philosophy. Callicles' ideal is of a good which consists in the pursuit of one's desires without limit. Socrates had already suggested that limitless desire is unsatisfiable desire; now he argues that the concept of good is necessarily bound up with the concept of observing a limit. And anything that is to count as a "way of living" will necessarily have some order or form, by which we can distinguish it from other ways of living. So any good which we desire can only be specified by specifying the rules which would govern the behavior which would be or procure that particular good.

Toward the close of the *Gorgias* there are two other important moments. One is when Socrates attacks bitterly the line of Athenian statesmen from Miltiades to Pericles whose expansionist policies taught the Athenians to have desires without teaching them the connection between the goods they might desire and the rule-governed order within which alone goods can be realized. The second is the discussion of the religious myth of judgment and punishment in the after-life; with this myth, Plato symbolizes what is at stake in the choice between different fundamental moral attitudes. Both the political and the religious attitudes exemplified here are recurrent features of Plato's thought which are treated very misleadingly if conceived of as external to his moral analyses. But in order to understand why this is so, we should have to examine the political and metaphysical background to the dialogues more fully, and before doing this, it is perhaps worth reiterating in summary form a number of conclusions toward which an inspection of the arguments in the *Gorgias* tends to push us.

The first of these is that the advice "Do whatever you want to" is necessarily useless except in a severely restricted context. When Socrates says that unquenchable desire is unsatisfiable desire, this is not just a matter of there being always something more that is desired. Rather it is that a desire is only satisfiable if it is given a specified object. When we say to people, "Do whatever you want," this makes sense where there are a number of clearly defined alternatives and we do not wish our preferences to weigh with the agent. But to say to the agent who asks the general moral questions, How shall I live? what shall I do?, "Do whatever you want to", specifies no goal to be pursued. The problem is to know which wants to pursue, which to discourage, and so on. The correct retort to the injunction "Gather ye rosebuds while ye may" is, Which rosebuds?

It is a companion error to suppose in any case that my wants are given, fixed, and determinate, while my choices are free. My wants are not simply determinative of my choices; they are often enough the material on which choice has to be exercised. This is blurred by conceiving of moral concepts as part of the realm of convention, but of desires as part of nature. Socrates does not of course pursue any of these points, and he does not answer his own question any more than Gorgias answered it. What he does is to state one necessary condition for an answer to the question, What does a good consist in? The answer is that if anything is to be a good, and a possible object of desire, it must be specifiable in terms of some set of rules which might govern behavior. The Calliclean injunction to break all rules—if you want to, that is—does not make sense. For a man whose behavior was not rule-governed in any way would have ceased to participate as an intelligible agent in human society.

This is brought out not only by the content of the *Gorgias* but also by its form. Even Callicles and Socrates share certain concepts, and the dialogue form brings out the way in which it is this sharing which enables Socrates to bring home to Callicles the internal incoherence of Callicles' view. This suggests that badness consists in a breach with a form of life in which certain goods can be attained, for to share concepts is always to share a form of life to some degree. And indeed Socrates affirms explicitly in the *Gorgias* that what the bad man lacks is an ability to κοινωνειν, to share a common life (κοινωνειν). Thus a necessary step forward in specifying what is good is to specify the kind of common life necessary for the good to be realized. This is the task of the *Republic*.

# 5

## PLATO: THE *REPUBLIC*

The *Republic* opens with a request for a definition of δικαιοσύνη, and the first book clarifies the nature of this request. The definition of justice as "telling the truth and paying one's debts" is rejected, not only because it may sometimes be right to withhold the truth or not to return what one has borrowed, but because no list of types of action could supply what Plato is demanding. What he wants to know is what it is about an action or class of actions which leads us to call it just. He wants not a list of just actions, but a criterion for inclusion in or exclusion from such a list. Again, a definition of justice as "doing good to one's friends and harm to one's enemies" is rejected not just because of the argument that to harm someone would be to make him worse—that is, more unjust—with the consequence that the just man would be involved in making men less just, but because any definition of justice in terms of "doing good" and the like is bound to be unilluminating. When Thrasymachus comes upon the scene he tells Socrates that Socrates is not to offer him a definition which tells him that justice is "the same as what is obligatory or useful or advantageous or profitable or expedient." Socrates retorts that this is like asking what 12 is and refusing to accept any answer of the form that it is twice 6, or 3 times 4, or 6 times 2, or 4 times 3. But Socrates does accept the task of offering a quite different kind of elucidation; it would be a mistake to suppose that when Socrates does offer us a formula, namely that justice is that state of affairs in which everyone has regard to his own concerns, this is in itself the answer that was being sought. This formula is unintelligible apart from the rest of the *Republic*, and Thrasymachus is right to suppose that the search for expressions synonymous with δικαιοσύνη would not be to the point. For to be puzzled about a concept is not like being puzzled about the meaning of an expression in a foreign language. To offer a verbal equivalent to an expression about whose meaning we are conceptually puzzled will not help us, for if what we are offered is a genuinely synonymous expression, then all that puzzled us originally will puzzle us in the translation. To understand a concept, to grasp the meaning of an expression, is partially, but crucially to grasp its functions, to understand what can and cannot be done with and through it. Moreover, we cannot decide what words are to mean, or what role concepts are to play, by fiat. We may on occasion wish to introduce a new concept and so legislate as to the meaning of a new expression; but what we can say in a given situation is limited by the common stock of concepts and the common grasp of their functions. No objection to the *Republic* is therefore more misconceived than that which would have been made by Humpty Dumpty ("When I use a word . . . it means just what I choose it to mean—neither more nor less")[14] and which was in fact made by Professor Karl Popper when he wrote, "But was Plato perhaps right? Does 'justice' perhaps mean what he says? I do not intend to discuss such a question. . . . I believe that nothing depends upon words, and everything upon our practical demands or decisions."[15] The point I have tried to make is that only those demands and decisions are open to us which there are concepts available to express, and that therefore the investigation of what concepts we either must or may use is crucial.

Thrasymachus' own elucidation of the concept of justice is as follows. He does not believe that "just" *means* "What is to the interest of the stronger"; but he does believe that, as a matter of historical fact, rulers and ruling classes invented the concept and the standards of justice for their own purposes, and that it is in fact more profitable to do what is unjust rather than just. Socrates' initial probing of Thrasymachus' position is highly reminiscent of the *Gorgias*. He questions the concept of "the stronger" just as he did before, and he argues that the τέχνη of ruling, on the analogy of the τέχνη of medi-cine, must, if it is true art, be practiced for the benefit of those upon whom it is exercised. Medicine is for the benefit of patients, not for that of doctors, and so ruling must be for the benefit of the people, not of the rulers. But this thoroughly ineffectual analogy only belongs to the preliminary sparring. The position that Socrates had finally restated in the *Gorgias* is one which can be strikingly attacked from Thrasyma-chus' premises, and is so attacked by Socrates' own disciples Glaucon and Adeimantus. But before Socrates completes the reiteration of his earlier attack on unlimited self-assertion—that restraint within the per-sonality and between people is a condition of their well-being—he invokes the concept of ἀρετή, and the notion that there is a specifically human virtue, to exercise which will be to be in a state of well-being or happiness. Ἀρετή belongs now not to a man's specific social function, but to his function as a man. The connection between virtue and hap-piness is written into this concept in what initially must seem an arbi-trary way; the rest of the argument of the *Republic* is an attempt to remove this arbitrariness.

The revival of Thrasymachus' case by Glaucon and Adeimantus runs as follows. Men in a state of nature are moved entirely by self-interest; the origin of laws lies in the moment when men discovered and agreed that clashes of self-interest were so damaging that it was more to their interest to forego doing injury to others than to continue in their natural way of life, so risking any injury that others might do to them. And ever since, men have obeyed the law only from fear of con-sequences; if men could avoid suffering the ill consequences of their actions, unlimited self-love would manifest itself openly instead of in law-abiding disguises. Suppose two men, one man now apparently just, the other unjust, were given a magic ring such as Gyges had to make himself invisible, so that both had complete liberty of action; then both would behave in the same way. They would, like Gyges, who seduced his queen and murdered his king, pursue the path of complete self-aggrandizement. That is, everyone prefers injustice to justice if he can be unjust successfully.

This example depends on that fallacious portrait of the presocial, natural man which I have already criticized. For Plato's suggestion is that perhaps Gyges with his ring is natural man. The superiority of the present case over that originally put into the mouth of Thrasymachus is that Plato now turns sharply toward the identification of self-interest as a trait in social and not merely in natural man. He makes Adeimantus stress that the conventionally virtuous and just citizen is on the side of Thrasymachus, not of Socrates. For the Greek equivalent of the bourgeois father teaches his children to pursue virtue and to flee vice precisely and only because vitrue brings rewards and vice has unfortunate consequences both in this world and in the next. But if these are the only reasons for praising virtue, how can justice in itself and apart from any rewards, be more profitable than injustice?

Plato's answer is to try to show what justice is, first in the state, and then in the soul. He outlines a state in which all basic needs are met. Three classes of citizen are required: artisans and laborers to produce the material needs of society; soldiers to defend the state; and rulers to organize its social life. The key transition here is from recognizing three functions which have to be discharged in social life to asserting that three distinct and separate classes of citizens are needed, one to discharge each function. Plato relies for this transition upon two beliefs, one not certainly true, and one certainly false. The belief which is not certainly true is that one man is better to stick to one job, that this form of the division of labor is under all possible circumstances the best form; the belief which is certainly false is that men are by nature divided up into men best suited for each of these functions. Of this belief it might just be noted that it is invoked most often by those who believe that people like themselves are well suited to rule, while others are not; and that it ignores the fact that most people have different capacities which do not exclude one another, let alone the fact that in existing societies most abilities of most people are unrealized. But Plato's beliefs on this point were powerfully reinforced by his doctrine of the tripartite soul.

The arguments for the tripartite soul are independent of those for the tripartite state, but it is necessary for the doctrine of the tripartite state that at least something like the doctrine of the tripartite soul should be true. That the soul has parts is shown, according to Plato, by the fact that it has conflicts. If a given man desires to drink (because he is thirsty) and does not desire to drink (because he suspects the condition of the water) at one and the same time, then, since the same predicate cannot both hold and not hold of the same subject in the same respect at one and the same time, there must be at least two different subjects, of one of which we are predicating the desire to drink and of the other of which we are predicating the desire not to drink. The assumption which underlies this argument is that a man cannot simultaneously desire to do something and desire not to do it, in the same sense in which a man cannot simultaneously move in a given direction and not move in that direction. But where desires are concerned a man may desire some end, envisaged under a particular description, and not desire it under some other description. So a man may want to drink the water, because he is thirsty, but want not to drink, in case he risks an illness. It might perhaps seem that the short way to escape Plato's argument here is to say that the man just does not have incompatible desires. He desires to quench his thirst, and he desires not to be ill, and it is merely a contingent fact that this water would both quench his thirst and make him ill. But to this the rejoinder might be that his desires remain incompatible: for what the man desires is *to drink this particular water* and what he fears is *to drink this same water.* Yet Plato is only right in a sense about these being incompatible desires, and that they are does not have any of the consequences which he supposes to follow. And this is because the incompatibility belongs to the possibility of satisfying both desires, not of having both desires. This is important because Plato uses his bad argument to expound a distinction between that part of the soul which is the appetites and that part which is the reason, a distinction which exerts enormous pressure upon some subsequent moral philosophy.

Plato's picture of the parts of the soul is not in fact coherent. Sometimes he speaks as though the rational part of the soul had one set of desires and the appetitive part another; at other times, as if the appetites were the desires, and reason essentially a check and restraint upon them. He speaks as though the desire to drink was a nonrational craving, the apprehension of danger from drinking an insight of reason. But in fact we do not first have desires and then afterwards reason about them; we learn—and we use our reason in learning—to desire certain things (Plato does not distinguish the biologically determined appetite from the conscious human desire), and the desire to quench one's thirst is as rational as the desire not to be injured by poison in the water. It is just not true that only our restraint upon ourselves derives from reflection; it is often upon reflection that we decide that we need to drink. An irrational fear of being poisoned might be checked by a reasonable desire to quench one's thirst, just as much as vice versa—an irrational desire to quench one's thirst might be inhibited by a rational fear of poison. What makes a desire reasonable or unreasonable is its relation to our other purposes and choices, possible as well as actual. A man may behave unreasonably by not allowing his desires play, and desire may on occasion correct an agent's would-be rational assessments. But these facts Plato, and a long tradition which is to follow him, rule out of court in order to maintain that rigid division between reason and the appetites in which reason is always to be in the right.

The original source of this distinction is of course not in Plato's own arguments from the alleged facts of conflict, but in his inherited Pythagorean and Orphic beliefs in the separation of an immortal soul from a body that is a prison and a tomb. But later writers, who might have been unimpressed by the religious doctrine, have still been content with the philosophical distinction. Plato himself gives a far more interesting and positive account of desire in the *Symposium*; but even here desire leads us away from this world in the end.

Plato's doctrinal allegiances lead him in the *Republic* not merely to draw false conclusions from the facts of conflict but also, as I have just suggested, to misdescribe them. The essence of conflict of desire is that it provides an occasion for choice on my part between my desires, even if I do not choose. But Plato's division of the soul into parts makes conflict a tug of war, which could not be an occasion for choice. "I" am not confronted with my desires. "I" am split between two autonomous parties, reason and appetite; or else "I" am reason, struggling against appetite. Nor is Plato consistent here with his other writings. The Greek word for *soul*, ψοχή, means originally simply that which makes the difference between life and death, between a man and a corpse. Some early Greek thinkers identify the soul with a material substance; the Pythagoreans with a harmony between the elements of the body, a balance. Plato argues against both in the *Phaedo* that the soul is an immaterial simple substance; that to be destroyed is to be divided up into parts; and that since the soul has no parts it must be immortal. Appetite in the *Phaedo* belongs to the body, so that the distinction between reason and appetite remains a constant element, pointing to the continuity of the religious background. But the *Phaedo* offers us no grounds for believing in the division into parts of the soul.

The division of the soul in the *Republic* is not just between reason and appetite; there is also the "spirited" part, which is concerned neither with rational standards of behavior nor with bodily desires, but with standards of honorable behavior, and with anger and indignation. Plato tells the story of Leontius, who, overcome with desire, stares at the corpses of executed criminals, cursing himself as he does so. The Platonic moral is that anger and appetite can conflict. The spirited part of the soul acts, when "it is not corrupted by a bad upbringing," as an agent of reason, being indignant when reason is overborne. So a man who has been wronged feels indignant, but a man who feels that he is in the wrong cannot find it in his nature to be indignant if he is made to suffer in turn. So Plato says.

Men therefore fall into three classes depending upon which part of the soul is dominant; this division is that required by the tripartite state. Into which class a man falls may in part be a matter of his early training, but cannot fundamentally be so determined. Plato believes that there are born shoemakers and born rulers. Justice in the state is a matter of everyone knowing his place. Of the four traditional virtues, courage belongs to the class of auxiliary guardians whose function is defense, and wisdom to the ruling guardians. Temperance is a virtue not of a class, but of the society as a whole because "the desires of the inferior multitude will be controlled by the desires and wisdom of the superior few." Justice belongs not to this nor to that class, nor to particular relationships between classes, but to the society's functioning as a whole.

Justice in the soul is likewise a matter of each part of the soul performing its proper and allotted function. An individual is wise in virtue of reason ruling in him and brave in virtue of the spirited part playing its role; an individual is temperate if his inferior bodily appetites are ruled by his reason. But justice belongs not to this or that part or relationship of the soul, but to its total ordering. The two questions then arise, What sort of man will be just? and, How could the just state come about? These questions are asked and answered together, and this is no accident. When, later on, Plato comes to discuss the corruption of state and soul he treats them as belonging together. Moreover, the just man will rarely exist except in the just state, where at least some men—the future rulers—are systematically educated in justice. But the just state cannot possibly exist except where there are just men. So the questions of how the state can come to be and of how the just man is to be educated have to be posed together. And so we reach the point where Plato brings on stage the ideal of the philosopher-king.

Plato defines a philosopher by setting out an account of knowledge and belief and then contrasting the philosopher, who knows, with the nonphilosophical man, who at best has only true belief or opinion. The argument begins from considering the meaning of pairs of predicates, and the examples used are beautiful and ugly, just and unjust, and good and bad. Plato says that "Since beautiful and ugly are opposite, they are two; and so each of them is one."[16] But many things exhibit beauty and many things are ugly. So that there is a difference between those who are aware of this or that object as beautiful and those who grasp what "beautiful itself" is. I use this expression "beautiful itself" ("αὐτὸ τὸ καλόν") to translate Plato's innovating use of *itself* to convert an adjective into an expression that names what the adjective is supposed to mean or stand for. And I use the expression "mean or stand for" not because I want to mislead the reader into supposing that "meaning" and "standing for" are the same, but because Plato makes just this mistake. The identification comes about in this way. Plato contrasts the man who uses the word beautiful in an ordinary, confused way with the man who has really grasped what beautiful means, and he interprets this contrast as the contrast between the man who happens to be acquainted with a number of beautiful objects and the man who is acquainted with that which beautiful stands for. The former man is in possession only of "belief"; his judgments are not reinforced by a well-grounded understanding of the meaning of the expression which he uses. The latter is in possession of knowledge; for he really understands what he says.

Knowledge (ἐπιστήμη) and belief or opinion (δόξα) can then be defined in terms of contrasting classes of objects. Belief is concerned with the world of sense perception and of change. Of this fleeting and evanescent realm we can have at best only true opinion. Knowledge is concerned with unchanging objects, about which we can have secure, rationally founded views. Plato's distinction between knowledge and belief is a complex one. In part it is a straightforward distinction between those convictions which, because they are acquired by reasoning and backed up by argument, are not at the mercy of clever orators (that is, knowledge) and those convictions which, being a matter of nonrational conditioning anyway, are liable to change whenever subject to the techniques of nonrational persuasion (that is, belief). But clearly this distinction has nothing to do with the subject matter of our beliefs. It concerns rather the different ways in which individuals may acquire and hold their beliefs. Why, then, should Plato suppose that his distinction is one of subject matter? The reason is that Plato thought himself to have independent grounds for believing that no secure, rationally grounded judgments could be made about the subject matter afforded by sense perception. Some of these grounds were derived from earlier philosophers. Both Heraclitus and Protagoras had emphasized the relativity of judgments of sense perception. But the point that Plato is concerned to make can be detached from the detail of their particular doctrines.

If I can say of quite different objects that they are beautiful, and of the same object at one time or from one point of view that it is beautiful and at another time or from another point of view that it is ugly, then the meaning of the predicates *beautiful* and *ugly* cannot be explained simply by referring to the objects to which they are applied. This is not just because, as Plato pointed out in the passage cited earlier, the objects are many and the meaning single; it is also because the judgments are liable to variation, and to contradiction by other judgments, whereas the one thing that does not vary is the meaning. To put it in a much later mode of speech, Plato is engaged in elucidating what is involved in describing two or more uses of an expression as instances of the use of one and the same predicate. The difference from Socrates is that Socrates saw only that the use of ethical predicates must be governed by criteria; whereas Plato supposed that if this is to be so, that if there are to be objective standards for the use of such predicates, it must be the case that such predicates are used to refer to objects, and objects belonging not to the multifarious, changing world of sense, but to another, unchanging world, apprehended by the intellect precisely through its dialectical ascent, whereby it grasps the meaning of abstract nouns, and of other general terms. These objects are the Forms, through the imitation of which or participation in which the objects of sense perception have the characters that they have.

The philosopher is the man who has learned through a training in abstraction to acquaint himself with the Forms. He alone therefore really understands the meaning of predicates, and he alone has genuinely founded moral and political views. His training is primarily in geometry and in dialectic. By dialectic Plato understands a process of rational argument which is a development from the dialogue of the Socratic interrogation. Beginning from some proposition which has been advanced for consideration, one ascends in one's search for justifications up a deductive ladder until one reaches the indubitable certainties of the Forms. What Plato presents in the *Republic* is a progress in rational argument, culminating in a vision of the Form of the Good (that is, in a vision of what the predicate *good* stands for—that in virtue of which it has meaning). In the *Republic* there is, too, a strongly religious attitude toward the supreme Form, the Form of the Good. The Form of the Good is not one among the other Forms we contemplate: they belong to the realm of unchanging existence—the Form of the Good dwells beyond existence. Just as it is that by virtue of the sun's light we see everything else, but if we look into the sun itself we are dazzled, so it is that in the intellectual light given out by the Form of the Good we grasp the other Forms, but we cannot contemplate the Form of the Good itself.

*Good*, then, for Plato—at least in the *Republic*—is only used properly when it is used as the name of a transcendent entity or when it is used to express the relation of other things to that entity. The difficulties in Plato's conception of Forms were first formulated by Plato himself in later dialogues; at the moment we need only note that to suppose that there are Forms does not in fact do anything to solve the problem which Plato is posing in the *Republic*—that of how a predicate with a single meaning can be applied in many different ways and to many different subjects. For to say that a predicate derives its meaning from one primary case leaves it entirely obscure as to how this predicate is then capable of being applied in other cases. But just this was what we wanted to know. Moreover, we are at once involved in logical oddity. For if this is how we answer our problem, we are involved in saying that the primary application of *beautiful* is to the Form of Beauty, that of *high* to the Form of Height, and so on. But to say that "Beauty is beautiful" or that "Height is high" is clearly not to speak with a clear meaning. This fact Plato himself brought out in later criticisms of his own position.

What is important is that the theory of meaning has been decisively brought on the scene. The logician has entered moral philosophy for good. But even though, from now on, the systematic and self-conscious logical analysis of moral concepts will be at the heart of moral philosophy, it can nonetheless never be the whole of moral philosophy. For we have to understand not only the logical interrelations of moral concepts, rules, and the like but also the point and purpose such rules serve. This involves us both in the theory of human purposes and motives and in the theory of society, since different kinds of wants and needs are dominant in different social orders. We can see all three interests, the epistemological, the psychological, and the political, meeting in the central parts of the *Republic*. For Plato's first theory, that we can understand what goodness is, what justice is, what courage is, and so on, by seeing them exhibited in a certain type of state and a certain type of soul, now has to be reconciled with Plato's second theory, that we can only understand what goodness, justice, and the rest of them are if we become acquainted with the relevant Forms. However, not only is a reconciliation not difficult, but it enables Plato to make his earlier contentions more cogent. The rulers of the just state, in whom the rule of reason is present, are rational in virtue of an education which has enabled them to apprehend the Forms. In the just state the philosopher is king; only he can bring into being and maintain in being a state in which justice is embodied *both* in the political arrangements *and* in the soul. It follows that the class division of the just society can, as Plato had earlier suggested, be maintained by *educating* some to be rulers, others to be auxiliaries, most to be ruled; the use of eugenic controls and selection methods is to insure that those fit for the education of rulers receive it. To make the common people content they will be told a story about the metals in the soul: precious in the souls of rulers, base in the souls of the ruled. Plato does not believe in a correlation between intelligence and some merely accidental property, such as a color of the skin, in the way that racists in South Africa and

Mississippi believe; he does, however, believe in the occurrence of inborn intelligence, or the lack of it, in the way that conservative educationalists do; and he believes that ingenious propaganda—the telling of what he calls "noble lies"—can insure that inferior people will accept the fact of their own inferiority.

Those of superior intelligence proceed to the vision of the Forms in ways that Plato delineates by means of two different parables, that of the Line and that of the Cave. The Line is divided horizontally; below the division lie the realms of imagining and perceiving, while above it lie those of mathematical entities—which for Plato are closely related to Forms—and of the Forms. The passages about the Cave picture men chained so that they cannot see the daylight; behind them a fire and a puppet show are so contrived that the prisoners see a procession of shadows on the wall. They believe that the words in their language refer to the shadows and that the shadows are the sole reality. A man who escaped from the Cave would slowly accustom himself to the light of the world outside. He would pick out, first, shadows and reflections; then physical objects; and finally, the heavenly bodies and the sun. This is for Plato a parable of the ascent to the Forms. The man who returns to the Cave will be unaccustomed to the darkness; he will not for some time identify the shadows in the Cave as well as do those of his former companions who never left the darkness; and he will cause great resentment by his subsequent claims that the shadows are devised and unreal and that the true reality lies outside the Cave. So great will the resentment be, that if the chained men could, they would kill this man from the outer world—precisely as the Athenians killed Socrates.

What, then, is the philosopher who has ascended to the Forms to do? It will only be at the rarest moments in history, and possibly it will never happen at all, that he will have the possibility of intervening to create the just state. Plato himself, first in his response to the Athenians' treatment of Socrates, and then in his own disillusionment with the tyrannical rulers of Syracuse, has a deep pessimism about political life. But if the ideal state can never become real, what was the point of depicting it? Plato's answer is that it provides a standard against which we can judge actual states. This is part of what Plato himself is doing when he pictures a series of stages of decline from the ideal state and from the just soul; in so doing he brings out further the intrinsic connection which he believes to hold between politics and psychology.

The first stage in decline is the timocratic state; here the military and the guardians have fallen out, and the state is based on the military values of honor with some infusion of the values of private property. The next stage, the oligarchical, is one in which the class structure is maintained only in the interest of the ruling class, and not at all in the interest of the whole state; the rich use the class structure to exploit the poor. In the third phase the poor revolt and create a democracy, in which every citizen is equally free to pursue his will and his personal aggrandizement, while finally the would-be despot is able to enlist from such a democracy enough dissatisfied malcontents to create a tyranny. Plato's aim here is at least twofold; he has placed the actual forms of constitution of Greek city-states upon a moral scale, so that even if we cannot have the ideal, we know that timocracy (traditional Sparta) is best, oligarchy (Corinth) and democracy (Athens) worse, and tyranny (Syracuse) worst of all. But his argument also brings out that one reason why they can be morally evaluated is because to each type of constitution a type of personality corresponds. In timocracy the appetites are restrained and ordered, but not by reason. Honor instead has this role. In oligarchy they are still disciplined, but only by the love of wealth and a regard for stability which springs from a regard for property. In democracy every taste, every inclination has equal sway in the personality. And in tyranny—in the men with despotic souls—the baser appetites, that is the bodily ones, exercise absolute and irrational control. Plato now uses this classification of personality types in order to return to the question of the justification of justice in the form in which Glaucon and Adeimantus had raised it. To do this Plato compares the external and opposed positions of the just man and the despotic man, who now turns out to be the extreme personality type of the unjust man.

Plato has three arguments to show that the just life is happier than the unjust one. The first is that the unjust man sets no curb upon his desires, and so his desires are without limit. But, being limitless, his desires can never be satisfied, and so he will always be discontented. The second argument is that only the philosopher is in a position to contrast the pleasures of reason with those of limitless appetite and sensuality, for he alone knows both sides. Finally, it is argued that the pleasures of intellect are genuine, while what the man of appetite takes to be pleasure is often merely a cessation of pain or discomfort (as eating relieves hunger) and at best far less real (in terms of the notion of the real as the unchanging and immaterial) than what the intellect delights in. These are bad arguments. The third depends for part of what it seeks to prove upon the arguments about the Forms, and it in any case ignores—with Plato's characteristic and utterly deplorable puritanism—the many genuine bodily pleasures; the second is simply false—even in Plato's terms the philosopher is no more acquainted with the pleasures of limitless desire than the sensualist is with the delights of rational control; while the first argument fallaciously infers from the premise that the sensualist will always have appetites which have not yet been satisfied the conclusion that he will always be and feel unsatisfied and dissatisfied. But it is not the badness of the particular arguments that is so important. Given Plato's psychology, only bad arguments were available to him. For the complete divorce of reason and desire in the soul entails that the contrast has to be between reason on the one hand and senseless and uncontrolled appetite on the other. These are the only alternatives available, given the Platonic psychology; but in fact they are not, of course, the only or even the most important alternatives. In order to vindicate justice against injustice, Plato accepts the criterion implied by Thrasymachus' exaltation of successful worldly, and especially, successful political ambition—the vulgar criterion of pleasure—and argues that the unjust but successful tyrant has less pleasure, is more discontented, than the just man, even than the just man unjustly done to death. But to do this, he has to equate the unjust man with the man who pursues pleasure limitlessly and senselessly. And Plato has to make this equation, since reason, in the Platonic scheme, can only dominate, not inform or guide, appetite, and appetite of itself is essentially irrational. The man who in fact threatens the prestige of justice is not the senseless sensualist or the unchecked tyrant, but much more often l'*homme moyen sensuel*, the man who is everything, including unjust and vicious, in moderation, the man whose reason restrains his vice today in the interests, not of virtue, but of vice tomorrow. This is the man who praises virtue for what he can get out of it in the way of wealth, office, and reputation, and this is the man whom Glaucon and Adeimantus had in mind. This was why the case that Glaucon and Adeimantus propounded was so much more of a threat to Plato than the case put by Thrasymachus. But Plato's conceptual scheme tempts him into considering this man, whom he observes and describes with tolerable accuracy in the oligarchical and democratic states, as merely a less extreme version of despotic man. But despotic man is drawn so extremely that what is described is no longer a possible moral type. I can be said to pursue pleasure only if I am pursuing identifiable goals and making choices between alternatives in terms of them. The man who can no longer make choices but passes on heedlessly and inevitably from one action to the next is not a possible normal human type, but rather a compulsive neurotic. And this may have been what Plato wished to describe, for he very strikingly connects the behavior of this man with the pursuit of those fantasies of which most men are conscious only in dreams, thus strikingly anticipating Freud. But any classification which entails making the way of life of *l'homme moyen sensuel* merely a moderate version of the compulsive behavior of the neurotic, and lumps both together in contrast with rationality, is thereby condemned as a classification. Nor does the myth with which the *Republic* closes help Plato. For the suggestion that in the realm after death the just will be rewarded and the unjust punished appropriately depends for its force upon the notion that justice is indeed superior to injustice, that the just man *deserves* his reward and the unjust his punishment. So that the question of the justification of justice is still left without a clear answer. A very brief reconsideration of the central arguments of the *Republic* makes it clear why on Plato's terms this has to be so.

The argument begins from the need for an understanding of the meaning of ethical predicates apart from their particular applications. This starting point will recur in the history of philosophy in writers as different from Plato as St. Augustine and Wittgenstein. When we inquire about what it is for something to be just or red or equal, the rational first move is to offer examples, to try and give a list of just actions or red objects or cases of equality. But such a list misses the point of the inquiry. What we want to know is not which actions are just, but what it is in virtue of which actions are just. What is it that enables us to mark off those cases which genuinely belong on our list from those that do not? We need a criterion. Wittgenstein will suggest that the criterion is embodied in a rule, and the rule in a socially established practice. Augustine will suggest that the criterion is given by an interior illumination which is a gift of God. Plato finds his criterion in the knowledge of the Forms. But knowledge of the Forms is accessible only to a few, and only to those few who have either enjoyed the educational disciplines of the as yet nonexistent ideal state or are among the very rare natures which are both philosophically capable and inclined and also not corrupted by the social environment. It follows not only that only these few will be able to perform the task of justifying justice but also that only to them will the justification be intelligible and convincing. Thus the social order which the Platonic concept of justice enjoins could only be accepted by the majority of mankind as a result of the use of nonrational persuasion (or force).

Everything therefore turns for Plato on the possibility of establishing, first, that there are Forms and that knowledge of them has the role which he claims, and second, that only a minority are capable of this knowledge. The latter is merely asserted and never argued for. The former depends upon arguments about which Plato himself, as we shall see, came to have serious doubts. But behind all Plato's explicit statements there lies a further assumption which must now be brought into the open.

We speak of justification in at least two radically different types of context. Within a discipline like geometry the justification of a theorem consists in showing how it follows validly from the axioms. There is no question here of what counts as a justification for one person not counting as a justification to another. Within the field of conduct, however, this is not so. To justify one course of action as against another is not only to show that it accords with some standard or conduces to some end but also to show this to someone who accepts the relevant standard or shares the particular end. In other words, justifications of this type are always justifications to somebody. Aristotle later tries to show how there are certain specifically human ends in the light of which policies of action can be justified to rational beings as such. But Plato restricts the class to whom his justifications can be addressed to those who have acquired knowledge of the Forms. When, subsequently, he discusses the justification of justice in terms independent of this knowledge, that is in the passages where he compares types of state and of soul, he in fact falls back on comparisons, half a priori, half empirical, which are bound on his own terms to founder—for they presumably belong to the world of opinion, of δόξα, not of ἐπιστήμη, of knowledge—except against the background of a transcendental knowledge which has been pointed to but never brought on the scene.

One root of Plato's mistake here is his confusion of the kind of justification which is in place in geometry with that which is in place in matters of conduct. To treat *justice* and *good* as the names of Forms is to miss at once one essential feature of justice and goodness—namely, that they characterize not what is, but what ought to be. Sometimes what ought to be is, but more often not. And it always makes sense to ask of any existing object or state whether it is as it ought to be. But justice and goodness could not be objects or states of affairs about which it would make sense to inquire in this way. Aristotle was to make very much this criticism of Plato; Plato's own blindness to it is one contributory factor to his curious combination of an apparent total certitude as to what goodness and justice are, and a willingness to impose his own certitudes upon others, with a use of profoundly unsatisfactory arguments to support his convictions.

# 6

---

# POSTSCRIPT TO PLATO

The difficulty of the *Republic* lies in part in the fact that Plato tries to achieve so much in so little space. The question, What is justice? is originally put as a simple request for a definition; but it becomes an attempt to characterize both a virtue which can be manifested in individual lives *and* a form of political life in which virtuous men will be at home, insofar as they can ever be at home in the world of change and of unreality. Both have already been described in the course of outlining the arguments of the *Republic*; what remains is to stress their internal connection. For in fact Plato's morals and Plato's politics are closely interdependent. Each logically requires to be completed by the other. We can best understand that this is so by examining the structure of two dialogues of Plato, one wholly devoted to the question of how the individual should live, and the other entirely concerned with politics. In each case we shall discover that the argument ends in mid-air, and that we are forced to look elsewhere for a complementary argument. The first of these dialogues is the *Symposium*, a work which belongs to the same middle period of Plato's life as the *Republic* does; the second is the *Laws*, which was written at the very end of Plato's life. Socrates is the central character of the *Symposium*, and this is moreover the pre-Platonic Socrates, the teacher of Alcibiades and the target for Aristophanes. By the time of the *Laws* Socrates is no longer present in the dialogue at all.

This in itself emphasizes the sharp contrast: the agnostic Socrates would never have set himself up as a legislator.

The *Symposium* is an account of a drinking party to celebrate Agathon's victory in a dramatic competition. The guests compete, too, in making speeches about the nature of ἔρως, sometimes translated as "love." But if it is so translated, one must recall that ἔρως hovers halfway between *love* and *desire*, and that the pre-Socratic philosophers had made it the name for whatever impulses drive all beings in nature toward their goals as well as for the specifically human impulses to grasp and to possess. In the *Symposium* Aristophanes explains ἔρως by an extended joke, a myth about human origins. Men originally had four arms, four legs, and so on—were, indeed, like two of our present human beings fastened together. Being far stronger and more adroit like this than they are now, they threatened the hegemony of the gods, who overcame this threat by an act of separation. Ever since, men, being but half-beings, have wandered through the world searching for the being who will complete them. The difference between hetero-sexual and homosexual love is explained with reference to the sort of being which was originally divided in two, and hence to the sort of being each individual needs to complete his nature. (We may note that this is also used to explain what is taken for granted by all the characters, the superiority of homosexual to heterosexual love).

Ἔρως is thus desire for what we do not possess. The lover is a man who is unsatisfied. But is love in fact such that we can only love what we do not have? Socrates in his speech recounts the doctrine into which he was initiated by the priestess Diotima.

Ἔρως, according to her account, is a desire which will not be satis-fied by any particular object in the world. The lover ascends from the love of particular beautiful objects and people to the love of αὐτὸ τὸ καλόν, beauty itself, and at this point the lover's search is accom-plished, because this is the good which the soul seeks. The object of desire is what is good, but *good* does not mean, is not defined as, "what the soul desires." "There is certainly a doctrine by which lovers are men searching for the other half of themselves; but on my view love is not desire either of the half or of the whole, unless that half or whole happens to be good." Good therefore is not just that which we happen to desire at any given moment; it is that which would satisfy us, and which would continue to satisfy us once we had made the ascent of abstraction from particulars to the Form of the Beautiful. This ascent has to be learned; even Socrates had to receive this account from Diotima. In the *Symposium* itself Plato draws no political morals from this; but what morals could be drawn if we were to accept what is said in the *Symposium*?

The good can be achieved only through an education of a particular kind, and if this education is to be available to more than a random selection of mankind, it will have to be institutionalized. What is more, the institutions of the educational system will have to be directed and controlled by those who have already made the prerequisite ascent from the vision of particulars to the vision of the Forms. Thus, from the *Symposium* with its entirely nonpolitical argument—the dialogue ends with everyone else drunk and asleep while Socrates explains at dawn to a barely awake Agathon and Aristophanes that the man with a genius for tragedy must also have a genius for comedy and vice versa—we can infer a picture of a society with an educational system directed from the top.

Everything of course depends upon the connection between good and the Forms. Plato's first correct insight is that we use the concept of good in order to evaluate and grade possible objects of desire and aspiration. Hence the also correct conclusion that *good* cannot simply mean "what men desire." His second correct insight is that the good must therefore be what is worth pursuing and desiring; it must be a possible and an outstanding object of desire. But his false conclusion is that the good must therefore be found among the transcendental, out-of-this-world objects, the Forms, and hence that the good is not something that ordinary people can seek out for themselves in the daily transactions of this life. Either knowledge of the good is communicated by a special religious revelation (as it is by the priestess Diotima to Socrates) or it is to be reached by a long intellectual discipline at the hands of authoritative teachers (as in the *Republic*).

The Forms are important to Plato both for religious and for logical reasons. They provide us both with an eternal world not subject to change and decay and with an account of the meaning of predicative expressions. Therefore, when Plato encountered radical difficulties in the theory of Forms he reached a point of crisis in his philosophical development. The most central of these difficulties appears in the dialogue called the *Parmenides* and is presented in the so-called Third Man argument. Where we have two (or more) objects to which the same predicate applies, because they share a common characteristic, we apply that predicate in virtue of the fact that both objects resemble a common Form. But now we have a class of three objects, the two original objects plus the Form, which must all resemble each other, and thus have a common characteristic, and hence be such that the same predicate applies to all three. To explain this we must posit a further Form; and so we embark on a regress, in which nothing about common predication is explained because a further explanation is always demanded, no matter how far we may go. These and kindred difficulties led Plato toward a series of logical inquiries which he himself never brought to a conclusion; some of his later lines of thought prefigure modern developments in logical analysis, while others anticipate Aristotle's published criticism of Platonic positions, and may even have resulted from the young Aristotle's spoken criticisms. Yet Plato himself quite clearly never abandoned belief in the Forms. His puzzlement about them may, however, explain a curious gap in the *Laws*.

The *Laws* is a work which reminds us that Plato has an independent interest in political philosophy. The *Laws* concerns the nature of a society in which virtue is universally inculcated. In the first parts of this very long work the emphasis is upon the nature of inculcation; in the later parts practical proposals for legislation to be enacted in the (imaginary) about-to-be-founded Cretan city of Magnesia are discussed. As with the society of the *Republic*, there is to be a hierarchical order of rulers and ruled in the city. As with the society of the *Republic*, true virtue is only possible for those who belong to the restricted class of the rulers. But in the *Republic* the whole emphasis was upon the education of the rulers. In the *Laws* there is nothing like this. The education of the rulers is discussed only in the last book, and then not at great length. And this can be understood in the light of Plato's mature puzzlement about the Forms. The rulers are certainly going to have to grasp the nature of the Forms; but Plato does not and perhaps cannot tell us just what it is that they are going to have to grasp. Certainly the education of the rulers is represented as going further and being more exacting than that of the mass of the citizens. But it is in what Plato has to say about the mass of the citizens and their education that the fascination of the *Laws* resides.

In the *Republic* the role of ordinary people in the state corresponds to that of appetite in the soul. But the relation between reason and appetite is depicted as a purely negative one; reason restrains and checks the nonrational impulses of appetite. In the *Laws* the positive development of desirable habits and traits takes the place of this restraint. The common people are encouraged live in accordance with virtue, and both education and the laws are to nurture them in this way of life. But when they live in accordance with the precepts of virtue, it is because they have been conditioned into and habituated to such a way of life, and not because they understand the point of it. That understanding is still restricted to the rulers. This emerges most clearly in discussion of the question of the existence of the gods or god. (For sophisticated Greeks of Plato's period singular and plural expressions about the divine appear to be interchangeable.) In the *Republic* explicit references to the divine are sporadic. Stories of the traditional gods, purged of immoral and unworthy actions, will have their part in education. But the only true divinity appears to be the Form of the Good. In the *Laws*, however, the existence of the divine has become the cornerstone of morals and politics. "The greatest question . . . is whether we do or do not think rightly about the gods and so live well." The divine is important in the *Laws* because it is identified with law; to be obedient before the law is to be obedient before god. The divine also seems to represent the general primacy of spirit over matter, soul over body; on this is founded the argument for the existence of god introduced in Book X.

The ordinary people are to be induced to believe in gods, because it is important that all men should believe in gods who attend to human affairs, and who are not subject to human weakness in that attention. But the rulers are to be men who have "toiled to acquire complete confidence in the existence of the gods" by intellectual effort. What others hold as a result of conditioning and tradition they have grasped by the use of rational proof. Suppose, however, that a member of the ruling group comes to think that he has found a flaw in the required proof—what then? Plato gives a clear answer in Book XII. If this doubter keeps his doubts to himself, then well and good. But if he insists on disseminating them, then the Nocturnal Council, the supreme authority in the hierarchy of Magnesia, will condemn him to death. The absence of Socrates from the dialogue is underlined by this episode. His prosecutors would have had an even easier task in Magnesia than they had in Athens.

Plato's determination to uphold a paternalistic and totalitarian politics is clearly independent of any particular version of the theory of Forms; for long after he has abandoned the version which in the *Republic* helps to sustain such a politics, he is prepared to advocate the political views which it sustained. But it is also clear that Plato's political philosophy is not merely only justifiable if, but is only intelligible if, some theory of values as residing in a transcendent realm to which there can be access only for an intellectually trained elite can be shown to be plausible. This is the connection between the nonpolitical vision of the *Symposium* and the entirely political vision of the *Laws*. But what is the turn in Plato's thought which transformed Socrates from hero into potential victim? We can distinguish at least two turning points.

The first is the rejection of the Socratic self-knowledge through the discovery of one's own ignorance; the second is the belief that to give true answers to the Socratic questions somehow imposes an obligation to incarnate these answers in social forms. This belief is a curious blend of political realism with totalitarian fantasy. That the possibility of living a virtuous life depends for most people upon the existence of the right kind of social structure does not entail that we ought to create a social structure in which virtue is imposed. Indeed, on Plato's own view virtue is not imposed: it is either rationally apprehended by the few, or it is impossible, its place being taken by an externally conforming obedience, for the many. But it does not follow that Plato did not believe in imposing virtue; but rather that the confusion imbedded in his beliefs obscured from him that this was what he believed in.

# 7

## ARISTOTLE'S *ETHICS*

"Every craft and every inquiry, and similarly every action and project, seems to aim at some good; hence the good has been well defined as that at which everything aims." The book which Aristotle opens with this trenchant sentence is traditionally known as the *Nicomachean Ethics* (it was either dedicated to or edited by Aristotle's son Nicomachus), but its subject matter is declared to be "politics." And the work which is called the *Politics* is presented as the sequel to the *Ethics*. Both are concerned with the practical science of human happiness in which we study what happiness is, what activities it consists in, and how to become happy. The *Ethics* shows us what form and style of life are necessary to happiness, the *Politics* what particular form of constitution, what set of institutions, are necessary to make this form of life possible and to safeguard it. But to say only this is misleading. For the word πολιτικός does not mean precisely what we mean by *political*; Aristotle's word covers both what we mean by *political* and what we mean by *social* and does not discriminate between them. The reason for this is obvious. In the small-scale Greek city-state, the institutions of the πόλις are both those in which policy and the means to execute it are determined and those in which the face-to-face relationships of social life find their home. In the assembly a citizen meets his friends; with his friends he will be among fellow members of the assembly. There is a clue here to the understanding of parts of the Ethics which later on we shall have to follow up. For the moment we must return to the first sentence.

Good is defined at the outset in terms of the goal, purpose, or aim to which something or somebody moves. To call something good is to say that it is under certain conditions sought or aimed at. There are numerous activities, numerous aims, and hence numerous goods. To see that Aristotle is completely right in establishing this relationship between being good and being that at which we aim, let us consider three points about the use of the word good. First, if I aim at something, try to bring about some state of affairs, that I so aim is certainly not sufficient to justify my calling whatever I aim at good; but if I call what I aim at good, I shall be indicating that what I seek is what is sought in general by people who want what I want. If I call what I am trying to get good—a good cricket bat or a good holiday, for example—by using the word good, I invoke the criteria characteristically accepted as a standard by those who want cricket bats or holidays. That this is genuinely so is brought out by a second point: to call something good and to allow that it is not a thing which anyone who wanted that sort of thing would want would be to speak unintelligibly. In this good differs from red. That people in general want or do not want red objects is a contingent matter of fact; that people in general want what is good is a matter of the internal relationship of the concept of being good and being an object of desire. Or to make the same point in a third way: if we were trying to learn the language of a strange tribe, and a linguist asserted of one of their words that it was to be translated by good, but this word was never applied to what they sought or pursued, although its use was always accompanied, say, by smiles, we should know a priori that the linguist was mistaken.

"If, then, there is some one goal among those which we pursue in our actions, which we desire for its own sake, and if we desire other things for its sake, and if we do not choose everything for the sake of something else—in that case we should proceed to choose ad infinitum, so that all desire would be empty and futile—it is plain that this would be the good and the best of goods."[17] Aristotle's definition of the supreme good leaves it open for the moment whether there is or is not such a good. Some medieval scholastic commentators, doubtless with an eye to theological implications, rewrote Aristotle as if he had written that everything is chosen for the sake of some good, and that therefore there is (one) good for the sake of which everything is chosen. But this fallacious inference is not in Aristotle. Aristotle's procedure is to inquire whether anything does in fact answer to his description of a possible supreme good, and his method is to examine a number of opinions which have been held on the topic. Before he does this, however, he issues two warnings. The first is to remember that every sort of inquiry has its own standards and possibilities of precision. In ethics we are guided by general considerations to general conclusions, which nonetheless admit of exceptions. Courage and wealth are good, for example, but wealth sometimes causes harm and men have died as a result of being brave. What is required is a kind of judgment altogether different from that of mathematics. Moreover, young men will be no good at "politics": they lack experience and hence they lack judgment. I mention these dicta of Aristotle only because they are so often quoted; certainly there is something very middle-aged about the spirit which Aristotle breathes. But we ought to remember that what we have now is the text of lectures, and we ought not to treat what are clearly lecturer's asides as if they are developed arguments.

Aristotle's next move is to give a name to his possible supreme good: the name εὐδαιμονία is badly but inevitably translated by *happiness*, badly because it includes both the notion of behaving well and the notion of faring well. Aristotle's use of this word reflects the strong Greek sense that virtue and happiness, in the sense of prosperity, cannot be entirely divorced. The Kantian injunction which a million puritan parents have made their own, "Do not seek to be happy, seek to be deserving of happiness," makes no sense if εὐδαίμων and εὐδαιμονία are substituted for *happy* and *happiness*. Once again the change of language is also a change of concepts. In what does εὐδαιμονία consist? Some say in pleasure, some say in wealth, some say in honor and reputation; and some have said that there is a supreme good over and above all particular goods which is the cause of their being good. Aristotle dismisses pleasure rather brusquely at this point—"The many in choosing a life fit for cattle exhibit themselves as totally slavish"—but later on he is to deal with it at great length. Wealth cannot be the good, for it is only a means to an end; and men prize honor and reputation not as such, but they prize being honored because they are virtuous. So honor is envisaged as a desirable by-product of virtue. Does happiness, then, consist in virtue? No, because to call a man virtuous is to talk not of the state he is in, but of his disposition. A man is virtuous if he would behave in such and such a way if such and such a situation were to occur. Hence a man is no less virtuous while asleep or on other occasions when he is not exercising his virtues. More than this, however, a man can be virtuous and wretched and such a man is certainly not εὐδαίμων.

Aristotle at this point challenges not merely the Kantians and the puritans to come, but also the Platonists. Plato in both the *Gorgias* and the *Republic* looked back to Socrates and asserted that "it is better to suffer tortures on the rack than to have a soul burdened with the guilt of doing evil." Aristotle does not confront this position directly: he merely emphasizes that it is better still both to be free from having done evil and to be free from being tortured on the rack. The fact that, strictly speaking, what Aristotle says and what Plato says are not inconsistent could be misleading. The point is that if we begin by asking for an account of goodness which is compatible with the good man suffering any degree of torture and injustice, the whole perspective of our ethics will be different from that of an ethics which begins from asking in what form of life doing well and faring well may be found together. The first perspective will end up with an ethics which is irrelevant to the task of creating such a form of life. Our choice between these two perspectives is the choice between an ethics which is engaged in telling us how to endure a society in which the just man is crucified and an ethics which is concerned with how to create a society in which this no longer happens. But to talk like this makes Aristotle sound like a revolutionary beside Plato's conservatism. And this is a mistake. For, indeed, Plato's memory of Socrates insures that even at his worst he has a deep dissatisfaction with all actually existing societies, while Aristotle is in fact always extremely complacent about the existing order. And yet Aristotle is at this point in his argument far more positive than Plato. "No one would call a man suffering miseries and misfortunes happy, unless he were merely arguing a case."

Plato's making goodness independent of any this-worldly happiness follows, of course, from his concept of the good as well as from his memories of Socrates. It is this concept of the good which Aristotle now proceeds to attack. For Plato the word *good*'s paradigmatic meaning is given by considering it as the name of the Form of the Good; consequently, *good* is a single and unitary notion. Of whatever we use it, we ascribe the same relationship to the Form of the Good. But in fact we use the word in judgments in all the categories—of some subjects, such as god or intelligence, of the mode of a subject, *how* it is, the excellence it has, its possession of the right amount of something, its existence in the right time or place for something, and so on. Moreover, on the Platonic view everything that falls under a single Form should be the subject of a single science or inquiry; but things that are good are dealt with by a number of sciences—such as, for example, medicine and strategy. Thus Aristotle argues that Plato cannot account for the diversity of uses of *good*. Moreover, the phrases Plato uses to explain the concept of the Form of the Good are not in fact explanatory. To speak of the good "itself" or "as such" does not clearly add anything to *good*. To call the Form eternal is misleading: that something lasts forever does not render it any the better, any more than long-enduring whiteness is whiter than ephemeral whiteness. Moreover, knowledge of Plato's Form is of no use to those in fact engaged in the sciences and crafts in which goods are achieved; they appear to be able to do without this knowledge perfectly well. But the heart of Aristotle's criticism of Plato is in the sentence: "For even if there is some unitary being which is the good, predicated of different things in virtue of something they share or existing separated itself by itself, plainly it would not be something to be done or attained by a man; but it is something which is just that which we are now looking for." That is, *good* in the sense in which it appears in human language, *good* in the sense of that which men seek or desire, cannot be the name of a transcendental object. To call a state of affairs good is not necessarily to say that it exists or to relate it to any object that exists, whether transcendental or not; it is to place it as a proper object of desire. And this brings us back to the identification of the good with happiness in the sense of εὐδαιμονία.

That happiness is the final end or goal, *the* good (and that more than a name is involved here), appears from considering two crucial properties which anything which is to be the final end must possess, and which happiness does in fact possess. The first of these is that it must be something which is always chosen for its own sake and never merely as a means to something else. There are many things which we *can* choose for their own sake, but *may* choose for the sake of some further end. But happiness is not among these. We may choose to pursue intelligence, honor, pleasure, wealth, or what we will for the sake of happiness; we could not choose to pursue happiness in order to secure intelligence, honor, pleasure, or wealth. What sort of "could not" is this? Clearly, Aristotle is saying that the *concept* of happiness is such that we could not use it of anything but a final end. Equally, happiness is a self-sufficient good; by self-sufficiency Aristotle intends that happiness is not a component in some other state of affairs, nor is it just one good among others. In a choice between goods, if happiness were offered along with one but not the others, this would always and necessarily tilt the scales of choice. Thus, to justify some action by saying "Happiness is brought by this" or "Happiness consists in doing this" is always to give a reason for acting which terminates argument. No further *why?* can be raised. To have elucidated these logical properties of the concept of happiness is not, of course, to have said anything about what happiness consists in. To this Aristotle turns next.

In what does the final end of a man consist? The final end of a flute player is to play well, of a shoemaker to make good shoes, and so on. Each of these kinds of man has a function which he discharges by performing a specific activity and which he discharges well by doing whatever it may be well. Have men therefore a specific activity which belongs to them as men, as members of a species, and not merely as kinds of men? Men share some capacities, those of nutrition and growth, with plants, and others, those of consciousness and feeling, with animals. But rationality is exclusively human. In man's exercise of his rational powers therefore the specific human activity consists, and in the right and able exercise of them lies the specific human excellence.

Aristotle advances this argument as though it were obvious, and against the background of the general Aristotelian view of the universe it is obvious. Nature is composed of well-marked and distinct kinds of being; each of these moves and is moved from its potentiality to that state of activity in which it achieves its end. At the top of the scale is the Unmoved Mover, thought unchangingly thinking itself, to which all things are moved. Man, like every other species, moves toward his end, and his end can be determined simply by considering what distinguishes him from other species. Given the general vision, the conclusion appears unassailable; lacking it, the conclusion appears highly implausible. But very little in Aristotle's *argument* is affected by this. For when he proceeds to his definition of the good, he depends only on the view that rational behavior is the characteristic exercise of human beings, in the light of which any characteristically human good has to be defined. The good of man is defined as the activity of the soul in accordance with virtue, or if there are a number of human excellences or virtues, in accordance with the best and most perfect of them. "What is more, it is this activity throughout a whole life. One swallow does not make a summer, nor one fine day. So one good day or short period does not make a man blessed and happy."

*Happy*, that is, is a predicate to be used of a whole life. It is lives that we are judging when we call someone happy or unhappy and not particular states or actions. The individual actions and projects which make up a life are judged as virtuous or not, and the whole as happy or unhappy. We can see, says Aristotle, the connection between happiness thus understood and all those things which are popularly thought to constitute happiness: virtue, though not man's final end, is an essential part of the form of life that is; pleasure is taken by a good man in virtuous activity, and hence pleasure rightly comes in; a modicum of external goods is needed for characteristic human well-being and well-doing; and so on.

We have two large questions on our agenda as a result of Aristotle's definition of the good for man. There is the question to be answered at the end of the *Ethics* as to the activity in which the good man will be chiefly employed. And there is the question of the excellences, of the virtues, which he has to manifest in all his activities. When Aristotle proceeds to the discussion of the virtues he subdivides them in accordance with his division of the soul. Aristotle's use of the expression *soul* is quite different from Plato's. For Plato soul and body are two entities, contingently and perhaps unhappily united. For Aristotle the soul is form to the body's matter. When Aristotle speaks of the soul we could very often retain his meaning by speaking of personality. Thus nothing peculiar to the Aristotelian psychology turns on his distinction between the rational and nonrational parts of the soul. For this is simply a contrast between reasoning and other human faculties. The nonrational part of the soul includes the merely physiological as well as the realm of feelings and impulses. These latter can be called rational or irrational insofar as they accord with what reason enjoins, and their characteristic excellence is to so accord. There is no *necessary* conflict between reason and desire, such as Plato envisages, although Aristotle is fully aware of the facts of such conflicts.

We therefore exhibit rationality in two kinds of activity: in thinking, where reasoning is what constitutes the activity itself; and in such activities other than thinking where we may succeed or fail in obeying the precepts of reason. The excellences of the former Aristotle calls the intellectual virtues; of the latter, the moral virtues. Examples of the former are wisdom, intelligence, and prudence; of the latter, liberality and temperance. Intellectual virtue is the consequence usually of explicit instruction; moral, of habit. Virtue is not inborn, but a consequence of training. The contrast with our natural capacities is plain: first we have the natural capacity, and then we exercise it; whereas with virtues we acquire the habit by first performing the acts. We become just men by performing just actions, courageous by performing courageous actions, and so on. There is no paradox here: one brave action does not make a brave man. But continuing to perform brave actions will inculcate the habit in respect of which we call not merely the action but also the man brave.

Pleasures and pains are a useful guide here. Just as they can corrupt us by distracting us from habits of virtue, so they can be used to inculcate the virtues. For Aristotle one sign of a virtuous man is that he gets pleasure from virtuous activity, and another is that he knows how to choose among pleasures and pains. It is this matter of virtue as involving choice that makes it clear that virtue cannot be either an emotion or a capacity. We are not called good or bad, we are not praised or blamed, by reason of our emotions or capacities. It is rather what we choose to do with them that entitles us to be called virtuous or vicious. Virtuous choice is choice in accordance with a mean.

This notion of the mean is perhaps the single most difficult concept in the *Ethics*. It will be most conveniently introduced by an example. The virtue of courage is said to be the mean between two vices—a vice of excess, which is rashness, and a vice of deficiency, which is coward-ice. A mean is thus a rule or principle of choice between two extremes. Extremes of what? Of emotion or of action. In the case of courage, I give way too much to the impulses which danger arouses when I am a coward, too little to them when I am foolhardy. Three obvious objec-tions at once arise. The first is that there are many emotions and actions for which there cannot be a "too much" or a "too little." Aristotle specifically allows for this. He says that a man "can be afraid and be bold and desire and be angry and pity and feel pleasure and pain in general, too much or too little"; but he says also that malice, shame-lessness, and envy are such that their names imply that they are evil. So also with actions such as adultery, theft, and murder. But Aristotle states no principle which will enable us to recognize what falls in one class, what in the other. We can, however, attempt to interpret Aristotle at this point and try to state the principle implicit in his examples.

If I merely ascribe anger or pity to a man, I thereby neither applaud nor condemn him. If I ascribe envy, I do so condemn him. Those emotions of which there can be a mean—and the actions which cor-respond to them—are those which I can characterize without any moral commitment. It is where I can characterize an emotion or action as a case of anger or whatever it is, prior to and independently of asking whether there is too much or too little of it, that I have a subject for the mean. But if this is what Aristotle means, then he is committed to showing that every virtue and vice are mean and extreme for some emotion or concern with pleasure and pain characterizeable and iden-tifiable in nonmoral terms. Just this is what Aristotle sets out to show in the latter part of Book II of the *Ethics*. Envy, for example, is one extreme, and malice another, of a certain attitude to the fortunes of others. The virtue which is the mean is righteous indignation. But this very example brings out a new difficulty in the doctrine. The righteously indignant man is one who is upset by the undeserved good fortune of others (this example is perhaps the first indication that Aristotle was not a nice or a good man: the words "supercilious prig" spring to mind very often in reading the *Ethics*). The jealous man has an excess of this attitude—he is upset even by the deserved good fortune of others; and the malicious man is alleged to have a defect here in that he falls short of being pained—he takes pleasure. But this is absurd. The malicious man rejoices in the ill-fortune of others. The Greek word for malice, ἐπιχειρεκακία, means this. Thus what he rejoices in is not the same as what the jealous and the righteously indignant man are pained by. His attitude cannot be placed on the same scale as theirs, and only a determination to make the schematism of mean, excess, and defect work at all costs could have led Aristotle to make this slip. Perhaps with a little ingenuity Aristotle could be emended here so as to save his doctrine. But what of the virtue of liberality? The vices here are prodigality and meanness. Prodigality is excess in giving, deficiency in getting, and meanness is excess in getting, deficiency in giving. So these are not after all excess or defect of the same emotion or action. And Aristotle himself half admits that to the virtue of temperance and the excess of profligacy there is no corresponding defect. "Men deficient in the enjoyment of pleasures scarcely occur." Thus the doctrine finally appears as at best of varying degrees of usefulness in exposition, but scarcely as picking out something logically necessary to the character of a virtue.

Moreover, there is a falsely abstract air about the doctrine. For Aristotle does not, as he might seem to, think that there is one and only one right choice of emotion or action, independent of circumstances. What is courage in one situation would in another be rashness and in a third cowardice. Virtuous action cannot be specified without reference to the judgment of a prudent man—that is, of one who knows how to take account of circumstances. Consequently, knowledge of the mean cannot just be knowledge of a formula, it must be knowledge of how to apply the rules to choices. And here the notions of excess and defect will not help us. A man who is suspicious of his own tendency to indignation will rightly consider how much envy and malice there is in it; but the connection of envy and malice with indignation is that in the one case I evince a desire to possess the goods of others, and in the other I evince a desire for the harm of others. What makes these wrong is that I desire that what is not mine should be mine, without thought for the deserts of others or myself, and that I desire harm. The viciousness of these desires is in no way due to their being excess or defect of the same desire, and therefore the doctrine of the mean is no guide here. But if this classification in terms of the mean is no practical help, what is its point? Aristotle relates it to no theoretical account of, for example, the emotions, and it therefore appears more and more as an arbitrary construction. But we can see how Aristotle may have arrived at it. For he may have examined everything commonly called a virtue, looked for a recurrent pattern, and thought that he had found one in the mean. The list of virtues in the *Ethics* is not a list resting on Aristotle's own personal choices and evaluations. It reflects what Aristotle takes to be "the code of a gentleman" in contemporary Greek society. Aristotle himself endorses this code. Just as in analyzing political constitutions he treats Greek society as normative, so in explaining the virtues he treats upper-class Greek life as normative. And what else could we have expected? To this there are two answers. The first is that it would be purely unhistorical to look in the *Ethics* for a moral virtue such as meekness, which enters only with the Christian gospels, or thrift, which enters only with the puritan ethics of work, or for an intellectual virtue such as curiosity, which enters self-consciously with systematic experimental science. (Aristotle himself, in fact, exhibited this virtue, but perhaps could not have envisaged it as a virtue.) Yet this is not good enough as an answer, for Aristotle was aware of alternative codes. There is in Aristotle's *Ethics* not merely a contempt for the morality of artisans or of barbarians, but also a systematic repudiation of the morality of Socrates. It is not just that the undeserved suffering of the good man is never attended to. But when Aristotle considers justice he so defines it that the enactments of a state are unlikely to be unjust provided that they are properly enacted, without undue haste and in due form. It cannot therefore—generally speaking—be just to break the law. Moreover, in the discussion of the virtues, the defect of the virtue of truthfulness is the vice of the self-deprecator which is named εἰρωνεία, irony. This is a word closely associated with Socrates' claim to ignorance, and its use can scarcely have been accidental. Thus at every point where a reference to Socrates occurs in Aristotle we find none of Plato's respect, although a deep respect for Plato himself is shown. It is difficult to resist the conclusion that what we see here is Aristotle's class-bound conservatism silently and partisanly rewriting the table of the virtues, and so from yet another point of view suspicion is cast upon the doctrine of the mean.

The detail of Aristotle's account of particular virtues is rendered with brilliant analysis and perceptive insight, especially in the case of courage. It is much more, as I have just suggested, the list of virtues which raises questions. The virtues discussed are courage, temperance, liberality, magnificence, greatness of soul, good temper or gentleness, being agreeable in company, wittiness, and lastly, modesty, which is treated as not a virtue, but akin to one. Of these, greatness of soul is to do in part with how to behave to one's social inferiors, and liberality and magnificence concern one's attitudes to one's wealth. Three of the other virtues have to do with what are sometimes called manners in polite society. Aristotle's social bias is thus unmistakable. This bias would not matter philosophically but for the fact that it prevents Aristotle from raising the questions, How do I decide what is in fact included in the list of the virtues? could I invent a virtue? is it logically open to me to consider a vice what others have considered a virtue? And to beg these questions is to suggest strongly that there just *are* so many virtues—in the same sense that at a given period there just are so many Greek states.

Aristotle's account of the particular virtues is preceded by an account of the concept of voluntary action, necessary, as he says, because it is only to voluntary actions that praise and blame are assigned. Hence, on Aristotle's own premise, only in voluntary actions are virtues and vices manifested. Aristotle's method here is to give criteria for holding an action to be nonvoluntary. (The usual translation for ἀκούσιος is *involuntary*, but this is a mistake. *Involuntary* in English usage is contrasted with "deliberate" or "done on purpose," not with "voluntary.") An action is nonvoluntary when it is done under compulsion or in ignorance. Compulsion covers all cases when the agent is really not an agent at all. The wind carries his ship somewhere, for example. Actions can also be nonvoluntary where other people have the agent in their power, but actions done under threat of one's parents or one's children being put to death are borderline cases. They satisfy the ordinary criteria of voluntary actions in that they are deliberately chosen. But no one apart from such special circumstances would deliberately choose to act as he would under such threats. In some cases we allow the circumstances to be an excuse, in others not. As an example of the latter, Aristotle cites our attitude to the character of Alcmaeon in Euripides' play, who murders his mother under threats.

Aristotle is careful to point out that the fact that I am motivated in some particular way never entails that I am compelled. If I could allow that my being moved by pleasure or for some noble end was enough to show that I was compelled, then I could not conceive of an action which could not be shown by this or a similar argument to be compulsory. But the whole point of the concept of being compelled is to distinguish actions which we have chosen on the basis of our own criteria, such as the pleasure we shall get or the nobility of the object, from those things we do in which our own choice was not part of the effective agency. Thus, to include too much under the heading of compulsion would be to destroy the point of the concept.

In the case of ignorance Aristotle distinguishes the nonvoluntary from the merely not-voluntary. For an action to be nonvoluntary through ignorance, the discovery of what he has done must cause the agent pain and a wish that he had not so acted. The rationale of this is clear. A man who, having discovered what he has unwittingly done, says, "But if I had known, that is just what I would have chosen to do" thereby assumes a kind of responsibility for the action, and so cannot use his ignorance to disclaim such responsibility. Aristotle next distinguishes actions done in a state of ignorance, such as when drunk or raging, from actions done through ignorance, and points out that moral ignorance—ignorance of what constitutes virtue and vice—is not exculpatory, but is indeed what constitutes vice. The ignorance which is exculpatory is that through which a particular action is done, which would otherwise not have been done, and it is ignorance as to the particular circumstances of the particular action. The examples of such ignorance are various. A man may not know what he is doing, as when someone tells of a matter which he does not know is a secret and so does not know that he is revealing something hidden. A man may mistake one person for another (his son for an enemy) or one thing for another (a harmless weapon for a deadly one). A man may not realize that a medicine is in this type of case deadly, or how hard he is hitting. All these types of ignorance are exculpatory, for it is a necessary condition of an action being voluntary that the agent knows what he is doing.

What is most worth remarking on here is Aristotle's method. He does not begin by looking for some characteristic of voluntary action which all voluntary actions must have in common. He rather looks for a list of characteristics any one of which would if present in an action, be sufficient to withdraw the title "voluntary" from it. An action is treated as voluntary unless done through compulsion or ignorance. Thus Aristotle never gets involved in the riddles of later philosophers about free will. He delineates the concepts of the voluntary and the involuntary as we possess them, and brings out the point about them that they enable us to contrast those cases where we admit the validity of excuses and those cases where we do not. Because this is so, Aristotle only raises marginally—in discussing our responsibility for our own character formation—the question which has haunted modern free-will discussions, Is it possible that all actions are determined by causes independent of the agent's deliberations and choices, so that no actions are voluntary? For Aristotle, even if all actions were somehow thus determined, there would still be a distinction between agents acting under compulsion or through ignorance and agents not so acting. And Aristotle would surely be right about this. We should not be able to escape his distinction no matter what the causation of action might be.

What does emerge about voluntary action in a positive sense is that choice and deliberation have a key role in it. The deliberation which leads up to action always concerns means and not ends. This is yet another Aristotelian saying which may mislead us if we read it ana-chronistically. Some modern philosophers have contrasted reason and emotion or desire in such a way that ends were merely the outcome of nonrational passions, while reason could calculate only as to the means to attain such ends. We shall see later on that Hume took such a view. But this view is alien to Aristotle's moral psychology. Aristotle's point is a conceptual one. If I in fact deliberate about something, it must be about alternatives. Deliberation can only be as to things which are not necessarily and inevitably what they are, and as to things which are within my power to alter. Otherwise there is no room for deliberation. But if I choose between two alternatives, then I must envisage something beyond these alternatives in the light of which I make my choice, that for the sake of which I shall choose one rather than another, that which provides me with a criterion in my deliberation. This will in fact be what in that particular case I am treating as an end. It follows that if I can deliberate about whether or not to do something, it will always be about means that I am deliberating in the light of some end. If I then deliberate about what was in the former case the end, I shall now be treating it as a means, with alternatives, to some further end. Thus, necessarily, deliberation is of means, not of ends, without there being any commitment to a moral psychology of a Humean kind.

The form of the deliberation involved Aristotle characterizes as that of the practical syllogism. The major premise of such a syllogism is a principle of action to the effect that a certain sort of thing is good for, befits, satisfies a certain class of person. The minor premise is a statement, warranted by perception, that here is some of whatever it is; and the conclusion is the action. An example which, although its content is mysterious, makes the form of the practical syllogism clear is given by Aristotle: Dry food is good for man—major premise; Here's some dry food—minor premise; and the conclusion is that the agent eats it. That the conclusion is an action makes it plain that the practical syllogism is a pattern of reasoning by the agent and not a pattern of reasoning by others about what the agent ought to do. (That is why a second minor premise—*e.g.*, And here is a man—would be redundant, and indeed misleading, since it would distract from the point.) Nor indeed is it a pattern of reasoning by the agent about what he *ought* to do. It is not to be confused with perfectly ordinary syllogisms, whose conclusion is a statement of that order. Its whole point is to probe the sense in which an action may be the outcome of reasoning.

A probable first reaction to Aristotle's account will fasten upon just this point. How can an *action* follow from premises as a conclusion? Surely only a statement can do that. To remove this doubt, consider some possible relations between actions and beliefs. An action can be inconsistent with beliefs in a way analogous to that in which one belief can be inconsistent with another. If I assert that all men are mortal, and that Socrates is a man, but deny that Socrates is mortal, I become unintelligible in my utterance; if I assert that dry food is good for man, and I am a man, and I assert that this is dry food, and I do not eat it, my behavior is analogously unintelligible. But perhaps the example is bad. For it may be that I can provide an explanation which will remove the apparent inconsistency. How? By making another statement, such as that I am not hungry, having just finished gorging myself on dry food, or that I suspect that this dry food is poisoned. But this strengthens, not weakens the parallel with ordinary deductive reasoning. If I allow that a warm front's approach causes rain, and that a warm front is approaching, but deny that it is going to rain, I can remove the appearance of inconsistency in this case also by making some further statement, such as that before the warm front reaches here it will be intercepted. So that actions can be consistent and inconsistent with beliefs in much the way that other beliefs can be. And this is because actions embody principles. It is in holding this that Aristotle lays himself open to the charge of "intellectualism." To understand this charge, let us consider it first in a crude form and then in a more sophisticated one.

The crude version of the attack is that made by Bertrand Russell.[18] It is because his actions embody principles, conform or fail to conform to precepts of reason in a way that those of no other species do, that Aristotle defines man as a rational animal. Russell's comment upon this is to invoke the history of human folly and irrationality: men just are not rational in fact. But this is to miss Aristotle's point massively. For Aristotle is in no sense maintaining that men always act rationally, but that the standards by which men judge their own actions are those of reason. To call human beings irrational, as Russell rightly does, is to imply that it makes sense and is appropriate to judge men as succeeding or failing in the light of rational standards, and when Aristotle calls men rational beings, he is simply pointing out the meaningfulness and appropriateness of the application of predicates which refer to such standards. However, Aristotle is committed to more than this. For he has to maintain that men characteristically act rationally, and what this implies is that the concept of human action is such that unless a piece of behavior fulfills some elementary criterion of rationality, it does not count as an action. That is, unless implicit in the behaviour there is a purpose of a recognizably human kind, unless the agent knows under some description what he is doing, and unless we can detect some principle of action in his behavior, what we have is not an action at all, but merely a bodily movement, perhaps a reflex, only to be explained in terms of other bodily movements, such as those of muscles and nerves. That Aristotle is right about this appears if we consider another kind of criticism of his intellectualism, implied in the injunctions of all those moralists who believe that reason is a misleading guide, that we should rely on instinct or on feeling. This appeal to feeling as a moral guide is central to the Romantic period; it emerges again in modern times in the appeal to dark, visceral emotion of D. H. Lawrence's Mexican period; and in its most detestable form it is expressed in the Nazi cry to think with the blood. But these injunctions are intelligible only because they are backed up by reasons; and these reasons are usually assertions to the effect that too much reasoning leads to a calculating, insufficiently spontaneous nature, that it inhibits and frustrates. In other words, it is argued that our actions, if the product of too much calculation, will exhibit undesirable traits or will produce undesirable effects. But to argue like this is to meet Aristotle on his own ground. It is to suggest that there is some criterion or principle of action which cannot be embodied in deliberate action, and thus that deliberate action would be to that extent irrational. And to argue thus is to accept, not to dissent from, a central thesis of Aristotle's rationalism.

Does Aristotle in any case believe that every human action is preceded by an act of deliberation? Clearly if he does believe this, what he believes is false. But he does not. It is only acts which are chosen (in a specially defined sense of *chosen* which involves deliberation) which are preceded by deliberation, and Aristotle says explicitly that "not all voluntary actions are chosen." What does follow from Aristotle's account is that we can assess every action in the light of what would have been done by an agent who had in fact deliberated before he acted. But this imagined agent cannot, of course, just be any agent. He has to be *ὁ φρόνιμος*, the prudent man. Once again translation raises difficulties. *Φρόνησις* is well translated in medieval Latin by *prudentia*, but badly in English by *prudence*. For later generations of puritans have connected prudence with thrift, and especially with thrift in monetary matters (it is the "virtue" embodied in life insurance), and so in modern English *prudent* has something of the flavor of "cautious and calculating in one's own interest." But *φρόνησις*, has no particular connection either with caution or with self-interest. It is the virtue of practical intelligence, of knowing how to apply general principles in particular situations. It is not the ability to formulate principles intellectually, or to deduce what ought to be done. It is the ability to act so that principle will take a concrete form. Prudence is not only itself a virtue, it is the keystone of all virtue. For without it one cannot be virtuous. A man may have excellent principles, but not act on them. Or he may perform just or courageous actions, but not be just or courageous, having acted through fear of punishment, say. In each case he lacks prudence. Prudence is the virtue which is manifested in acting so that one's adherence to other virtues is exemplified in one's actions.

Prudence is not to be confused with a simple faculty for seeing what means will bring about a given end. Aristotle denominates that particular faculty *cleverness* and holds that it is morally neutral, since it is of equal use to the man who pursues praiseworthy and to the man who pursues blameworthy ends. Prudence includes cleverness; it is the cleverness of the man who possesses virtue in the sense that his actions always flow from a practical syllogism whose major premise is of the form "Since the end and the best thing to do is. . . ." It is a conjunction of a grasp of the true $τέλος$ of men with cleverness. For Aristotle the role of intelligence is to make articulate principles on which a man whose natural dispositions are good will have already been acting unconsciously, so that we are less likely to make mistakes; the role of prudence is to know how a given principle (which will always be of a certain degree of generality) applies in a given situation. There is, therefore, after all a point in the argument at which Aristotle clashes with irrationalists such as D. H. Lawrence and with Tolstoy. For Aristotle holds that an explicit and articulate grasp of principle will help to insure the right sort of conduct, while Lawrence's praise of spontaneity and Tolstoy's adulation of peasant ways of life rest on the contention that being explicit and articulate about principles is morally crippling. This clash has more than one root. To a certain extent Aristotle and Lawrence or Tolstoy disagree as to what the right sort of conduct is; and to a certain extent they disagree about what the actual consequences of being articulate are. But once again we must note that although one can be a Lawrentian or a Tolstoyan without inconsistency, what one cannot consistently do is to offer an explicit and articulate rational defense of their doctrines. And the fact that both Lawrence and Tolstoy exhibited all the intellectualism which they used their intellectual resources to condemn strongly suggests that an Aristotelian position of some sort is unavoidable. Moreover, it is only when one is explicit and articulate about principle that one is able to mark clearly the cases where one has failed to do what one should have done. And because this is such a strong point in favor of Aristotle's position, we may well be puzzled that for Aristotle failure constitutes a problem. But it does.

Aristotle begins from Socrates' position, discussed in an earlier chapter, that nobody ever fails to do what he thinks to be best. If a man does anything, then his doing it is sufficient to show that he thought it the best thing to do. Consequently moral failure is logically impossible. This, says Aristotle, flies in the face of the facts. But, for Aristotle, that men should fail to do what they believe they ought to do still constitutes a problem. His explanations are several. A man may, for example, know what he ought to do, in the sense of being committed to a principle of action, but ignore his principle because he is not exercising his knowledge, as may happen when a man is drunk or mad or asleep. So a man carried away may do what in one sense he knows he ought not to do. Or a man may fail to recognize an occasion as one appropriate to the application of one of his principles. What we need to underline here is, however, not the adequacy of Aristotle's explanations. We can set out a wide range of different kinds of case in which there is a gap between what an agent professes and what he does. What is interesting, however, is that Aristotle, and in this he is very close to Socrates, feels that there is something special to be explained in the facts of moral weakness or failure, that such weakness or failure constitutes a problem. This suggests strongly that Aristotle's initial assumption is that men are rational beings in a much stronger sense than we have hitherto ascribed to him. For the suggestion is that if men always did what they thought best, there would be nothing to explain. Yet any account of men as agents which only introduces the facts of weakness and failure by a kind of afterthought is bound to be defective. For human desires are not straightforward drives to unambiguous goals in the way that biological instincts and drives are. Desires have to be given goals, and men have to be trained to reach them, and the point of having principles is in part to detect and diagnose failure in the attempt to reach them. Thus fallibility is central to human nature and not peripheral to it. Hence the portrait of a being who was not liable to error could not be the portrait of a human being. The portrait of the Jesus of the Gospels needs the temptations in the wilderness and the temptation in Gethsemane in order that we can be shown, at least in the intention of the authors, not merely a *perfect* man, but a perfect *man*.

Aristotle's halfhearted admission of fallibility is connected not merely with a philosophical blindness to the importance of this human characteristic but also with a moral attitude to prosperity of a kind that can only be called priggish. This emerges clearly in the course of his account of the virtues. Aristotle's list of virtues falls clearly into two parts, a division obviously not perceived by Aristotle himself. There are, on the one hand, traits such as courage, restraint, and agreeableness which it is hard to conceive of as not being valued in any human community. Even these, of course, fall on a scale. At one end of this scale there are norms and traits which could not be disavowed totally in any human society, because no group in which they were absent could fall under the concept of a society. This is a matter of logic. When Victorian anthropologists sailed round the world they reported the recurrence of certain norms in all societies as an empirical generalization, just as a comparative anatomist might report similarites in bone structure. But consider the case of truth telling. It is a logically necessary condition for any group of beings to be recognized as a human society that they should possess a language. It is a necessary condition for a language to exist that there should be shared rules, and shared rules of such a kind that an intention to say that what is, is can always be presumed. For if when a man said, "It is raining" we could not have such a presumption, then what he said would not communicate anything to us at all. But this presumption, necessary for language to be meaningful, is only possible where truth telling is the socially accepted and recognized norm. Indeed, lying itself is only possible where and on the assumption that men expect the truth to be told. Where there is no such expectation, the possibility of deception disappears too. Thus the recognition of a norm of truth telling and of a virtue of honesty seems written into the concept of a society. Other virtues, although not logically necessary to social life, are obviously causally necessary to the maintenance of such life, given that certain very widespread and elementary facts about human life and its environment are what they are. Thus the existence of material scarcity, of physical dangers, and of competitive aspirations bring both courage and justice or fairness on the scene. These are virtues which, given such facts, appear to belong to the form of human life as such. Other virtues again appear unavoidable for recognition by any society in which fairly widespread human desires are present. There can be exceptions, but as a matter of fact they will be rare. So agreeableness is a general human virtue, although we may come across an occasional people, such as the bad-tempered Dobuans, who may not rate it as such. But toward the other end of the scale there are virtues which are more or less optional, so to speak, which belong to particular contingent social forms, or which are matters of purely individual choice. The non-Aristotelian, but Christian virtues of loving one's enemies and of humility, with the practice of turning the other cheek, appear to belong in the latter category; the English and much more Aristotelian public school virtue of being "a gentleman" in the former. These differences Aristotle does not recognize, and so we find side by side in Aristotle's list virtues which anyone would find it hard not to recognize as virtues and alleged virtues which are difficult to comprehend outside Aristotle's own social context and Aristotle's own preferences within that context.

The two Aristotelian virtues which demand attention in this respect are those of "the great-souled man" ($\mu\varepsilon\gamma\alpha\lambda\acute{o}\mu\nu\chi o\varsigma$) and of justice. The great-souled man "claims much and deserves much." It is for Aristotle a vice to claim less than you deserve, just as much as it is to claim more. It is particularly in relation to honor that the great-souled man claims and deserves much. And since the great-souled man has to deserve most, he must have all the other virtues too. This paragon is extremely proud. He despises honors offered by common people. He is gracious to inferiors. He repays benefits so as not to be put under obligations, and "when he repays a service, it is with interest, for in this way the original benefactor will become the beneficiary and debtor in turn." He speaks his mind without fear or favor, because he has a poor opinion of others and would not care to conceal his opinion. He runs into few dangers, because there are few things which he values and would wish to preserve from harm.

It is because Aristotle conceives of him as not failing that Aristotle endows the great-souled man with no sense of his own fallibility. The great-souled man's characteristic attitudes require a society of superiors and inferiors in which he can exhibit his peculiar brand of condescension. He is essentially a member of a society of unequals. In such a society he is self-sufficient and independent. He indulges in conspicuous consumption, for "he likes to own beautiful and useless things, since they are better marks of his independence." Incidentally, he walks slowly, has a deep voice and a deliberate mode of utterance.

He thinks nothing great. He only gives offense intentionally. He is very nearly an English gentleman.

This appalling picture of the crown of the virtuous life has an almost equally distressing counterpart in one aspect of Aristotle's account of justice. Much of what Aristotle says about justice is illuminating and far from objectionable. He distinguishes between distributive justice— fairness—and the corrective justice which is involved in redress for a harm done. He defines distributive justice in terms of the mean: "To do injustice is to have more than one ought, and to suffer it is to have less than one ought," and justice is the mean between doing injustice and suffering it. But when Aristotle comes up against the use of δίκαιος as meaning either "fair" or "right," or "in accordance with the laws," he asserts without argument that although everything unlawful is unfair, everything unfair is unlawful. It is less clear in the Ethics than it is in the Politics[19] that Aristotle is prepared to believe that the positive laws of existing states can be more than marginally at variance with what is fair and right. "The laws aim either at the common interest of all, or at the interest of those in power determined in accordance with virtue or in some such way; so that in one sense we call just anything that effects or maintains the happiness or the components of the happiness of the political community." Aristotle goes on to describe the law as enjoining virtue and forbidding vice, except where it has been carelessly enacted. And this must remind us of Aristotle's complacency with the existing social arrangement. It is perhaps no accident that he also believes that some men are slaves by nature.

By contrast, Aristotle appears to advantage in his inclusion of friendship as among the necessities of the man who achieves or is to achieve the good. He distinguishes the varieties of friendship—those between equals and unequals; those based on shared pleasure, mutual usefulness, or common virtue—and produces a typical catalogue, whose details perhaps matter less than the fact that the discussion is there at all. But the self-sufficiency of Aristotle's ideal man deeply injures and deforms his account of friendship. For his catalogue of types of friend presupposes that we can always ask the questions, On what is this friendship based? for the sake of what does it exist? There is therefore no room left for the type of human relationship of which it would miss the point totally to ask on what it was based, for the sake of what it existed. Such relationships can be very different: the homosexual love of Achilles for Patroclus, or of Alcibiades for Socrates; the romantic devotion of Petrarch to Laura; the marital fidelity of Sir Thomas More and his wife. But none of these could be included in the Aristotelian catalogue. For the love of the person, as against the goodness, pleasantness, or usefulness of the person, Aristotle can have no place. And we can understand why when we remember the great-souled man. He admires all that is good, so he will admire it in others. But he needs nothing, he is self-contained in his virtue. Hence friendship for him will always be a kind of moral mutual admiration society, and this is just the friendship which Aristotle describes. And this again illuminates Aristotle's social conservatism. How could there be an ideal society for a man for whom the ideal is as ego centered as it is for Aristotle?

The exercise of virtue is, of course, for Aristotle not an end in itself. Virtues are dispositions which issue in the types of action which manifest human excellence. But the injunctions "Be virtuous," "Be courageous," "Be great-souled," "Be liberal" do not tell us what to do in the sense of what to aim at; they rather tell us how we should behave in the pursuit of our aim, whatever it is. But what should that aim be? What, after all this, does εὐδαιμονία consist in? What is the τέλος of human life? A claim which Aristotle takes with immense seriousness, but nonetheless finally dismisses, is that of pleasure. On this subject he has to argue against two kinds of opponent. Speusippus, who was Plato's immediate successor as head of the Academy, had argued that pleasure was in no sense a good. Eudoxus the astronomer, who was also a pupil of Plato, held by contrast that pleasure was the supreme good. Aristotle wished to deny the position of Speusippus without laying himself open to Eudoxus' arguments. His arguments for the goodness of pleasure, or at least for the goodness of some pleasures, are partly a refutation of Speusippus' position. To argue, for example, that pleasures are bad because some are harmful to health is like arguing that health is an evil because sometimes the pursuit of health conflicts with the pursuit of wealth. More positively, Aristotle points to the fact that everyone pursues pleasure as evidence that it is a good, and he advances another argument to the effect that pleasure is taken in what he calls unimpeded activity. By unimpeded activity he means activity which achieves its end, which is well done. Everybody, he argues, takes pleasure in unimpeded activity; everybody wishes his activities to be unimpeded; everybody therefore must see pleasure as a good. But in fact pleasure appears to be common to all forms of activity, and to be the only factor common to all; Aristotle finds himself for a moment close to the position of Eudoxus, and some scholars have held that in Book VII of the Ethics this is the position which he in fact takes. But, in Book X at any rate, he produces arguments against this Eudoxian position, although even here he is clearly puzzled by the relation of pleasure to the τέλος of human life. The reason why he is puzzled is evident. Pleasure clearly satisfies some of the criteria which anything which is to play the role of such a τέλος must satisfy, but equally clearly it fails to satisfy others. We take pleasure in what we do well (unimpeded activity again), and thus taking pleasure in an activity is a criterion of doing it as we wish to do it, of achieving the τέλος of that action. A τέλος must be a reason for acting, and that we would get pleasure is always a reason for acting, even if not always a finally conclusive one. Pleasure, too, is not only sought by almost everybody, and therefore appears to be a universal τέλος; but it cannot be a means to anything else. We do not seek pleasure for the sake of anything further to be got out of it. At the same time, pleasure has characteristics that make it appear not to be a τέλος. It does not complete or terminate an activity; that is, the pleasure we get from doing something is not a sign that we have reached our goal and should therefore stop. Rather, getting pleasure is a reason for continuing the activity. Moreover, there is no particular action or set of actions which can be specified as ways of getting pleasure. Pleasure comes from many different kinds of activity, and so to say that pleasure was the τέλος would not of itself ever give us a reason for choosing one of those kinds of activity rather than another. But to do this is the function of a τέλος. And finally the pleasure that we take in an activity cannot be identified separately from the activity itself; to enjoy or take pleasure in doing something is not to do something and to have an accompanying experience of something else which is the pleasure. To enjoy playing a game is not to play the game, and in addition, to experience some sensations, say, which are the pleasure. To enjoy playing a game is simply to play well and not to be distracted, to be, as we say, thoroughly involved in the game. Thus we cannot identify pleasure as a τέλος external to the activity, to which the activity is a means. Pleasure, says Aristotle, in a memorable but unhelpful phrase supervenes on the τέλος "like the bloom on the cheek of youth."

Different activities, different pleasures; which activities then? The activities of the good man. But which will these be? "If happiness consists in activity in accordance with virtue, it is reasonable that it should be activity in accordance with the highest virtue; and this will be the virtue of what is best in us." What is best in us is reason and the characteristic activity of reason is θεωρία, that speculative reasoning which deals with unchanging truths. Such speculation can be a continuous and pleasant—it is, Aristotle says brusquely, "the pleasantest"—form of activity. It is a self-sufficient occupation. It has no practical outcome, so it cannot be a means to anything else. It is an activity of leisure and peacetime, and leisure is the time when we do things for their own sake, since business affairs are for the sake of leisure and war is for the sake of peace. Above all, since it is concerned with what is unchanging and timeless, it is concerned with the divine. Aristotle follows Plato and much else in Greek thought in equating changelessness and divinity.

Thus, surprisingly, the end of human life is metaphysical contemplation of truth. The treatise which began with an attack on Plato's conception of the Form of the Good ends not so far away from the same attitude of contempt for the merely human. External goods are necessary only to a limited extent, and the wealth required is only moderate. Thus the whole of human life reaches its highest point in the activity of a speculative philosopher with a reasonable income. The banality of the conclusion could not be more apparent. Why then is it reached? One clue is in Aristotle's concept of self-sufficiency. A man's activities in his relations with other men are for Aristotle in the end subservient to this. Man may be a social-cum-political animal, but his social and political activity is not what is central. Yet who can live with this degree of leisure and wealth and this degree of disengagement from affairs outside himself? Clearly only a few people. This however could not appear as an objection to Aristotle: "For it is the nature of the many to be moved by fear, but not a sense of honor, to abstain from what is bad not on account of its baseness but for fear of the penalties; for, living on their emotions, they pursue the appropriate pleasures and the means to these pleasures, and avoid the opposite pains, but they lack even a concept of the noble end of true pleasure, never having tasted it." So, Aristotle concludes, they could not be attracted or changed by ethical theorizing. The tone is that of Plato's *Laws*.

Aristotle's audience, then, is explicitly a small leisured minority. We are no longer faced with a τέλος for human life as such, but with a τέλος for one kind of life which presupposes a certain kind of hierarchical social order and which presupposes also a view of the universe in which the realm of timeless truth is metaphysically superior to the human world of change and sense experience and ordinary rationality. All Aristotle's conceptual brilliance in the course of the argument declines at the end to an apology for this extraordinarily parochial form of human existence. At once the objection will be made: this is to judge Aristotle against the background of our values, not of his. It is to be guilty of anachronism. But this is not true. Socrates had already presented an alternative set of values in both his teaching and his life; Greek tragedy presents other, different possibilities; Aristotle did not choose what he chose for lack of knowledge of alternative views of human life. How, then, are we to understand this union in the *Ethics* of philosophical acumen and social obscurantism? To answer this we must look at his work in a wider perspective.

# 8

---

# POSTSCRIPT TO GREEK ETHICS

The division of labor and the differentiation of function in early societies produces a vocabulary in which men are described in terms of the roles they fulfill. The use of evaluative words follows hard upon this, since any role can be filled well or ill, and any customary mode of behavior conformed to or broken away from. But evaluation with a wider scope is only possible when traditional role behavior is seen in contrast with other possibilities, and the necessity of choice between old and new ways becomes a fact of social life. It is not surprising therefore that it is in the transition from the society which was the bearer of the Homeric poems to the society of the fifth-century city-state that *good* and its cognates acquired a variety of uses, and that it is in the following decades that men reflect self-consciously about those uses. Greek philosophical ethics differs from later moral philosophy in ways that reflect the difference between Greek society and modern society. The concepts of duty and responsibility in the modern sense appear only in germ or marginally; those of goodness, virtue, and prudence are central. The respective roles of these concepts hinge upon a central difference. In general, Greek ethics asks, What am I to do if I am to fare well? Modern ethics asks, What ought I to do if I am to do right? and it asks this question in such a way that doing right is made something quite independent of faring well. A writer thoroughly imbued with the modern spirit in ethics, the Oxford philosopher H. A. Prichard[20] could accuse Plato of falling into error simply by attempting to justify justice at all. For to justify justice is to show that it is more profitable than injustice, that it is to our interest to be just. But if we do what is just and right because it is to our interest, then, so Prichard takes almost for granted, we are not doing it because it is just and right at all. Morality indeed cannot have any justification external to itself; if we do not do what is right for its own sake, and whether it is to our interest or not, then we are not doing what is right.

The assumption made by Prichard is that the notion of what is to our interest, of what is profitable to us, is logically independent of the concept of what it is just and right for us to do. If what is profitable is also just, this, so far as ethics is concerned, is merely coincidental, a happy accident. Doing what we want and getting what we want is one thing; doing what we ought is another. But Prichard here misses the point not only of Plato but of the implications of the Greek moral vocabulary which Plato uses. The Greek moral vocabulary is not so framed that the objects of our desires and our moral aims are necessarily independent. To do well and to fare well are found together in a word like εὐδαίμων. From such purely linguistic considerations, of course, little of substance follows. It still remains to ask whether it is modern ethics which is clarifying a valid distinction that the Greek moral vocabulary fails to observe or Greek ethics which is refusing to make a false and confusing distinction. One way of answering this question would be as follows.

Ethics is concerned with human actions. Human actions are not simply bodily movements. We can identify as instances of the same human action deeds which are executed by means of quite different bodily movements—as the movements involved in shaking a hand and those involved in putting out a flag may both be examples of welcoming somebody. And we can identify as the same bodily movements those which exemplify very different actions—as a movement of the legs may be part of running a race or of fleeing in battle. How, then, do I exhibit a piece of behavior as an action or part of a sequence of actions rather than as mere bodily movement? The answer can only be that it is by showing that it serves a purpose which constitutes part or the whole of the agent's intention in doing what he does. What is more, the agent's purpose is only to be made intelligible as the expression of his desires and aims.

Consider now how modern post-Kantian ethics emphasizes the contrast between duty and inclination. If what I do is made intelligible in terms of the pursuit of my desires, if my desires are cited as affording me reasons for doing what I do, it cannot be that in doing what I do I am doing my duty. Hence when I am doing my duty what I do cannot be exhibited as a human action, intelligible in the way that ordinary human actions are. So the pursuit of duty becomes a realm of its own, unconnected with anything else in human life. To this the reply of a writer like Prichard would be that indeed this is so, and that to suppose it could be otherwise would be an error. But we can now more fruitfully approach Prichard's position in another way, and exhibit its historical roots. If we do so, we shall see a gradual attenuation of the concept of duty and of kindred concepts, in which there is a progress from a notion of a duty as consisting in the requirement to fulfill a specific role, the fulfillment of which serves a purpose which is entirely intelligible as the expression of normal human desires (consider the duties of a father, seaman, or doctor as examples); the next step is perhaps the concept of duty as something to be done by the individual whatever his private desires; finally, we reach the concept of duty as divorced from desire altogether. If we could not explain Prichard's concept of duty historically, I think we should be very much in the position of anthropologists who come across a new and incomprehensible word, such as, for example, *tabu*, a word which is puzzling because it appears not simply to mean "prohibited" but to give a reason for the prohibition, without its being clear what reason. So when someone like Prichard says it is our "duty" to do something, he does not just tell us to do it, as though he uttered an injunction "Do that," but he appears to give us a reason. Consequently, just as we may ask of Polynesians why we should refrain from doing something because it is tabu, so we shall want to ask Prichard why we should do something because it is our duty. And in each case the answer will be similar, and similarly incomprehensible: "Because it is tabu," "Because it is your duty." The lack of connection with other aims, purposes, and desires produces in the end unintelligibility. Yet the concept which Prichard elucidates is one in common use. " 'Why ought I to do that?'

'You just ought'" is not uncommon as a form of moral dialogue in modern society. Thus the philosophical elucidation raises interesting problems about the role of the concept in our social life. But rather than pursuing these at this stage, we must instead return to the Greeks. The crucial point for the immediate discussion is that it may now be clearer why we could not use the moral words which express the modern concept of duty in translating Greek moral words; for these retain the connection with the vocabulary of desire in terms of which they can be made intelligible.

The function of evaluative terms in Greek is, then, to grade different possibilities of conduct in terms of our desires; but in terms of which of our desires? Both Plato and Aristotle criticize the simple sophistic picture of human desires. We have to ask not only what we do now in fact happen to want, but what in the long run and fundamentally we want to want. And this implies a picture of man, made explicit, in different ways, in both Plato and Aristotle, in which certain satisfactions are objectively higher than others. The use of the word *objectively* implies the existence of an impersonal, unchosen criterion. What is it? That there is some such criterion follows from treating the question, What is the good for man? or even just, What is good for man? as an intelligible question at all. For unless there is some criterion by which to judge between possible answers, all possible replies are on a level and the question ceases to have point. It does not, of course, follow that there must be such a criterion (or criteria), but only that the question and the criterion stand or fall together. Plato's transcendentalism springs in part from his grasp of this point. He believes that there must be a criterion. It cannot be derived from existing social structure and institutions, for we use our evaluative concepts to criticize these. It cannot be derived either from our desires just as they are, for we use our evaluative concepts to criticize and to grade our desires. Hence it is easy to conclude that it must be derived from an order existing apart from human life as it is. Where Plato sees the criterion as transcendent, Aristotle sees it as embedded in one particular sort of practice and social arrangement. Both assume that if the chain of justifications which are constituted by answers to questions about the good for men is to be a chain of rational arguments, there must be essentially only one such chain and there must be one essential point at which it reaches a final conclusion (the vision of the Form of the Good or eudaemonistic contemplation). This is of course a mistake, and it is a mistake which both Plato and Aristotle make because they do not understand the conditions which have to be satisfied for there to be available the kind of criteria the existence of which they take for granted—even if they are sometimes in doubt as to their precise nature.

If I treat any form of inquiry as rational, I presuppose that there is some criterion by which to determine whether the answers to its questions are correct or incorrect. In speaking of a criterion I speak of a standard which the individual is not free to accept or reject as he wills or chooses. He may reject a given criterion on rational grounds, such as that its falsity is entailed by some more fundamental or more generally applicable criterion; or he may find a proposed criterion unintelligible upon closer scrutiny. Consider two quite different kinds of example.

Arithmetic is a rational, because rule-governed, discipline. The rules which govern simple arithmetical operations enable us to determine whether the answer to a given sum is correct or incorrect. Anyone who understands the meaning of the words *one, two, plus, equals,* and *three* has no choice over whether to admit the truth of "One plus two equals three." But a condition of there being an agreed meaning for the words in question is that there should be a socially established practice of counting. We can imagine a tribe lacking number concepts because they lack the practice of counting. I do not mean by this that counting as a social, teachable practice is logically prior to the possession of number concepts, for counting itself in turn presupposes such possession. But I can only appeal to a rule to settle a disputed arithmetical question in a community where number concepts are intelligible, and they will only be intelligible where counting is an established and recognized practice.

Consider now how similar evaluative terms are, in this one respect at least, to arithmetical. We are more accustomed to think of arithmetic as a rational discipline than we are of the criticism of cricket and football, chess and bridge. (This is partly because in our study of Greek culture we usually overrate Plato and underrate the Olympic games about which we could learn from Lucian. Plato thinks of "gymnastic," of games playing, as merely a means to an end, as part of an educational discipline whose point lies in a final end-product of a quite different kind. This is also the doctrine of the English public schools, for whom the point of games is that they produce "character.") But a study of the concepts used in the criticism of games for their own sake is philosophically revealing, even about Plato. Consider the concept of a good batsman. The questions of whether a batsman is a good batsman and how good a batsman he is are intelligible because there are established criteria: variety of strokes, ability to improvise, moral stamina in crises. We have these criteria because we have criteria of success or failure in cricket in general, and in the role of a batsman in particular; and the winning of matches is not, of course, the sole criterion. How you win them also enters into it. But these criteria can only be appealed to because there is an established practice of games playing and can only be appealed to by those who share the social life in which this practice is established. Imagine a people who did not share the concept of a game and therefore could not acquire the relevant criteria. All that they would and could grasp would be that the word good was generally being used in contexts where approval of some sort was being indicated. Their philosophers would naturally enough construct theories about the meaning of good to the effect that its use is to express approval. And these theories would necessarily miss a large part of the point.

In Greek ethics something analogous to this imagined situation actually occurs. We begin with a society in which the use of evaluative words is tied to the notion of the fulfillment of a socially established role. We can indeed imagine a society of which this is true in a far stronger sense than it is of the imaginary society depicted in or the real societies reflected in the Homeric poems. Here the nouns and verbs to which evaluative adjectives and adverbs are attached would always invariably be those which name roles and role-fulfilling activities. In consequence, all the uses of good will belong with that class of adjectives whose meaning and force are dependent upon the meaning of the noun or noun-phrase to which they are attached. We can understand this class by contrasting it with the class of adjectives whose meaning and force is not so dependent. Such are, for example, color words. We can render them meaningless by attaching them to a noun or noun-phrase which cannot allow them any sense if it is used with its normal meaning (consider "pink rational number"), but when they are attached to any noun in such a way as to form a meaningful phrase their meaning is independent of that of the noun. Because of this, I can in such cases validly deduce from "This is an XY," both "This is an X" and "This is a Y." (So from "This is a red book" it follows that "This is red" and "This is a book.") But there are also the adjectives of which this is not true, where the force of the adjective is dependent upon the meaning of the particular noun to which it is attached, because the criteria for the correct application of the adjective vary with and are determined by the meaning of the noun. Such is *good* in those uses which connect with role-fulfillment. The criteria for the correct application of the expressions "good shepherd" and "good general" and "good flautist" are determined by the criteria for the application of the expressions *shepherd, general*, and *flautist*. In learning how to describe social life one also learns how to evaluate it. Moreover there are a variety of uses of *good* where such impersonal and objective criteria can be found: "good at" used of skills and "good for" used of medicines or instruments, of means efficient for given ends, are two examples. In a society restricted to these uses, all evaluation would be a matter of the application of criteria about which the individual was not free to exercise choice.

Such a society's evaluative usage resembles the usage of those who criticize performances in a game. In both cases there are accepted standards; in both cases to acquire the vocabulary necessary to describe and to understand the game is logically inseparable from acquiring these standards. In both cases the fact that the standards are objective and impersonal is consistent with evaluative disagreements and even with disagreements which are incapable of resolution. This is because there are a number of criteria in terms of which we judge performances or exercises of ability and not just one single criterion for each role or skill. So we may in evaluating a batsman differ in the weight that we give to ability to improvise as against the possession of a particular stroke, and in evaluating a general differ in the weight we give to ability to organize supply lines as against tactical brilliance on the field.

Just as in the case of the criticisms of games we could imagine a social group in which the use of evaluative words was lost, so we can imagine a society in which traditional roles no longer exist and the consequent evaluative criteria are no longer used, but the evaluative words survive. In both cases all that remains of evaluation is the sense of approval attached to the words. The words become used as signs that the individual speaker is indicating his tastes, preferences, and choices. If we conceived of philosophical analysis as an analysis of how different concepts are in fact used in common speech, as a study of the logical features of *usage*, then we might well fall into an interesting trap at this point. For if we were to insist upon treating as the meaning of the word *good* only features of its use which were present on every occasion of its use, then we should naturally conclude that the essential meaning of the word is given by laying down its function of commending or expressing approval or indicating choice or preference, and so on; and that its association with criteria of an impersonal and objective kind is secondary, contingent, and accidental. Or we might fall into the opposite trap of supposing that since the word *good* is in many standard cases only used intelligibly if it is applied in accordance with impersonal and objective criteria, all uses in which it is divorced from such criteria are too unimportant to be taken seriously. In fact however, unless we see these two uses as constituting two successive phases in a historical narrative, we shall miss a large part of the point about the word *good*. When I speak of a historical narrative I mean one in which the later part is unintelligible until the former is supplied, and in which we have not understood the former until we see that what followed it was a possible sequel to what had gone before. The use of the word *good* when it is used only or primarily as an expression of approval or choice is unintelligible except as a survival from a period when criteria of an impersonal, unchosen kind governed its use, because it has no distinctive use or function to distinguish it from a simple imperative or expression of approval. What would be being said when something is called *good* would be no more or other than would be said by someone who said, "Choose one of that kind," or, "That is the kind I prefer." This apparent redundancy of *good* might be explained away by pointing to its propagandistic possibilities. The use of the word *good* actually *says* no more than is said by the man who straightforwardly announces his choice or preference, but a man may contrive to give the impression of saying more, and by so doing attach prestige to his announcement by the use of *good*. *Good* is a status symbol for expressions of choice, on this view. But this theory, in fact, discloses its own weakness, for why should *good* have this kind of status? why should it carry this type of prestige? The answer can only be that it carries with it a distinction derived from its past, that it suggests a connection between the speaker's individual choices and preferences and what *anyone* would choose, between *my* choice and the choice which the relevant criteria dictate.

It would be equally mistaken however to suppose that the word *good* could not become detached from the particular criteria which have governed its use, and still remain intelligible. What gives the word *good* its generality is partly the fact that a connection with choice and preference is present from the outset. To call something *good* is to say that anyone who wanted something of that kind would be satisfied with this particular specimen. We bring into the picture more than our own individual choice and preference; we point to more than our own individual choice and preference: we point to a norm for choice. And in a society where traditional roles and the corresponding traditional evaluation of behavior have broken down or disappeared, the sequel to unsuccessful attempts to use the word *good* as a simple expression of choice or preference may well be an attempt to re-establish norms for choice. And there is no reason at all why *good* should not acquire new criteria of application.

I have tried to delineate in the argument so far an ideal historical sequence. Such a sequence is useful for two different types of reason. It brings out the connection between historical intelligibility and logical relationships. I cannot understand the logical structure of a given philosophical theory, for example, unless I understand the problems to which it is intended to be a solution. But in a great many instances I cannot hope to understand what those problems are unless I know what problems were posed by the philosophical predecessors of the theory and how the historical context imposes limits upon solutions to their problems. It is always possible and usually useful to abstract both problem and solution, question and answer, from their particular context and to examine matters of logic without too much reference to their *actual* history. (This is what idealist philosophers, and particularly R. G. Collingwood, sometimes failed to see; but what they succeeded in seeing and saying on this point is more illuminating than most later writing.) But more than this, the concepts which furnish the materials for philosophical investigation are, as we have already noticed, liable to change. Thus what may appear at first misleadingly as two rival elucidations of the same concept, between which we have to choose, may be envisaged more usefully as two successive analyses of a concept in process of transformation, between which there is no question of a choice. Both are needed and so is their interrelationship, so that we may not lose sight both of the continuity and of the change in the concept.

Moreover, to analyze concepts in terms of ideal historical sequences may be useful for another reason. In abstracting certain characteristics of the sequence, and thus lending it an ideal character, we acquire a method for noting similar sequences embedded in quite different historical processes. And in noting similarity we may also note differences. Consider both the resemblances and the differences between what happened to *ἀγαθός* in Greek usage and what happened to duty in English. Just as *ἀγαθός* is originally tied to performance of a role, so is duty. We still talk of the duties of a policeman or a probation officer, and in a society where the moral life is exhaustively conceived in terms of role description, the duties of a father or a king may be as vigorously delimited by custom as those are which are now defined by statute. It is when we detach a man from his roles, but still leave him with the concept of "duty," that the concept is necessarily transformed. This detachment is a consequence of a sufficiently radical change in established social structure and does not have to occur to a whole society all at once in a once-for-all kind of way. It can occur for part of a society, and it will occur in such a way as to be modified by other moral beliefs. So for part of English society in the eighteenth century the concept of duty became generalized in association with the concept of vocation. Originally we have a society of well-defined occupational roles and functions, hierarchically arranged, and to this arrangement there corresponds a belief in different stations in life to which God is pleased to call men. When the occupational roles become more important, the notion of a calling by God, but not to any one particular "station," remains. The duties which were tied to a particular office are replaced by the duty one owes to God simply as a man. In such a situation the content of duty will be blurred. This kind of situation provides part of the background to the kind of moral dilemma which is examined in some of Jane Austen's novels. Her characters cannot simply conceive of morality in terms of the adequate fulfillment of a well-established role. Edmund Bertram in *Mansfield Park* can be open to Mary Crawford's criticism of his intention to become a clergyman: he can be forced to ask himself whether it will make him more or less of "a man." Being a landowner and being "in trade" no longer carry a sense of clearly defined status in the heirarchy of duties. That this is so is highlighted by one remarkable exception. The person of the naval officer provides a touchstone of virtue in Jane Austen precisely because of his professionalized sense of duty. And she is able to speak of duty in this context far more clearly than elsewhere because the link between duty and duties has not been broken.

The history of ἀγαθός in Greek and of duty in English (or German) are of course as different as the history of the breakdown of traditional Greek society is from the history of the transformations of preindustrial England. But in both cases we get a move from the well-defined simplicities of the morality of role fulfillment, where we judge a man *as* farmer, *as* king, *as* father, to the point at which evaluation has become detached, both in the vocabulary and in practice, from roles, and we ask not what it is to be good at or for this or that role or skill, but just what it is to be "a good man"; not what it is to do one's duty as clergyman or landowner, but as "a man." The notion of norms for man emerges as the natural sequel to this process, and opens new possibilities and new dangers.

At this point, however, does not the argument involve us in apparent paradox? We can understand why Plato and Aristotle (and why, in the later context, Price and Kant) look for norms independent of the structure of this or that particular social framework. But the cost of doing this is to suggest the truth of exactly the kind of relativism which they were seeking to overcome. If the kind of evaluative question we can raise about ourselves and our actions depends upon the kind of social structure of which we are part and the consequent range of possibilities for the descriptions of ourselves and others, does this not entail that there are no evaluative truths about "men," about human life as such? Are we not doomed to historical and social relativism?

The answer to this is complex. The first part of the answer has already been suggested in the course of discussing Aristotle. It is that there are certain features of human life which are necessarily or almost inevitably the same in all societies, and that, as a consequence of this, there are certain evaluative truths which cannot be escaped. But, put simply like this, this point can be misleading. We cannot, as I have already argued, conceive of a group of beings who would satisfy the minimal conceptual conditions necessary for us to characterize them correctly as a human group where there was not rule-governed behavior, and where the norms which governed that behavior did not entail a norm of truth telling, a norm of ownership and justice and the like. In any human group some notions of truth and justice necessarily find some foothold. Moreover, as I have also argued, in any human group it is almost inconceivable that certain qualities such as friendliness, courage, and truthfulness will not be valued, simply because the range of ends possible for the activities of those who do not value such qualities is far too restricted. But this kind of argument might be quite wrongly held to provide us with a kind of transcendental deduction of norms for all times and all places; it might be held to provide a guide to conduct for men, irrespective of the nature of the society in which they find themselves. Not only is this a mistaken conclusion, but it derives from a misunderstanding of the import of the premises from which it is derived. Just because human society as such either has to have or will usually have certain norms as part of the ineliminable logical framework of its actions and its discourse, so all choices of different evaluative possibilities arise within this framework and within the context of the norms in question. It follows that these norms cannot provide us with reasons for choosing one out of the set of possibilities rather than another. To put this concretely, human society presupposes language; language presupposes rule following; and such rule following presupposes a norm of truth telling. Lying as a form of human action, it is often pointed out, logically presupposes a norm of truth telling. But although the liar therefore vindicates in his practice the existence of the very norm which his practice violates, he thereby shows that the existence of the norm opens up possibilities both of lying and of truth telling; the existence of the norm entails nothing in the way of guidance on any particular occasion of perplexity as to whether we should lie or whether we should tell the truth. And not only different individual choices but very different codes of honesty lie within the range of possibilities open to us. Thus anyone who claims that the elucidation of the norms governing human activity as such provides a guide to how to live is making a fundamental mistake.

It is in outlining the concrete personal and social alternatives in a particular situation and the possibilities of good or evil inherent in them that we in fact frame practical questions and answers. In this task the alleged alternatives of "historical relativism" and "norms for men as such" scarcely arise. For certainly in asking for criteria to govern my choices I am asking for criteria and not for something else; I am asking for guidance of an impersonal kind, not just for me, but for anyone— anyone, that is, in my situation. But the more that I particularize my situation the more I ask for guidance for people who belong specific-ally to my time and place—or to other times and places of a sufficiently and relevantly similar sort. I am always going to be faced with two dangers. If I abstract sufficiently, I shall be able to characterize my situation in terms quite apart from any specific time and place, but by so doing I shall not solve my problem but relocate it. For the highly general form of problem and solution then has to be translated back into concrete terms, and the real problem becomes how to do this. If I do not abstract sufficiently, I shall always be in danger of making myself the victim of what is taken for granted in a particular situation. I shall be in danger of presenting what is merely the outlook of one social group or part of the conceptual framework for men as such.

Both Plato and Aristotle suppose that from the elucidation of the necessary conceptual framework for human life they can draw practical guidance; and this mistake is both camouflaged and reinforced by their adapting forms of description at once used in and well-suited to char-acterizing the social life of the Greek πόλις to serve as forms of descrip-tion for human life as such. This is not only a weakness. Some later writers on moral philosophy have supposed that the problems can be posed in a vocabulary which is somehow independent of any social structure. This supposition is one of the roots of the belief that there are two distinct spheres of life, one for "morals," the other for "politics." But, in fact, every set of moral evaluations involves either neutrality toward or assent to or dissent from the social and political structure within which it is made. And insofar as dissent is concerned, the moral evaluations will involve some degree of commitment to an alternative. What is striking about Plato and Aristotle is the unity of morals and politics in their writings. Yet this very unity in the end betrays their ideals.

Both Plato and Aristotle take for granted, naturally enough, the social structure of the πόλις, with the slaves excluded from the political structure, the artisans and farmers coming out at the bottom, a richer class above them, and some kind of elite ruling. Because the questions they pose, and sometimes the concepts they employ, presuppose the πόλις and its social unity, neither of them faces up to the actual decline of the πόλις. Because they are spokesmen for its unity, they ignore or dislike the heterogeneity of Greek society. The concept of a common interest is taken for granted. The conservatism of Aristotle is of course quite different from that of Plato. Plato's idealization of a πόλις utterly different from that of fourth-century reality means that politics becomes a hit-or-miss affair of the philosopher king happening to turn up at the right time and the right place. Those modern critics of Plato who have castigated him as a fascist have missed the point very badly. For the essence of fascism is that it glorifies and upholds some existing ruling class: the essence of political Platonism was that it excoriated every actual political possibility. Plato's own political failure at Syracuse, where successive visits met a blank wall in political reality, was grounded not merely in the conditions of Syracuse in particular or in the city-state in general, but in Plato's own doctrine. Plato may be conceded the title of either reactionary or conservative, but if all reactionaries were Platonists, revolutionaries would have an easy time.

With Aristotle it is different. We are much closer to actual states and constitutions in Aristotle's empirically based *Politics*. But in two respects Aristotle faces up to the realities of the πόλις even less than Plato does. The δῆμος, the mass of ordinary people, appear in Plato as governed by desires which have no room for expression in the just state; in the *Republic* the desires are to be repressed, in the *Laws* they are to be remolded. But throughout Plato the natural clash of desires between rulers and ruled figures prominently in the political picture. Both Plato and Aristotle see the desires of the rulers as the characteristic of "man," those of the ruled as nearer the merely animal. But in the *Nicomachean Ethics* the baser passions, characteristic of the ruled, appear merely as sources of error and distraction. There is nothing of Plato's at times nearly hysterical picture of what he takes to be the anarchy of desire.

Since all norms belong within the just state, and desire of an untrammeled kind has no place in it, this picture of desire as anarchic is inevitable. But by recognizing that there are desires which cannot be legitimated and allowed expression within his form of ideal state, Plato also recognizes implicitly that those whose desires they are would find in them a criterion for criticizing his state and life in it as "less profitable" than the pursuit of what his state would characterize as injustice. Plato is at times a candid partisan of a ruling class, even if only of an imaginary ruling class.

Aristotle is in this respect uncandid. The Aristotelian ideal of the leisured and perfected life of abstract contemplation is only accessible to an elite; and it presupposes a class structure which excluded the mass of ordinary men both from political power and from the moral idea. But every desire is allowed expression in a form that will either satisfy it or purge it. This explains the difference between Plato and Aristotle on the subject of tragedy. The values of Greek tragedy express the conflicts of Greek society as much as the values of Plato and Aristotle express or attempt to depict Greek society as a unified structure. In the *Oresteia* tribal and urban values conflict; in *Antigone* those of the family and those of the state; in *The Bacchae* those of reason with those of the passions. They present to the mass audience of the πόλις rival allegiances for their desires in an aesthetic mode calculated to arouse passion. Plato rightly sees that they do not present the kind of consistent, single moral ideal he believes in and that they run contrary to his attempt to suppress the desires of the mass audience. Hence his consistent advocacy of censorship and repression. But Aristotle sees that the aesthetic evocation of pity and terror may purge us of them. Far from providing us with motives for action, the drama may evacuate us of otherwise dangerous desires and emotions, and in so doing, it will stabilize the existing social order. Hence Aristotle has none of Plato's enthusiasm for censorship.

In fact, Aristotle is much more of a quietist in relation to political activity. Provided only that there is room for the contemplative elite, the *Nicomachean Ethics* does not provide for a condemnation or an endorsement of any social structure; and the *Politics* uses criteria of stability to judge between types of state which have only this negative connection—of making room for an elite—with the arguments of the

Ethics. In fact, by his own practice as the tutor of the young Alexander, and by his advocacy of the life of contemplation, Aristotle, as Kelsen pointed out, sided with the powers which were about to destroy the πόλις as a political entity. For the exaltation of the contemplative life is an exaltation of it as a form of life for those men who have hitherto composed the political elite. It provides a rationale for their withdrawal to the status of citizen, "good citizens" in Aristotle's sense, but not rulers. And this is just what the absolutism of Macedon, the first of the new large-scale states, required the rulers of what had hitherto been city-states to become. As Kelsen puts it, "the glorification of the contemplative life, which has renounced all activity and more especially all political activity, has at all times constituted a typical element of the political morality set up by the ideologies of absolute monarchy. For the essential tendency of this form of state consists in excluding the subjects from all share in public affairs."[21]

The facts of the decline of the πόλις and the rise of the large-scale state have immensely more important consequences for the history of moral philosophy than any gravitational pull that they may have exerted upon Aristotle's analyses. The milieu of the moral life is transformed; it now becomes a matter not of the evaluations of men living in the forms of immediate community in which the interrelated character of moral and political evaluation is a matter of daily experience, but of the evaluations of men often governed from far off, living private lives in communities which are politically powerless. In Greek society the focus of the moral life was the city-state; in the Hellenistic kingdoms and the Roman empire the sharp antithesis between the individual and the state is inescapable. The question now is not, In what forms of social life can justice express itself? or, What virtues have to be practiced to produce a communal life in which certain ends can be accepted and achieved? but, What must I do to be happy? or, What goods can I achieve as a private person? The human situation is such that the individual finds his moral environment in his place in the universe rather than in any social or political framework. It is salutary to observe that in many ways the universe is a more parochial and narrow moral environment than Athens was. The reason for this is very simple. The individual who is situated in a well-organized and complex community, and who cannot but think of himself in terms of the life of that community, will have a rich stock of descriptions available to characterize himself, his wants, and his deprivations. The individual who asks, What do I desire, as a man, apart from all social ties, in the frame of the universe? is necessarily working with a meager stock of description, with an impoverished view of his own nature, for he has had to strip away from himself all the attributes that belong to his social existence. Consider in this light the doctrines of Stoicism and Epicureanism.

The remote ancestor of both is Socrates, the Socrates who is essentially the critic, the outsider, the private foe of public confusions and hypocrisies. Plato sees that if one asks seriously for answers to the Socratic questions, one necessarily becomes the partisan of one sort of social order against others, and in so doing, one has to abandon the role of the merely private person and critic. But among Socrates' disciples there were some who retained this mode, who stylized the Socratic way of life and drew their moral code from this style of life rather than from reflection on the character of definition. Independence and self-sufficiency become for them the supreme values; the only way to avoid injury from changing circumstance is to make oneself radically independent of circumstance. Antisthenes, the logician, rejects as goods not merely wealth and honors, but anything that might provide the satisfaction for a desire. Virtue consists in the absence of desire and is sufficient by itself for happiness. The man who is virtuous in the sense of desiring nothing has nothing of which to fear the loss; he is able to bear even slavery without injury. Antisthenes sees conventional politics and conventional religion only as sources of illusion. Not the state, but the universe is the habitation of the virtuous man; not the local gods of the state, but the one good is his god, and the only service of god is the practice of virtue. What independence of this sort could mean is shown in Diogenes' life in his tub and in his reply to Alexander's question of whether there was anything that Alexander could do for him: "Yes, get out of the light." It is Diogenes' expressed wish to live with the simplicity of an animal and his chosen self-title, "The dog" (ὁ κύων), that won for moralists of this school the title "Cynics." (The link with the English word cynicism lies in the Cynic claim to see through all conventional values).

Aristippus of Cyrene begins from the assumption of the identity of the pursuit of virtue and the pursuit of εὐδαιμονία. He identifies εὐδαιμονία with pleasure; but holds that excess of pleasure leads to pain and that the limitation of desires is a condition of their satisfaction. Among Aristippus' disciples, called Cyrenaics, perhaps the most significant figure was Hegesias, who stressed this latter point to the extent of holding that the absence of pain rather than the promotion of pleasure is the aim of life. What is more, he believed that abstention from actual pleasure was a condition of such absence. When Hegesias lectured at Alexandria, it is said that the effect was such on his hearers that many of them committed suicide, and in the end he was not allowed to give lectures.

Even in the thought of the Cynics and Cyrenaics we can discern a tendency which will be much more strongly exemplified in Stoics and Epicureans. For both Plato and Aristotle, although the relation of virtue to happiness may constitute a problem, that there is a connection between them waiting to be elucidated is a fundamental assumption. Unless virtue somehow leads to happiness, it lacks a τέλος, it becomes pointless; unless happiness is somehow bound up with the practice of virtue, it cannot be happiness for the kind of beings men are, it cannot constitute a satisfaction for a moralized human nature. Happiness and virtue are neither simply identical nor utterly independent of each other. But in the case of both Cynics and Cyrenaics we see the tendency to reduce one to the other, and to in fact operate either with the concept of virtue alone or with that of happiness alone. This separation of virtue and happiness is interestingly accompanied by a large stress upon self-sufficiency, upon avoiding disappointment rather than seeking for positive goods and gratifications, upon independence from contingent bad fortune, and this stress perhaps provides the very clue which we need to understand their separation. The sense one gets in reading the records of post-Socratic philosophy which survive in writers such as Diogenes Laërtius and Cicero is of a disintegrated social world in which there are more puzzled rulers than ever before, in which the lot of the slaves and the propertyless is very much what it was, but in which for many more middle-class people insecurity and an absence of hope are central features of life.

This suggests interestingly that the possibilities of connecting virtue and happiness are dependent not solely upon the features of two concepts which remain unchanged and hence have an unchanging relation, but upon the forms of social life in terms of which these concepts are understood. Let me suggest two extreme models. The first is of a form of community in which the rules which constitute social life and make it possible and the ends which members of the community in question pursue are such that it is relatively easy to both abide by the rules and achieve the ends. A well-integrated traditional form of society will answer to this description. To achieve the personal ideals of the Homeric hero or the feudal knight or the contemplative and to follow the social rules (which themselves invoke a respect for rank and religion) cannot involve fundamental conflict. At the other end of the scale, we might cite as an example the kind of society which still sustains traditional rules of honesty and fairness, but into which the competitive and acquisitive ideals of capitalism have been introduced, so that virtue and success are not easily brought together. Or there may well be intermediate types of society in which for some groups only is it true that their ends and the rules of the society are discrepant. From the vantage point of each of the different kinds of society the relation between virtue and happiness will look very different. At the one extreme we shall find virtue and happiness regarded as so intimately related that the one is at least a partial means to or even constitutive of the latter. At the other extreme we shall find a total divorce, accompanied by injunctions by the would-be moralists to regard virtue rather than happiness, and by the would-be realists (illuminatingly called "cynics" by the moralists) to regard happiness rather than virtue. Even though both *words* remain, the one will come to be defined in terms of the other. But inevitably in such a situation both the concept of virtue and the concept of happiness will become impoverished and will lose their point to a certain extent. To understand this situation we must look at the relationship between rules and ends, and to do this we must first make clear the distinction between them.

There are rules without which human life recognizable as such could not exist at all, and there are other rules without which it could not be carried on in even a minimally civilized form. These are the rules connected with truth telling, promise keeping, and elementary fairness. Without them there would not be an arena in which distinctively human ends could be pursued, but these rules by themselves in no way provide us with ends. They tell us how to behave in the sense of telling us what not to do, but they provide us with no positive aims. They provide norms to which any action we may perform is required to conform, but they do not tell us which actions to perform. Which actions we should perform depends upon what ends we pursue, what our goods are. In general *happiness* is a rubric relating to ends, *virtue* one dominating rules. It would be a mistake to suppose that in identifying this distinction between rules and ends we are also demarcating the public and the private domains in morality. For while it is true that ends may admit of private choices in a way that rules do not, it is also true that there are societies in which there are publicly established and agreed or imposed ends, as well as societies which leave alternative ends open to a great degree to individual preference. Moreover, there may be private innovations in the realm of rules as well as in that of ends. What does remain true, however, is that the dissociation of rules and ends will inevitably have repercussions on the relationship between private and public life. For where the observance of rules has no or relatively little connection at all with the achievement of ends, the observance of rules will become either pointless or an end in itself. If it becomes an end in itself, then the observance of rules may become a private ideal for the individual as well as a requirement of social morality. If the achievement of ends is in the same type of situation, as it will be, relatively independent of the observance of rules, then ends become dissociated from the requirements of the public domain. They provide other and rival private ideals. It will be natural in this situation to conceive of the pursuit of pleasure and the pursuit of virtue as mutually exclusive alternatives. Moreover, in each case, long-term projects, which tend to depend upon the possibility of relying on a widespread public congruence of rules and ends, will appear far less viable than short-term. Moral advice will most naturally be either of the "Gather ye rosebuds *while ye may*" kind or of the "Do what is right regardless of the consequences" kind. "*Fiat justitia, ruat coelum*" is a slogan that is pointless rhetoric except when it seems quite possible that the heavens *will* crumble. We can see these alternatives embodied in private moralities by the Cynics and the Cyrenaics. They rise to the level of universal codes in Stoicism and Epicureanism.

For the successive founders and refounders of Stoicism, Zeno,

Cleanthes, and Chrysippus, morals become unintelligible apart from cosmology. The universe is at once material and divine. The primary material of the universe, fire, is transmuted into various physical states by the activity of a universal rational principle, the Logos, which is the deity. In the transmutation of the universe a regular cycle recurs, returning again and again to a cosmic conflagration in which the original fire brings to an end one period and begins another. Each of these cyclical periods is identical, and every event in the universe therefore recurs indefinitely. Since man is an integral part of the universe, this eternal recurrence is also true of human history. Indefinitely often in the past and indefinitely often in the future I have written and shall write these words, and you have read and will read them, just as you do at this present moment.

Since human nature is part of cosmic nature, the law which governs the cosmos, that of the divine Logos, provides the law to which human action ought to be conformed. At once an obvious question arises. Since human life proceeds eternally through an eternally predetermined cycle, how can human beings fail to conform to the cosmic law? What alternatives have they? The Stoic answer is that men as rational beings can become conscious of the laws to which they necessarily conform, and that virtue consists in conscious assent to, vice in dissent from, the inevitable order of things. What this answer means can be better understood by considering the Stoic answer to the problem of evil.

Since everything is formed by the action of the divine principle, and that principle is entirely and unquestionably good, it follows that no evil can occur in the world. But evil does occur. How so? The Stoic rejoinder is, in effect, that evil does not *really* occur. A variety of arguments, which later on are to reappear in Christian theology, take the stage for the first time in Stoic costume. Chrysippus argued that of a pair of contraries, neither could be conceived to exist without the other, so that good and evil each require the existence of the other. Evil, being therefore a necessary condition for the occurrence of good, is in terms of a larger scheme not really evil at all. From this, Chrysippus deduces the impossibility of pleasure without pain and of virtue without vice. Courage could not occur did not cowardice; justice, did not injustice. Indeed we call actions cowardly or unjust not with reference to the act itself, but with reference to the agent's intention. The same action, in the sense of the same physical behavior, can be cowardly if done with one intention (the agent aims only to save himself) and courageous if done with another (the agent aims to prevent a struggle, even at the cost of his own reputation for courage).

We can now understand why the Stoics think it possible to combine determinism with a belief that men can either assent to or dissent from the divine law. What is determined is the entire physical world, including human beings insofar as they are part of that world; what apparently escapes determination is human assent or dissent to the course of things expressed in the form of intention. Even if I dissent from and rebel against the predetermined course of nature, my physical behavior will still conform to it. "*Ducunt volentem fata, nolentem trahunt,*" wrote Seneca later on.

In what form does the divine law to which my assent is invited present itself? As the law of nature and of reason. *Nature* now becomes a term quite other than what it was in either Plato or Aristotle. It refers to the cosmic status of the moral law; as such, it still contrasts with *convention* in the sense of what is merely established for local observance. But somehow the moral law and the physical universe now share a source, a prefiguring again of Christianity. What nature and reason invite us to is the observance of the four traditional virtues, prudence, courage, temperance, and justice. But one cannot, for the Stoics, possess one of these without possessing all. Virtue is single and indivisible. One cannot possess it in part; either one is virtuous, or one is not. There is a single dividing line among men. Above all, virtue is to be sought only for its own sake. "Virtue," as Diogenes Laërtius regards it, "is a rational disposition, to be desired in and for itself and not for the sake of any hope, fear, or ulterior motive."[22] Pleasure, by contrast, is not to be sought at all. Cleanthes thought that it was positively to be shunned; most of the Stoics that it was merely to be disregarded. Desire, hope and fear, pleasure and pain are against reason and nature; one should cultivate a passionless absence of desire and disregard of pleasure and pain. This the Stoics called *apathy*.

What then does one *do*? How does one actually behave? One disregards all attractions of external goods; one is therefore not exposed to the pain of their loss. Peace of mind is thereby secured. (Hence the later use of the adjective *stoical*). In the world at large, one disregards those differences between men which are merely a consequence of externals. There is one divine universe, one rational human nature, and therefore one appropriate attitude to all men. The Stoic is a citizen of the κόσμος, not of the πόλις.

It we turn not to Epicureanism expecting a sharp contrast, we find that what is striking about Epicureanism is in the end not the contrast with, but the resemblance to Stoicism. Superficially the differences are what stand out. Morality exists in a universe which is alien to it, and not, as with the Stoics, in a universe of which it is the highest expression. The atomism which Epicurus inherits from Democritus and bequeaths to Lucretius is a theory of blind physical determination. The moral consequences of atomism are negative; the gods do not control or interest themselves in human life. They dwell apart and indifferent, and natural phenomena have physical, not theological explanations. Plagues are not punishments, and thunderbolts are not warnings. Morality is concerned with the pursuit of pleasure, and not, as with the Stoics, with the pursuit of virtue independently of pleasure. Indeed, for Epicurus, virtue is simply the art of pleasure. But Epicurus then proceeds to argue that many pleasures, if heedlessly pursued, bring great pains in their wake, while some pains are worth tolerating for the ensuing or accompanying pleasures. He argues further, as the Cynics did, that the absence of pain is a greater good than positive pleasures; he argues, moreover, that a moderation in external goods is the only guarantee of not being pained by their loss; and he argues finally that freedom from intense desire is a condition of pleasure. All the conventional virtues are reinstated as means to pleasure and the gulf between Stoic apathy and Epicurean tranquillity (ἀταραξιά), verbally wide, is practically narrow. Epicurus' practical atheism makes him less pompous than the Stoics, and his high valuation of friendship makes him attractive as a person, but the regard for a quiet life, and detachment of the individual from the Platonic-Aristotelian morality of social life is as complete as it is in the Stoics.

Both Epicureanism and Stoicism are convenient and consoling doctrines for private citizens of the large impersonal kingdoms and empires of the Hellenistic and Roman worlds. Stoicism provides a better rationale for participation in public life, Epicureanism for withdrawal from it. Both place the individual in the context of a cosmos, not of a local community. Both have a function in a world in which pain is to be avoided rather than pleasure sought. In the Roman world especially, each has a function which is left unfulfilled by Roman religion. Roman religion is essentially an integrative cult in which the gods of the hearth, the gods of the formerly independent nations, and the gods of the empire express by their unity the single hierarchy of familial and imperial deities. The earliest Roman rulers speak from within their roles as fathers and consuls; if they use a religion to manipulate the plebeians, it is at least a religion which they share. But relatively early this ceases to be so. Polybius could write that "it is the very thing which among other peoples is an object of reproach, I mean superstition, which maintains the cohesion of the Roman state. These matters are clothed in such pomp and introduced to such an extent into their public and private life that nothing could exceed it, a fact which will surprise many. My own view at least is that they have adopted this course for the sake of the common people. It is a course which perhaps would not have been necessary had it been possible to form a state composed of wise men, but as every multitude is fickle, full of lawless desires, unreasoned passion, and violent anger, the multitude must be held in by invisible terrors and suchlike pageantry."[23]

Where religion is thus manipulative, the members of the middle and upper classes become unable to share the religion which they use for political purposes. They need beliefs which are rational by their own standards and will justify what *Romanitas* itself once justified or which will justify the withdrawal from public duty. These needs were admirably met by Stoicism and Epicureanism. Seneca and Marcus Aurelius exemplify the public side of Stoicism; Lucretius the liberating qualities of Epicureanism.

The doctrines of the Roman upper classes are, however, vulnerable in one crucial respect. The doctrines of apathy and ataraxia are useless as advice to those who already are propertyless and in no position to become hedonists. Exposed to poverty, disease, death, and to the will of those who are their rulers and often enough their owners, they still question how they are to live and what virtue and what happiness might be in their case. For some of these the mystery religions provided an answer. For even more an answer was to be given with the coming of Christianity.

# 9

## CHRISTIANITY

"God cannot talk about anything but Himself." Léon Bloy's remark about the Bible is an important half-truth. The Bible is a story about God in which human beings appear as incidental characters. That which is omitted by Bloy's epigram is the rich foreground of tribal saga, Middle Eastern kingship, prophesying and ritual, eating, drinking, sex, and death, which constitute the incidents. But that these constitute only the foreground becomes obvious if we remove God from the story: for what is then left is a jumble of characters and events in which all connection is lost. It is easy to underestimate this unity of the Bible; one way to bring out its importance is to reconsider some sociological theses about religion.

Myths, as anthropologists tell us, exhibit social pattern and structure. Myth and ritual together provide a means whereby men can exhibit to themselves the forms of their collective life. If we ask the key question of a society, What is holy to whom? we shall lay bare the different norms that inform social life. This is the thought that inspired Durkheim and his pupils in their work on religion, and especially on relatively primitive religion. It is a thought equally applicable to modern American religion, if we consider the way in which American religion acquired its hegemony by its key role in the work of imposing the norms of American homogeneity upon immigrant variety, and how, in filling this role, it transformed its own content. But it is equally clearly a source of great misunderstanding, if we suppose that this kind of analysis could afford us an exhaustive understanding of religion in the case of those religions which outlast a single people or society. In such religions we find built up a set of beliefs and ways of behaving which become relatively independent of particular, specific forms of social life. For this very reason we shall expect to find built into such religions enormous flexibility and adaptability with regard to behavior. We shall expect to discover a great capacity for coming to terms with quite different sets of moral standards in different times and places.

If this is the kind of expectation that we ought to have about religions which have a longer history than had the societies they outlasted, then it is pre-eminently the kind of expectation that we ought to form of the Judaeo-Christian tradition. We shall not be disappointed. The successive expression of the forms of life of Hebraic tribalism, Hellenistic monarchy, the Roman imperial proletariat, Constantinian bureaucrats, and the long list of their successors results in a theology which can accommodate a wide range of views in ethics. To an age which, like our own, has been continually exhorted to find the solutions to its own problems in Christian morality, it will perhaps come as a relief to consider that the whole problem of Christian morality is to discover just what it is. What bishops and journalists suppose to exist somewhere—if not on tables of stone, at least in materials of undoubted durability—turns out to be almost as elusive as the snark. And yet in speaking of a continuous tradition and of a single religion we appear to presuppose some sort of unity. This unity consists in certain themes which, although they can provide a context for very different sorts of norm and behavior, still furnish an entirely distinctive context. These themes are essentially as follows.

God is our father. God commands us to obey him. We ought to obey God because he knows what is best for us, and what is best for us is to obey him. We fail to obey him and so become estranged from him. We therefore need to learn how to be reconciled to God so that we can once more live in a familial relationship with him. These themes are of course susceptible of doctrinal development in a number of quite different directions. But what every such development necessarily embodies is the problem of reconciling two quite different models for understanding moral concepts and moral precepts.

The first of these conceives of moral precepts in terms of commandments and of moral goodness in terms of obedience. Why should I do that? "Because God says so." This at once raises the question, But why should I do what God commands? and to this there are three possible kinds of answer. The first points to God's holiness, the second to his goodness, the third to his power. I may answer "Just because he is God," and refuse to amplify this in any way. By this refusal I remain within the closed circle of religious concepts. The presupposition of the use of such concepts is that worship is a rational activity ("our reasonable service," as it is called in the New Testament) and *God* is defined as an adequate object of worship. Since worship involves a total abasement before and a total obedience to its object, in calling something or someone *God* I commit myself to obey its or his commandments. But it does not follow from this, as might be thought, that once I have accepted the practices of worship I am irremediably committed to an incorrigible religious dogmatism. For I can ask of any proposed object of worship, Is this an adequate object? Among the criteria of adequacy both the power and the knowledge that can be credibly ascribed to the object will appear, and since for any finite identifiable object it will be possible to conceive of some object that is more powerful and knows more, it will always be the case that any finite object is a less worthy object of worship than some other which can be conceived to exist. The ascent of this particular scale continues indefinitely to the point at which worshipers realize that only a nonfinite object, not identifiable as a particular being, is secure from displacement as God and characterization as mere idol. But, of course, by losing particularity, by becoming in the religious sense infinite, God becomes also questionable. For existence and particularity appear inextricably bound together. The leap from theism to monotheism prefigures the leap from theism to atheism; but, happily for religion, usually by some thousands of years.

Up to this point I have intentionally avoided remarking that among the criteria of adequacy by which the object of worship is judged, moral criteria normally appear. For at this point the first type of answer to the question, Why should I do what God commands? passes over into the second type of answer, "Because he is good." Since this answer has to function as a reason for obedience to God, it follows that *good* must be defined in terms other than those of obedience to God if we are to avoid a vacuous circularity. It follows that I must have access to criteria of goodness which are independent of my awareness of divinity. But if I possess such criteria, I am surely in a position to judge of good and evil on my own account, without consulting the divine commandments. To this the believer will correctly reply that if God is not only good, but also omniscient, his knowledge of effects and consequences will make him a better moral guide than anyone else. What one should note about this reply is that although it provides us with a reason for doing what God commands, if we act only for this reason, we shall be in the position of taking God's advice rather than of being obedient to him. But this is normally impossible in actual religions on other specifically religious grounds. For, first of all, God does not only know better than we what the outcomes of alternative courses of action will be; it is he who makes these alternative outcomes be what they are. And where, as often, God makes it a condition of a favorable outcome for us that we obey him, he provides us with quite another sort of reason for obeying him. If God's goodness makes it reasonable to do what he commands, his power makes it reasonable to do this in a spirit of obedience. But at this point we have already passed on to the third type of answer to the question, Why should I do what God commands?—namely, "Because of his power."

The power of God is both a useful and a dangerous concept in morals. The danger lies partly in this: if I am liable to be sent to hell for not doing what God commands, I am thereby provided with a corrupting, because totally self-interested, motive for pursuing the good. When self-interest is made as central as this, other motives are likely to dwindle in importance and a religious morality becomes self-defeating, at least insofar as it was originally designed to condemn pure self-interest. At the same time, however, the power of God is a useful, and for certain periods of history, morally indispensable concept. I have already suggested that the connection between virtue and happiness is one which can be made out more or less plausibly depending upon the rules and the ends which are advanced in a particular form of society. When social life is so organized that virtue and happiness appear in fact to have no connection, the conceptual relationships will be altered, for it will become impossible to argue that the appropriate form of justification for the conventional and established rules of virtue is to appeal to the happiness or the satisfaction to be obtained by following them. At this point either some justification is found for the conventional rules of virtue (for example, that they are to be followed "for their own sake") or the rules are abandoned. The danger lies in the possibility that all sight of the connection will be lost, that virtue appear independent of and even contrary to happiness, and that desires become primarily material for repression. The utility of the concept of the power of God is that it may help to keep alive belief in and an elementary understanding of the connection in social conditions where any relationship between virtue and happiness appears accidental. In a society where disease, famine, hunger, and death at any early age are among the staple components of human life, as they have been for the vast majority of people throughout history, belief in the power of God to make happiness coincide with virtue, at least in another world, if not in this, keeps open the question of the point of moral rules. Even this usefulness of the concept has of course its concomitant danger: that belief in the power of God should breed a belief that the connection between virtue and happiness is made only in heaven, and not on earth. It at best belongs to the class of desperate remedies for morality in impoverished and disordered societies; but this should not obscure the fact that it has provided such a remedy.

This view of the role of the concept of the power of God may suggest that religious conceptions of morality are intelligible only insofar as they complement or otherwise elaborate upon existing secular conceptions. This suggestion is surely correct. If religion is to propound a set of rules or a set of goals successfully, it must do so by showing that to live in the light of such rules and goals will be productive of what men can independently judge to be good. It would be absurd to deny that the world religions, and more especially Christianity, have been the bearers of new values. But these new values have to commend themselves by reason of the role that they can have in human life. There is, for example, no reason to quarrel with the contention that Christianity introduced even more strongly than the Stoics did the concept of every man as somehow equal before God. Even if, from St. Paul to Martin

Luther, this conviction appeared compatible with the institutions of slavery and serfdom, it provided a ground for attacking those institutions whenever their abolition appeared remotely possible. But insofar as the notion of the equality of men before God has moral content, it has so because it implies a type of human community in which nobody has superior rights of a moral or political kind to anyone else, but need is the criterion of one's claim upon other people, and the type of community is to be commended or otherwise insofar as it provides a better or worse framework within which men's ideals for themselves and for others can be realized.

In fact, the distinctive values of equality and of the criteria of need which Christianity in large part begot could not possibly commend themselves as general values for human life until it began to appear possible for the basic material inequalities of human life to be abolished. So long as men produce such a small economic surplus that most men have to live at or near subsistence level and only a few can enjoy much more than this, so long must the form of the consumption entrench an inequality of rights in social life. Equality under such conditions has to be a vision at best, and to give that vision religious sanction is the only way of maintaining it. It is only in small, separated communities that values of fraternity and equality can be incarnated; they cannot provide a program for society as a whole.

The paradox of Christian ethics is precisely that it has always tried to devise a code for society as a whole from pronouncements which were addressed to individuals or small communities to separate themselves off from the rest of society. This is true both of the ethics of Jesus and of the ethics of St. Paul. Both Jesus and St. Paul preached an ethics devised for a short interim period before God finally inaugurated the Messianic kingdom and history was brought to a conclusion. We cannot, therefore, expect to find in what they say a basis for life in a continuing society. Moreover, Jesus is, in any case, concerned not to expound a self-sufficient code, but to provide a corrective for the Pharisaic morality, a corrective which is partly a matter of bringing the point of the Pharisaic rules into the picture and partly a matter of showing how the rules must be construed if the coming of the kingdom is imminent. Hence the only form of prudence is to look to the kingdom. To take thought for the morrow, to lay up treasure on earth, not to sell all you have and give to the poor—these are essentially imprudent policies. You will lose your own soul if you pursue such policies, precisely because the world you gain is not going to last. The appeal of the Gospels to self-love, and their assumption of a basic self-love in human nature, is frank. The command to love one's neighbor as oneself could scarcely have force otherwise. Equally, St. Paul is misunderstood if he is taken to be issuing injunctions on other than an interim basis; St. Paul's dislike of marriage as other than an expedient ("It is better to marry than to burn") is not so inhumane as unhistorically minded secularists have made it out to be, if it is understood in terms of the pointlessness of satisfying desires and creating relationships now which will hinder one from obtaining the rewards of eternal glory in the very near future. But this kind of apology for St. Paul is, of course, more fatal to Pauline ethics than the conventional secularist attack. For the crucial fact is that the Messianic kingdom did not come, and that therefore the Christian church ever since has been preaching an ethics which could not find application in a world where history had not come to an end. Modern sophisticated Christians tend to be highly contemptuous about those who assign a date to the Second Coming; yet their own, not only dateless, but undatable, conception of that Coming is far more foreign to the New Testament.

It is therefore not surprising that insofar as Christianity has propounded moral beliefs and elaborated moral concepts for ordinary human life, it has been content to accept conceptual frameworks from elsewhere. We should notice three main examples of this. The first is the borrowing from feudal social life of concepts of hierarchy and role. When St. Anselm[24] explains man's relationship to God he does so in terms of the relationship of disobedient tenants to a feudal lord. When he explains the different services owed to God by angels, monastics, and laity, he compares them respectively to the services of those who hold a fief permanently in return for services, of those who serve in the hope of receiving such a fief, and of those who are paid wages for services performed but have no hope of permanence. It is crucial to note that a Christianity which in order to provide norms, has to be expressed in feudal terms thereby deprives itself of every opportunity for criticizing feudal social relations. But this is not the whole story. The theories of atonement and redemption, not only in Anselm but in other medieval theologians, depend on their conception of obedience or disobedience to the will of God. How are the values which God enjoins to be understood? The unsurprising answer is that the medieval God is always a compromise between the commanding voice of Jahweh upon Sinai and the god of the philosophers. Which philosophers? Either Plato or Aristotle.

The Platonic dichotomy between the world of sense perception and the realm of Forms is Christianized by St. Augustine into a dichotomy between the world of the natural desires and the realm of divine order. The world of the natural desires is that of his love for his mistress before his conversion and that of the *Realpolitik* of the earthly as against the heavenly city ("What are empires but great robberies?"). By an ascetic discipline, one ascends in the scale of reason, receiving illumination not from that Platonic anticipation, the Form of the Good, but from God. The illuminated mind is enabled to choose rightly between the various objects of desire which confront it. *Cupiditas*, the desire for earthly things, is gradually defeated by *caritas*, the desire for heavenly, in what is essentially a Christianized version of Diotima's message in the *Symposium*.

The Aristotelianism of Aquinas is far more interesting, for it is concerned not with escaping from the snares of the world and of desire, but with transforming desire for moral ends. It differs from the Aristotelianism of Aristotle in three main ways. $\Theta\varepsilon\omega\rho\acute{\iota}\alpha$ becomes that vision of God which is the goal and satisfaction of human desire; the list of the virtues is modified and extended; and both the concept of the $\tau\acute{\varepsilon}\lambda o\varsigma$ and that of the virtues are interpreted in a framework of law which has both Stoic and Hebraic origins. The natural law is that code to which we incline by nature; the supernatural law of revelation complements but does not replace it. The first injunction of the natural law is self-preservation; but the self which has to be preserved is the self of an immortal soul whose nature is violated by irrational slavery to impulse. The virtues are both an expression of and a means to obedience to the commandments of the natural law; and to the natural virtues are added the supernatural virtues of faith, hope, and charity. The key difference between Aristotle and Aquinas lies in the relationship which each takes to hold between the descriptive and the narrative elements of his analysis. Aristotle describes the virtues of the πόλις, and takes them to be normative for human nature as such; Aquinas describes the norms for human nature as such, and expects to find them exemplified in human life in particular societies. Aquinas cannot treat the descriptive task with the confidence of Aristotle because he has a belief in original sin; human nature as it ought to be, not human nature as it is, is the norm. But because he has neither the earlier Augustinian nor the later Protestant belief in the wholesale corruption of human desires and choices, he can treat human nature as it is as a tolerably reliable guide to human nature as it ought to be. As a Christian he, unlike Aristotle, although like the Stoics, treats human nature as one in all men. There are no slaves by nature. Moreover the table of the virtues is different. Humility takes its place; and so does religion in the sense of a disposition to perform the practices of due worship. But what is important in Aquinas is not so much the particular amendments which he makes to the Aristotelian scheme as the way in which he exhibits the flexibility of Aristotelianism. Aristotle's concepts can provide a rational framework for moralities very different from Aristotle's own. Aquinas, in fact, shows us how the conceptual links between virtue and happiness forged by Aristotle are a permanent acquisition for those who want to exhibit these links without admiring the great-souled man or without accepting the framework of the fourth-century πόλις.

Aquinas' theological ethics is such as to preserve the nontheological meaning of the word good. "Good is that to which desire tends." To call God good is to name him as the goal of desire. Thus the criterion of goodness is essentially nontheological. The natural man, without revelation, can know what is good, and the point of moral rules is to achieve goods, that is to achieve what satisfies desire. So "God is good" is a synthetic proposition, and to cite God's goodness is to give a reason for obeying his commandments. This view is replaced in the later Middle Ages by a quite different doctrine. Rapid transformation of the social order is always apt to make earlier formulation of natural law doctrine seem inapplicable. Men begin to look for the end of their life not within the forms of human community, but in some mode of individual salvation outside them. Natural religion and natural law are replaced by an appeal to divine revelation and to mystical experience.

The distance between God and man is emphasized. Man's finitude and sinfulness entail that he can have no knowledge of God but what he receives by grace, and man is held to possess by nature no criteria by which he can judge what God says, or is alleged to say. Good is defined in terms of God's commandments: "God is good" becomes analytic, and so does "We ought to do what God commands." The rules which God enjoins upon us can have no further justification in terms of our desires. Indeed, both in social life and in the conceptual scheme, the opposition between rules and desires becomes paramount. Asceticism and overasceticism (which Aquinas had characterized as "giving stolen gifts to God") become prominent in religion. The reasons for obeying God have to be in terms of his power and his numinous holiness rather than of his goodness.

The most notable philosopher who makes God's commandment the basis of goodness, rather than God's goodness a reason for obeying him, is William of Occam. Occam's attempt to base morals upon revelation is the counterpart of his restriction in theology upon what can be known by nature. Philosophical skepticism about some of the arguments of natural theology combines with theological fideism to make grace and revelation the sources for our knowledge of God's will. The oddity of Occam's critical rationalism is that it leaves the divine commandments as arbitrary edicts which demand a non-rational obedience. In Aquinas' Christianity room is left for an Aristotelian rationality; in Occam's there is none. The conclusion is perhaps that on an issue of this kind it matters more what kind of Christian or of non-Christian morality we are offered than whether the morality is Christian or not. And this view is not itself incompatible with a Thomist Christianity which exhibits more of a kinship with certain kinds of secular rationalism than with certain kinds of Christian irrationalism.

Nonetheless, this very fact makes it difficult to give an adequate account of the contribution of theism to the history of ethics. If one abstracts, for example, Abelard's early analysis of rightness (right action depends wholly on intention) or Grotius' later development of Aquinas' view of natural law into a law for the nations, one picks out what is not specifically theistic. If one develops in detail the morality of Augustinianism, one is expounding theology which appeals to revelation rather than a philosophical ethics. Hence one must err on the Middle Ages either by being encyclopedic or by being marginal. If, as I have done, one chooses the latter error, it is not as the lesser, but as the more manageable of two evils.

# 10

## LUTHER, MACHIAVELLI, HOBBES, AND SPINOZA

Machiavelli and Luther are morally influential authors about whom books on moral philosophy rarely contain discussions. This is a loss, because it is often in books such as these, rather than in those by more formally philosophical writers, that we discover the concepts which philosophers treat as the given objects of their discussion in the course of manufacture. Machiavelli and Luther were authors much in vogue among the Victorians. Hegel and Carlisle, Marx and Edward Caird, all recognized in them the masters of their own society; and in this they were right. Machiavelli and Luther mark in their different ways the break with the hierarchical, synthesizing society of the Middle Ages, and the distinctive moves into the modern world. In both writers there appears a figure who is absent from moral theories in periods when Plato and Aristotle dominate it, the figure of "the individual."

In both Machiavelli and Luther, from very different points of view, the community and its life are no longer the area in which the moral life is lived out. For Luther the community is merely the setting of an eternal drama of salvation; secular affairs are under the rule of the prince and the magistrate, whom we ought to obey. But our salvation hangs on something quite other than what belongs to Caesar. The structure of Luther's ethics is best understood as follows. The only true moral rules are the divine commandments; and the divine commandments are understood in an Occamist perspective—that is to say, they have no further rationale or justification than that they are the injunctions of God. To obey such moral rules cannot be to satisfy our desires; for our desires are part of the total corruption of our nature, and thus there is a natural antagonism between what we want and what God commands us to perform. Human reason and will cannot do what God commands because they are enslaved by sin; we therefore have to act against reason and against our natural will. But this we can do only by grace. We are saved not by works, for none of our works are in any way good. They are all the product of sinful desire.

We could not be further away from Aristotle; he is, said Luther, "that buffoon who has misled the church." The true transformation of the individual is entirely internal; to be before God in fear and trembling as a justified sinner is what matters. It does not follow from this that there are not actions which God commands and others which he forbids. But what matters is not the action done or left undone, but the faith which moved the agent. Yet there are many actions which cannot be the fruit of faith; these include any attempt to change the powers that be in the social structure. Luther's demand that we attend only to faith and not to works is accompanied by prohibitions uttered against certain types of work. He condemned peasant insurrection and advocated the massacre by their princes of peasant rebels against lawful authority. The only freedom he demands is the freedom to preach the gospel; the events that matter all occur in the psychological transformation of the faithful individual.

Although Luther had medieval Catholic predecessors on many individual points of doctrine, he was and boasted that he was unsurpassed in his upholding of the absolute rights of secular authority. In this lies his importance for the history of moral theory. This handing over of the secular world to its own devices is made the easier by his doctrine of sin and justification. For since in every action we are at the same time totally sinners and totally saved and justified by Christ, the nature of this action as against that does not come into the picture. To suppose that one action can be better than another is to be still using the standards of the law, from bondage to which Christ delivered us. Luther once asked his wife, Katharina, if she was a saint, and when she replied, "What, a great sinner such as me a saint?" reproved her and explained that everyone justified by faith in Christ was equally a saint. In such a perspective it is natural that the word *merit* should be expunged from the theological vocabulary, for it becomes impossible to raise the question of the merit of one action as against another.

The law of God becomes, therefore, only a standard against which we judge ourselves guilty and in need of redemption; and the commandments of God become a series of arbitrary fiats for which to demand any natural justification is at once impious and meaningless. *Good* and *right* are defined in terms of what God commands; and the tautologous character of "It is right to obey God" and "God is good" is not thought to be a defect, but rather to redound to God's glory. "God is all-powerful" remains, of course, a synthetic proposition; what God can do is all that the most powerful man can do and far more. So God is not only an omnipotence, but an arbitrary omnipotence. Aquinas had almost civilized Jahweh into an Aristotelian; Luther turns him into Nobodaddy for good. And at this point the resemblances between Luther and Calvin are more important than the differences.

For, firstly, Calvin too presents a God of whose goodness we cannot judge and whose commandments we cannot interpret as designed to bring us to the τέλος to which our own desires point; as with Luther, so with Calvin, we have to hope for grace that we may be justified and forgiven for our inability to obey the arbitrary fiats of a cosmic despot. Secondly, even where Calvin appears most at odds with Luther, in his treatment of the realm of the secular, there is an inner identity. Luther took St. Paul's attitude to the bureaucrats of the Roman empire as the model for his own attitude to the Elector of Saxony; Calvin took the attitude of the prophets to the kings of Israel and Judah as his model in dealing with the magistrates of Geneva. But although Calvin's theocracy makes clergy sovereign over princes, it sanctions the autonomy of secular activity at every level where morals and religious practice do not directly conflict with such activity. Provided that sex is restrained within the bounds of marriage and that churchgoing is enforced on Sundays, political and economic activity can proceed effectively unchecked by any sanctions whatsoever. Only the most obviously outrageous are ever condemned, and the history of Calvinism is the history of the progressive realization of the autonomy of the economic. Luther, like Calvin, bifurcated morality; there are on the one hand the absolutely unquestionable commandments, which are, so far as human reason and desires are concerned, arbitrary and contextless, and on the other hand, there are the self-justifying rules of the political and economic order.

"The individual" is the subject of both realms; individual precisely because he is defined as against the God who creates him and as against the political and economic order to which he is subordinated. "For the first time," wrote J. N. Figgis of the period immediately after the Reformation, "the Absolute Individual confronts the Absolute State."[25] The state becomes distinct from society; in the Middle Ages social ties and political ties have a unity, just as they did for the Greeks, even if the unity of feudalism and the unity of the πόλις were quite different. A man is related to the state not via a web of social relations binding superiors and inferiors in all sorts of ways, but just as subject. A man is related to the economic order not via a well-defined status in a set of linked associations and guilds, but just as one who has the legal power to make contracts. Of course this social process of transition from status to contract is not only slow and uneven, it never takes place once for all. Time and again, different sections of the community experience the shock of the dissolution of patriarchal ties; time and again, consciousness of the free market and the absolute state is sharpened. But in every case, what emerges is a new identity for the moral agent.

In traditional societies, and even in the Greek πόλις or under feudalism, a man defines himself in terms of a set of established descriptions by means of which he situates and identifies himself vis-à-vis other men. One reason why it is highly misleading to talk of a logical gulf between value and fact is that it suggests that in *every society* it is equally true that we can first set out the facts of the social order, and then as a second, logically independent task, inquire how in this society one ought to behave. But this could only be true for all societies if it was always necessarily the fact that one could describe a social order without making use of the concepts of duties and obligations; whereas in fact for many societies we cannot provide a specification of the minimal social identity of an individual (as son of a chief, or a villein, or member of such-and-such class or family), let alone of his full social role, without specifying him as having such-and-such obligations or duties. To this the reply will be that the fact that in such a society such a man is held to have certain duties can only be a fact about that society. It does not commit us to say that the man ought to perform them. But this is again highly misleading. For it implies that it is possible to say, for example, "It is not true that a son of a chief ought to do such and such"; but in the language of the tribe this is simply a false evaluative statement, and in the language which we use to describe the tribe it is simply a false descriptive statement. What, of course, is true is that we can characterize the life of the tribe without accepting their values; but this implies, not that we can discuss independently of their stock of social description how in this kind of society one ought to behave, but rather that we can always raise the additional question of whether this kind of society's continuance is a good or bad thing. What we often cannot do is characterize their social life in their factual terms and escape their evaluations.

There are, of course, many societies where the language of factual description is such that it avoids commitment to evaluation in this way, and the transition from the traditional forms of precapitalist society in western Europe to the individualist and mercantile society of early capitalism is a transition of this kind. It is, therefore, not just that Aquinas' Christian Aristotelianism and Luther's Christian fideism are based on alternative and competing metaphysical schemes; it is also the case that they are providing an analysis of and insight into different moral vocabularies. Of course, in the case of Luther particularly, the analysis which is implicit in his preaching is causally efficacious; Luther makes sense of the moral experience of his hearers, and in so doing, leads to the acceptance of a framework in which their experience comes to be interpreted in stock Lutheran ways. The crucial feature of the new experience is that it is the experience of an individual who is alone before God. When Luther wants to explain what an individual is he does so by pointing out that when you die, it is you who die, and no one else can do this for you. It is as such, stripped of all social attributes, abstracted, as a dying man is abstracted, from all his social relations, that the individual is continually before God.

Thus the individual no longer finds his evaluative commitments made for him, in part at least, by simply answering the question of his own social identity. His identity now is only that of the bearer of a given name who answers as a matter of contingent fact to certain descriptions (red haired or blue eyed, laborer or merchant), and he has to make his own choice among the competing possibilities. From the facts of his situation as he is able to describe them in his new social vocabulary nothing at all follows about what he ought to do. Everything comes to depend upon his own individual choice. Moreover, the sovereignty of individual choice is not only a consequence of his social vocabulary, but of the theorizing derived from theology.

In Aristotelian ethics, as in the less explicitly formulated moralities of traditional societies, human needs and wants, understood in various ways, provide the criteria for judging human actions. The Aristotelian account of the practical syllogism is a model here, where the major premise is always of the form that someone desires (or needs, or would benefit from) something. Practical reasoning begins at this point. But the facts of human desires and needs can in the sixteenth century no longer provide a criterion for the choices of the moral agent, or a major premise for his reasoning, at least if he takes seriously the charge of Lutherans and Calvinists alike that his desires are totally depraved. Even the popular theology of the Counter Reformation takes a much blacker view of human nature than Aquinas did. Because all desires are corrupt (although as always, sex usually takes the worst beating, with political rebellion its only close competitor) choice remains open. Between salvation and damnation, between profit and loss, between the multitude of competing policies which claim his attention, the individual has to choose.

Three main concepts of moral import therefore emerge from the Reformation period: that of moral rules as being at once unconditional in their demands but lacking any rational justification; that of the moral agent as sovereign in his choices; and that of the realm of secular power as having its own norms and justifications. It is not surprising either that the new concepts of rules and of the agent take on a new look when placed in this secular context. Moreover, the secular context had already found its own Luther. The author who is the Luther of secular power is Machiavelli. Like Luther, he has his medieval anticipators. Within the context of natural law medieval theologians had often argued that certain political ends justified means that were normally not permitted; the removal of tyrants by assassination is a common example. Powicke has explained how, from Frederick II and Philip the Fair onward, "The next step was to identify the natural law of necessity with the natural impulses of a political community, its rights to natural frontiers and self-assertion, or even to identify necessity not with natural law but with the dictates of history." This trend, so far as *Realpolitik* is concerned, was already adequately embodied in the medieval state, and the modern state has merely worsened *Realpolitik* by being more powerful. But Machiavelli is its first theorist.

A great deal of effort has been expended to show that, contrary to the Elizabethan dramatists, and in spite of his notorious admiration for Cesare Borgia, Machiavelli was not a bad man. This is partly because his was clearly an attractive personality, and it is widely although incorrectly felt that somehow one cannot be both bad and attractive. But more importantly it is because Machiavelli's private and personal preferences were certainly for democracy (in his sense of the word—that is, *extended* limited rule, with small masters sharing power with large merchants, excluding of course servants and propertyless men), for generosity, honesty, and candor. But none of this must be allowed to confuse the issue. For Machiavelli the ends of social and political life are given. They are the attainment and holding down of power, the maintenance of political order and general prosperity, and these latter, in part at least, because unless you maintain them, you will not continue to hold power. Moral rules are technical rules about the means to these ends. Moreover, they are to be used on the assumption that all men are somewhat corrupt. We may break a promise or violate an agreement at any time if it is in our own interest so to do, for the presumption is that, since all men are wicked, those with whom you have contracted may at any time break their promises if it is in their interest. Men must act not as in some abstract way they think they ought to act, but as other men act; since other men *are* influenced to some extent by generosity, clemency, and the like, these have their place. But still they only have their place as well-designed means to the ends of power.

Machiavelli's is the first ethics, at least since some of the sophists, in which actions are judged not as actions, but solely in terms of their consequences. He is therefore committed to the view that consequences are calculable, and most of *The Prince* and the *Discourses on Livy* is devoted to explaining how this is so. The study of history yields empirical generalizations from which we can derive causal maxims. The use of these maxims is to influence other people. Here again Machiavelli is both an heir of the sophists and an anticipator of modern writers. He must understand our evaluations as means to influence other people, rather than as answers to the question, What am I to do? It follows also that Machiavelli treats human behavior as governed by laws, and by laws of which the agents themselves are usually unconscious. For Machiavelli it is possible to take a very simple view of these laws, since he is prepared to treat human nature, its motives and aspirations, as timeless and unchanging. Generalizations derived from the ancient Romans can be applied without difficulty to sixteenth-century Florence. Nonetheless, "the individual" appears as starkly in Machiavelli as in Luther. He appears thus because society is not only the arena in which he acts but also a potential raw material, to be reshaped for the individual's own ends, law-governed but malleable. The individual is unconstrained by any social bonds. His own ends—not only those of power, but also those of glory and reputation—are for him the only criteria of action, apart from the technical criteria of statecraft. Thus we meet in Machiavelli for the first time what will become a familiar crux: the combination of an assertion of the sovereignty of the individual in his choices and his aims with the view that human behavior is governed by unchanging laws. It is true that Machiavelli distinguishes between those whom he considers in the one capacity (ruler or potential rulers) and those whom he considers in the other (the ruled). But he is unconscious of any possible contradiction.

Although he pays verbal obeisances to the distinction between ethics and politics, he makes clear the irrelevance of drawing it too sharply. Such a distinction depends upon there being a distinction between private and public life of such a kind that I can consider what it is best for me to do without considering in what political order it is requisite for me to live, either because I treat the political order as a given and unalterable context of private action, or because I think the political order irrelevant for some other reason. Machiavelli resembles Plato in making it clear on how many occasions ethics and politics merge. Because from his age onward it becomes increasingly possible for more and more people to play a part in altering or modifying political institutions, the political order is less and less often a given and unalterable context. Because the power of the state continually grows, that power impinges more and more upon the private citizen and upon the alternatives between which he has to make his moral choices.

Finally there is a lesson to be learned from Machiavelli's example as much as from his explicit teaching. In periods in which the social order is relatively stable all moral questions can be raised from within the context of the norms which the community shares; in periods of instability it is these norms themselves which are questioned and tested against the criteria of human desires and needs. Both Plato and Aristotle, although they lived out the decline of the πόλις, take its form and its institutions more for granted than Machiavelli does the forms and institutions of the Italian city-state. Machiavelli is more aware of the external threats to Florence from the larger powers than Aristotle ever was of the threat of Macedon to Athens. Living in an age of flux, Machiavelli understood the transience of political orders, and it is this which in one way makes his appeal to the permanence of human nature so striking. For the counterpart to a belief in the transience of political and social orders might easily not have been a belief in a timeless human nature with permanent needs against which these orders can be measured and in terms of which they can be explained.

It is, by now at any rate, clear that following the age of Luther and Machiavelli, we should expect the rise of a kind of moral-cum-political theory in which the individual is the ultimate social unit, power the ultimate concern, God an increasingly irrelevant but still inexpungeable being, and a prepolitical, presocial timeless human nature the background of changing social forms. The expectation is fully gratified by Hobbes.

"Being in a Gentleman's Library, Euclid's Elements lay open, and 'twas the El. libri I. He read the Proposition. By G . . . , sayd he (he would now and then sweare an emphaticall Oath by way of emphasis), this is impossible! So he reads the Demonstration of it, which referred him back to such a Proposition; which proposition he read. That referred him back to another, which he also read. Et sic deinceps (and so on) that at last he was demonstratively convinced of that trueth. This made him in love with Geometry."[26] The writer is John Aubrey, the subject is Thomas Hobbes, and the year of the episode referred to is

1629. Hobbes was already forty-one. His intellectual background to this date is symbolized by his rejection of Aristotle and his translation of Thucydides. The Aristotle who is rejected is the Aristotle of late, degenerate scholasticism. The complaint against this Aristotle is that he confuses the investigation of the meaning of words with the investigation of the things for which words stand. And with this complaint Hobbes rejects the whole Aristotelian epistemology of matter and form, essence and existance. In doing so, he believes that he is avoiding obfuscation; he is leaving himself with a universe composed only of concrete individuals, words and the bodies which they signify. Yet, in fact, Hobbes' own investigations assume—and necessarily assume—the form of a conceptual inquiry; for he wishes to lay bare the notions of right, justice, sovereignty, and power. He finds a non-Aristotelian model for his inquiries in Euclid's *Elements*. The impulse for these inquiries was that which sent him to Thucydides.

Thucydides' *History of the Peloponnesian War* was written, as Machiavelli's works were, in the belief that history can be instructive. It exhibits the downfall of Athens through the misdeeds of the Athenian democracy. The moral is the political corrosiveness of democracy, the villain Cleon the tanner, the archetype of envious and aspiring men. The England of the 1620s was full of envious and aspiring men. Not surprisingly, since the great price revolution which had begun in the previous century had destroyed the traditional economic patterns of the English land-holder. Fortunes were made and lost; individuals rose in standing through adroit use of money; the relationships of small and large gentry, of great noblemen and their lesser dependents, were in flux. England stood on the edge of a market economy in which the feudal and aristocratic ties were in danger of being displaced by the cash nexus. The state power embodied in the crown stood in new and uncertain relationship to its subjects. The particular strand in the cash nexus which taxation represents was the point at which the crown's assertion of what it claimed were traditional duties met the subjects' assertion of what they claimed were traditional rights. (It is always a sobering thought that the income-tax accountant searching for legal loopholes for his business clients is the spiritual descendant of Pym and Hampden.) Hobbes foresees danger in the claim to rights *against* the crown and translates Thucydides as a solemn warning against the threat to sovereignty of rival and warring social factions. It is as the loyal subject of the Stuart kings that Hobbes translates the admirer of Pisistratus and Pericles.

Yet Hobbes is entirely untypical in the manner of his intervention in the quarrels between the sovereign and his subjects. The hierarchical society of an earlier England is one in which personal, social, and political loyalties intermingle and support one another. Rights and duties are defined within a single, if complex, system. The justification of any particular move in the feudal game lies either in referring to the positions of the actors or to the rules of the game. What the economic revolutions, and particularly, in England, the price revolution of the sixteenth and seventeenth centuries bring about is a breaking of these ties. Most of the traditional social landmarks remain; what is questioned is their interrelationship. God is still believed in, and the priest is still in his parish. But one can question in a more radical way what links the priest to God. The elements of feudal society are all present—servants and other propertyless men, small gentry, nobility, the king; what is in question is the mode of their interrelation. The age is ripe for theories of authority; and the two most popular sources of theorizing are the scriptures and history. The doctrine of the divine right of kings, with its model of King David, vies for Biblical warrant with Presbyterian doctrines of ecclesiocracy disguised as theocracy. The appeal to historical precedent is used to prop up both the doctrine of divine right and the doctrine that the sovereign is dependent on Lords and Commons. Hobbes appeals to neither. He breaks with the whole discussion by his appeal to a new method, learned from Galileo, which will enable him not merely to understand the elements of social life, but to estimate the worth of appeals to history or to scripture.

The method is that of resolving any complex situation into its logically primitive, simple elements and then using the simple elements to show how the complex situation could be reconstructed. In doing this we shall have shown how the situation is in fact constructed. This is the method which Hobbes took Galileo to have employed in the study of physical nature. In the case of physical nature, of course, the theoretical reconstruction of complexity out of simplicity has no moral function; but in the case of human society the rectification of our understanding may provide a rectification of how we conceive our place in society and consequently of our beliefs as to how we ought to live.

When society is resolved into its simple elements, what do we find? A collection of individuals, each of which is a system whose end is its own self-preservation. The fundamental human motives are the desire to dominate and the desire to avoid death. "Men from their very birth, and naturally, scramble for everything they covet, and would have all the world, if they could, to fear and obey them."[27] "Continually to be outgone, is misery. Continually to outgo the next before, is felicity. And to forsake the course, is to die."[28] The only limitations upon a "perpetual and restless stirring of power after power" are death and the fear of death. The individuals who are driven by these motives know no rules except those precepts which instruct them in how they may preserve themselves. Before society exists there is nothing but competition for domination, a war of each against all. Of this situation it is true that "Where there is no common power, there is no law: where no law, no injustice. Force and fraud are in war the two cardinal virtues." Nonetheless reason instructs the individual that he has more to fear than to hope for from this war; death is a more certain outcome than domination. To avoid death, he must exchange peace for war, agreement for competition; and those articles of agreement which reason urges as prudent even in a state of nature constitute the Laws of Nature. The first is "that every man ought to endeavour peace, as far as he has hope of obtaining it; and when he cannot obtain it, that he may seek, and use, all helps, and advantages of war"; the second, "that a man be willing, when others are so too, as far-forth, as for peace, and defence of himself he shall think it necessary, to lay down this right to all things; and be contented with so much liberty against other men, as he would allow other men against himself"; and the third, "that men perform their covenants made."[29]

Yet this is clearly not enough to assuage the fear of death. For while we may agree with other men in order to make ourselves mutually secure from each other's aggression, how can we be sure that others will abide by these agreements and not merely use them to lull us into a false sense of security so that they may then attack us more effectively? In the state of nature there are no sanctions by means of which contracts may be enforced. "And covenants, without the sword, are but

words, and of no strength to secure a man at all."[30] To give the covenants the backing of a sword there has to be an initial contract by which
men transfer their power to a common power which becomes sovereign among them. This social contract effects the creation of "that great
LEVIATHAN, or rather, to speak more reverently, of that mortal God, to
which we owe under the immortal God, our peace and defence."[31]

The commands of the sovereign power, whatever the political nature
of that power—democratic, oligarchic, or monarchical—furnish a
second set of precepts which demand obedience. The only limitations
upon the obedience which the sovereign may demand is at the point
where the motive for assenting to the transfer of power to the sovereign in the original contract, that is, the fear of death, becomes a
motive for resisting the sovereign himself, namely at any point at
which the sovereign threatens to take away one's life. Otherwise the
only point at which one may cease to owe the sovereign obedience is
that at which the sovereign ceases to be able to perform the very
function for which he was given the power in the first place, that of
protecting the lives of his subjects. That is, the sovereign who becomes
powerless is no longer owed obedience, is no longer indeed a sovereign. Rebellions are always wrong while they are unsuccessful. Successful rebellion however is the assumption of sovereignty and has all the
justification of sovereignty behind it. It is, because successful, not
rebellion.

The rules which bind the individual are therefore of two kinds,
pre- and post-contract, natural and social. To use the word *social* is to be
reminded of one of the oddest of Hobbes' confusions, that he appears
not to distinguish the state and society, to make political authority not
dependent upon the prior existence of, but constitutive of, social life.
There *are* of course situations where the disappearance of the state's
power of repression may lead to the rise of anarchic violence. But there
are and have been plenty of situations where an orderly social life
continues without such a power being present. Indeed if one contrasts
eighteenth-, nineteenth-, and twentieth-century urban life, where the
state's repressive power is close at hand, with the moral life of those
other periods where it is often absent or far away, one might draw the
conclusion that the state's presence is a demoralizing factor. This would
be—at any rate, so far as the argument has taken us already—as

ill-founded, because as one-sided, a conclusion as Hobbes'. But it underlines Hobbes' error.

According to Hobbes the social rules are rules which we obey for two kinds of reason: first, because they are enforced by the sanctions of the sovereign; and second, because our desires are such that we prefer to obey the sovereign, in order to escape death at the hands of others, except where we are liable to incur it at the hands of the sovereign. The rules which constitute the law of nature we obey simply because they are precepts which tell us how to get what we want (domination) and avoid what we do not want (death). Both sets of rules are of the form, "If you want to get X, you must do Y." They are thus factual statements which may be true or false; and they are selected out of the set of such statements for inclusion in the list of natural and social precepts because the desires named in the antecedent clauses are the desires which all men do, as a matter of contingent fact, have.

Hobbes' position on this point has been attacked on two kinds of ground. The first of these attacks is misconceived. It is that moral rules are not the kind of prudential, factual statement that Hobbes makes them out to be, that moral rules are simply of the form "You ought to do so-and-so" and contain no reference to desires or inclinations. What is quite true is that in some societies (notably in modern Western ones, such as our own) this form of moral rule has been predominant; but it is not at all clear why the adjective moral should be restricted to this form of rule. To this it may be replied by Hobbes' critics that the moral rules in fact used by Hobbes' contemporaries were of this form and that Hobbes has simply misrepresented and misanalyzed them. The difficulty with this version of their contention is that it is difficult to know how to interpret utterances of the form "You ought . . ." where the absence of any hypothetical clause referring to desires may be due either to the fact that no such reference is intended or to the fact that such a reference is so clearly and commonly shared that it does not need to be made explicit. But it is important to note that Hobbes, in giving desires a central place in the moral picture, is at one with his predecessors; it is only gradually that Protestantism and other influences cause morality and desire to appear to be sharply contrasted. Hence this attack on Hobbes is perhaps slightly anachronistic.

That Hobbes did, however, misrepresent and misanalyze his contemporaries' use of moral rules remains true. Aubrey has a story of how, outside St. Paul's Cathedral, an Anglican clergyman who had seen Hobbes give alms to a poor man tried to improve the occasion by asking of Hobbes (who was reputedly impious and atheistic) if he would have given the alms, had not Christ commanded it. Hobbes' reply was that he gave the alms because not only did it please the poor man, but it pleased him to see the poor man pleased. Thus Hobbes tries to exhibit his own behavior as consistent with his theory of motives, namely that human desires are such that they are all self-interested. The kind of lie told by Hobbes according to this anecdote is a kind of lie indulged in more often by philosophers than by other men, a lie told in the interests of saving the face of a theory. It remains a lie and a culpable lie, although one that Hobbes needed to tell. For the root of his error is here. Human nature and human motives are not and cannot be what he says they are.

According to Hobbes any regard for the welfare of others is second-ary to a regard for, and indeed is only a means to, my own welfare. In fact, both in ourselves and in others we find other-regarding and self-regarding motives side by side. What could justify us in representing the former as a secondary offspring of the latter? What justifies Hobbes is his view of the contract as intervening between the state of nature and social life. But what justifies his view of the contract? Not any historical or anthropological evidence that man ever is or was like this. Hobbes does in passing refer to the American Indians, but his whole argument is based on a method that makes him independent of histor-ical evidence. He is resolving timeless human nature into its timeless elements, not recounting an evolutionary progress. The story of the contract must then be read as an extended metaphor; but it can only function, even as a metaphor, if it is an intelligible story, if it satisfies certain elementary requirements of logical coherence. This it fails to do.

The Hobbesian contract is the foundation of social life in the sense that prior to the contract there are no shared rules or standards; indeed, the story of the contract functions as some kind of explanation of how men came to share social norms. But any exchange of words, written or spoken, between men which it would be appropriate to characterize as a contract or agreement or making of promises can only be so characterized in virtue of there already existing some acknowledged and shared rule according to which the use of the form of words in question is understood by both parties to be a binding form of words. Apart from such an already acknowledged and accepted convention, there could be nothing which could be correctly called a contract, agreement, or promise. There could perhaps be expressions of intention; but in a Hobbesian state of nature there would be every reason to suspect that these were designed to mislead. The only available standards for interpreting the utterances of others would prevent any conception of agreement. Thus Hobbes makes two incompatible demands of the original contract: he wishes it to be the foundation of all shared and common standards and rules; but he also wishes it to be a contract, and for it to be a contract, there must already exist shared and common standards of the kind which he specifies cannot exist prior to the contract. The concept of an *original* contract is therefore ruined by internal self-contradiction and cannot be used even to frame a metaphor of a coherent kind.

If this is so, does not the whole Hobbesian case founder? It does. Hobbes wishes to picture a transition from a state of affairs where aggression and fear are the only motives and force is the only effective instrument to a state of affairs where there are acknowledged standards and legitimate authority. Clearly such transitions are sometimes made; an authority comes to be regarded as legitimate and is obeyed although originally imposed by force in at least this sense: the question of who is the legitimate authority in any state and the question of who has the power there do not necessarily receive the same answer. It is quite clear that Dutch William and the German "fools and oppressors called 'George'!"—Byron's description for them—had the power in Britain after 1689, when the legitimate authority rested with King James II and his descendants. But this also makes it clear that the concept of legitimate authority has application only within a context of socially accepted rules, practices, and institutions. For to call an authority legitimate is to appeal to an accepted criterion of legitimacy. Where there is no such criterion there can only be power or rival powers—as when an occupying army imposes its rule on a defeated country; and whether there is such a criterion or not is a matter of the acceptance by people in general of the criterion. *De facto* power can become *de jure* legitimacy.

It was Hobbes' insight to see this; indeed every inhabitant of England saw it in the transition from the *de facto* power of the Cromwellian army to the *de jure* legitimacy of the Commonwealth. But what Hobbes failed to see was that the acceptance of an authority is in fact the acceptance of rules which give others and ourselves the right to act in certain ways or the duty to act in certain ways, and that to have right is not to have power, while to have a duty is not to act from fear of the power of others. Hobbes equates "having a right to" with "having the power to" for at least two reasons. He saw correctly that authority is usually enforced by power, that authority often relies on the sanction of force. And he has such a limited view of human motives that he cannot provide any other explanation for acceptance of authority than the fear of such sanctions. But in fact an authority accepted *only* because men feared the consequences of not accepting it, or *only* because they feared the sanctions which it deployed, could not function with the effectiveness with which most political authorities do function. Political institutions only have the stability they have because most men most of the time grant a willing obedience to their authority, and men do this because they see their own desires and those the satisfaction of which the authority safeguards coinciding. So does Hobbes. But he has such a limited conception of human desires that he necessarily has a limited conception of political authority.

This limited conception of motives, desires, and activity insures that most of the substance of human life goes unmentioned in Hobbes. We have a sovereign power so that our lives may continue securely; but what are we to do with our lives within the framework of order thus secured? Hobbes does say that men are inclined to peace rather than to continuance in a state of nature not only by the fear of death, but also by "desire of such things as are necessary to commodious living; and a hope by their industry to obtain them." But what is commodious living? Hobbes has already said that "there is no such *finis ultimus*, utmost aim, or *summum bonum*, greatest good, as is spoken of in the books of the old moral philosophers," and his reason for saying this is his view that human felicity consists in "a continual progress of the desire from one object to another, the attaining of the former being still but the way to the latter," and that men are driven on by "a perpetual and restless desire of power after power that ceaseth only in death." This is a picture in which men are driven from desire to desire without the question, What kind of life do I want? ever arising. Hobbes' conception of the possible objects of desire is as limited as his conception of motives. Why?

The root of the trouble is perhaps twofold. Hobbes' theory of language commits him to the view that all words are names and that all names are names of individual objects or of collections of individual objects. Hence all objects of desire must be individual. At the same time, Hobbes' determinism, with its theological reinforcement (for Hobbes believes in God, a material though invisible deity, not the God of Christian orthodoxy, but the author of nature, who expresses his will in the precepts which in fact govern our natures), leads him to treat our desires as given and unalterable. The criticism of our desires and their rational remolding have no place in the Hobbesian system. It follows that, inevitably, our desires are for one individual object after another; and thus desires cannot include the desire for a certain kind of life, the desire that our desires should be of a certain kind.

Nonetheless, we owe to Hobbes a great lesson. This is that a theory of morals is inseparable from a theory of human nature. Just because Hobbes commits himself to a conception of a timeless human nature he commits himself to an unhistorical answer to the question of what had destroyed political order in England in the 1640s, replacing it by the question of what social and political order as such consist in. But although this question is dangerously overgeneral, it is a type of question which increasingly invades and must invade the domain of moral philosophers. In particular, we cannot hope to ask and answer questions about freedom without specifying the nature of the social background to the moral life. But this is a class of question which Hobbes himself never asks. He discusses the freedom of the will only in order to stress that all human acts are determined; and he discusses political freedom only within the limits allowed by the limitless power of the sovereign. That this should be so perhaps requires explanation. It is remarkable that Hobbes should be as impressed as he was by the fact of civil war and as unimpressed as he was by the declared and avowed aims of those who fought that war. But he *was* unimpressed and he was so because his theory of motives led him to suppose that high-minded ideals were necessarily but a mask for the drive to domination. Consequently he takes no stock in the appearance of freedom as an ideal and a goal, and in this he is blind to the most important social change in the history of this time. Certainly the appeal for freedom often did mask religious intolerance and economic ambition. But did it always? Could men have in fact specified their desires and their objects of desire in the kind of social order that was then emerging without invoking the concept of freedom? That Hobbes can ignore this question reinforces the view of him as a backward-looking philosopher. He remains preoccupied with the vanishing bonds of a former pattern of social life which is falling apart. In private life he himself was as concerned to escape dangers as to pursue more positive ends; when he saw the Civil War coming he went to France, "the first," as he says himself, "of those that fled." But if he feared death, he showed no signs at all of aspiring to domination. There is thus a crucial gap even between the values exhibited in his own quiet life at Malmesbury and those which he claims to pervade human life.

Hobbes is at every point a contrast to his only peer as a moral philosopher in his own century, Spinoza. It is not just that Spinoza's life unites philosophy and practice, that Spinoza manifests that very impersonal love of truth which he proclaims in his writings as the highest human value. It is also that he brings together a set of concepts which are forward-looking in that they are going to be constitutive of much of later human life: freedom, reason, happiness. The state exists to promote positive human goods, not merely as a bulwark against human disasters. Religion is a matter of truth primarily and of the magistrates only secondarily.

In the ordinary practice of pursuing moral judgments Spinoza sees two errors embodied. The first is that our standard of judgment is arbitrary and capricious. When we criticize a man as defective in some way, as being or doing what he ought not to be or do, we judge him, so Spinoza argues, against some picture we have formed of a proper or ideal man. But this picture is inevitably an arbitrary construction, put together of our own limited and chance experiences. Moreover, when we judge a man we say that he ought not to be as he is in a way that implies that he could be something other than he is. But this implies an illusory notion of freedom. Since everything is determined, nothing can be other than it is. Our ordinary state of mind, then, in which we pass everyday moral judgments, is one of confusion and illusion. How so? Spinoza's answer is that ordinary sense experience, and the ordinary uses of language which embody that experience, are inevitably a matter of conditioning, of association, of blurred meaning. Contrast the clarity of a mathematical system where every symbol has one clear and distinct meaning, and where it is therefore unambiguously obvious what propositions are entailed by and entail what other propositions. Thought becomes rational as it approaches the condition of geometry, geometry now being conceived of as the embodiment of the only possible approach to rigor and clarity. The ideal of a deductive system is not, however, merely an ideal for knowledge; this ideal mirrors the nature of the universe. The universe is a single web in which the whole determines every part. To explain any state of affairs is to understand that and how it must necessarily be as it is, given that other things are as they are. If we try to envisage anything apart from the system, we are trying to envisage something whose occurrence could not be made intelligible, since to be intelligible is to be exhibited as part of the system. The name of this single system is "*Deus, sive Natura*" (God or Nature).

There is therefore no good distinct from or apart from the totality of things. The attributes of God, infinity and eternity, belong to the single substance which is at once Nature and God. Is Spinoza here simply an atheist retaining the name *God*? Or is he a serious pantheist? Novalis was to call him the "god-intoxicated man"; Plekhanov was to hail him as the ancestor of materialist unbelief. There is a twofold answer. The first part of it is that compared with traditional Judaic or Christian theology Spinoza is an atheist; he believes in a single order of nature, and miraculous intervention is ruled out. The natural scientist need not reckon with supernatural irruptions or disturbances. The importance of this belief in the seventeenth century scarcely needs to be stressed. But, nonetheless, Spinoza did not simply dismiss the theological vocabulary; he treated it, as he treated ordinary language, as a set of expressions which needed reinterpretation to be made rational. He is thus the ancestor of all those skeptics who have treated religion not as simply false, but as expressing important truths in a misleading way. Religion needs not so much to be refuted as to be decoded. What is the relevance of this to morals?

The ordinary Jewish or Christian believer thinks of God as a being apart from the universe, and of the divine commandments as external precepts which he ought to obey. Spinoza did not undervalue the utility of what he saw as this superstitious morality of external obedience for ordinary uncritical people. But the counterpart of understanding God as identical with Nature is understanding ethics as the study not of divine precepts but of our own nature and of what necessarily moves us. Our nature as human beings is to exist as self-maintaining and self-preserving systems; this is true of the nature of all finite beings, which are subsystems of nature itself. Our unity as beings is disguised from us by our manner of thinking of ourselves as a unity of two quite distinct types of substance, body and mind. Those who believe in the duality of body and mind have, according to Spinoza, an insoluble problem on their hands as to how these can be related. But this problem disappears when we understand body and mind as simply two modes or aspects under which we have to conceive ourselves. We are a unity of body and mind. This is perhaps one point in the argument when we cannot avoid asking whether what Spinoza says is true. But where we ask this, we realize that the difficulty with Spinoza's system lies both in its form and in the use of some of the key terms. The form is of a deductive system in which all truths can be known by sufficiently careful reflection upon the meaning of the terms used in the propositions which express them. Consider Spinoza's claim that all men pursue their own interests or his assertion that all events have causes. These look at first sight like factual claims which could be refuted by citing counterexamples, whether that of a man who neglects his own interests to care for those of others, or that of a particular event without a cause. But Spinoza holds his positions to be true simply because they follow from the axioms of his deductive system, the axioms being propositions which he thinks no rational being could deny, because their denial appears to entail a contradiction. And the meaning of the key terms is such that we are left with no language in which counterexamples could be presented.

Spinoza's difficulty here is that he wants his propositions to have the content of factual truths, but to be guaranteed in the way in which the propositions of logic and mathematics are guaranteed. These wishes are incompatible. Factual assertions have the content that they have because their truth excludes some possible states of affairs from being actual. If it is true that it is raining, then it cannot be the case that it is not raining. But the assertions of logic and mathematics are compatible with any and every possibility in the world of fact. They cannot be falsified by the world being other than they assert it to be. To say that they are true is simply to say that they are framed in accordance with the appropriate rules. (I say nothing here about the status of such rules). This is why they possess the kind of certainty and the kind of clarity which Spinoza wishes his propositions to have. But he also wishes these propositions to be factual. He wants to be able to use his propositions as truths about man and nature with a factual content. Is the whole system then just a product of confusion?

The only fruitful way to approach Spinoza's ethics is to ignore the geometrical mode as far as is possible. We have to treat Spinoza's contentions as a mixture of factual claim and conceptual analysis, and we often have to ignore obscurities rooted in terms which are never satisfactorily explained. So it is with Spinoza's treatment of the unity of body and mind. But what we can draw out from his scheme is an important attempt to understand the relation between reason, the passions, and freedom.

For Hobbes man is simply driven by his passions. Deliberation has the role simply of intervening between passion and action as a middle link in the chain. The role of reason is simply to note facts, to calculate, and to understand; reason cannot move to action. For Spinoza this is a perfectly good description of man in his ordinary, unenlightened state. For in this state human beings are systems interacting with other systems, but unaware of the nature and causes of this interaction. By these encounters men are caused pleasure or pain, depending on what affected them at what time and the state they were then in. Objects which become associated with pleasure are desired; those associated with pain become objects of aversion. In pursuing pleasure and pain we are therefore being affected by causes outside rational knowledge and control; and so also with those complex evocations of pleasure and pain, the emotions of pride, joy, pity, anger, and so on. But this non-rational realm only dominates us for as long as we remain unconscious of its nature and power. As we form adequate notions of our emotions we cease to be passive in relation to them. We recognize ourselves for what we are, we understand that we cannot be other than we are; but to have understood is to have been transformed from what one was. One no longer sees oneself as an independent being confronting this, but as part of the system of necessity. To have seen this is to be free. Self-knowledge and only self-knowledge liberates.

Why does knowledge free us? Because, as we know more, we recognize that what we desire, hate, love, take pleasure or find pain in, has been the result of chance and accidental association and conditioning. To know this is to break the association. We recognize that pleasure and pain arise from our "power and perfection" as self-moving, self-preserving beings. We do not blame others, and we do not blame ourselves. Envy, hate, and guilt therefore vanish. External causes are not hindrances, for if they are real, the wise man knows them to be necessary and does not treat them as hindrances. He is therefore not frustrated. The joy of the man who has freed himself through knowledge of nature and of himself as part of nature is happiness. Genuine virtue is simply the realization of this state in which knowledge, freedom, and happiness are combined.

The possession of freedom in Spinoza's sense is of course compatible with being unable to do a great many things, provided that it is impossible that what hinders and prevents one should be altered. Spinoza thinks it impossible that one should rage against what could not be otherwise, for one can frame no conception of the impossible and hence cannot desire it; and if it is impossible that things should be other than they are, we cannot possibly desire that they should be. If we do so desire, we are irrational and our desire is not informed by genuine knowledge and adequate ideas. About this Spinoza is clearly wrong; knowledge is not a sufficient condition of being free. But it is often a necessary condition. I am not free merely because I get what I want, if I am not free to understand the causes and nature of my wants and reassess them. Spinoza's first great importance is that he sees the emotions and desires not as merely given, but as transformable. Aristotle had envisaged us as controlling and ordering our emotions and desires, but for Spinoza human nature appears even more malleable and transformable, and the largest transformation is that from being patients to being agents, from being those whose lives are determined by factors of which they are unaware to being those who are molded by themselves. The development of human powers becomes the end of the moral and political life. In this light both politics and theology are reinterpreted.

Spinoza agrees with Hobbes in seeing the need for the state as arising from the fact that all men pursue their own interests and seek to extend their own power. But for Hobbes the reasoning which justifies me in handing over myself and my rights to the sovereign is purely negative—only thus shall I escape being over-powered and killed by others. For Spinoza obedience to the sovereign is justified because thus civil order is procured and men are left free to pursue knowledge and self-liberation. Spinoza agrees with Hobbes in equating "having a right to" with "having the power to"; but he has a quite different picture of what enlightened men have the power to do and desire to do. It is not just that they desire an end of hate, envy, and frustration in themselves; but they will be gravely impeded unless they can diminish hate, envy, and frustration in others. Spinoza's enlightened man is therefore cooperative with others in the search for knowledge, and this cooperation is based not on fear, as all cooperation in Hobbes is, but on a common interest in the goods of self-knowledge and knowledge. Thus although Spinoza confuses "having a right to" with "having the power to" as much as Hobbes does, his picture of society is not disturbed in the same way, just because he recognizes human goals of a different kind. The state is for Spinoza at best a means; politics is an activity to procure the prerequisites for the pursuit of rationality and freedom. Spinoza is thus the first philosopher to make central to ethics two concepts which are defined to express the distinctively new values of modern society, those of freedom and reason.

# 11

## NEW VALUES

Both Hobbes and Spinoza struck their contemporaries as outrageous innovators; to both the label of "atheist"—which was used in seventeenth-century Europe with almost as much accuracy as the label "communist" is used in twentieth-century America—was attached. Spinoza was expelled from the synagogue; Hobbes was attacked by the Anglican clergy. And just because they stand so far from their contemporaries, it is only in a relatively indirect way that they give expression to the common and shared dilemmas of their society. But the questions which they ask, and the values which they embody—different as these are—soon become questions and values which inform a whole way of social life. And in a variety of ways philosophical questions and practical questions come into a closer relationship. In a variety of ways, for differing social circumstances provide relevantly different contexts for the relationship. In France, for example, philosophy in analyzing the concepts of the existing social and political order, those of sovereignty, law, property and the like, becomes critical of those concepts, and so an instrument for criticism of the established order. In England philosophy, in analyzing the concepts of the existing order, often provides a justification for these concepts. The differences between France and England are partly to be explained by the fact that the English social order provides many

French writers in the eighteenth century with a model in terms of which to criticize their own society; whereas within England no such model as yet exists, although by the end of the century the French Revolution had enabled France to return the compliment.

Nonetheless, in England we can mark the stages by which one moral scheme was transformed into a largely different one. We can use this history to partially explain how philosophical criticism can have quite different relations to social change in different types of period. There may be forms of society in which a variety of criteria are employed to justify and explain moral, social, and political standards. Do we obey the current rules and seek the current ideals because God authorizes them? Or because they are prescribed by a sovereign with legitimate authority? Or because obeying them is in fact a means to the most satisfying forms of human life? Or because, if we do not, we shall be punished or otherwise harmed by those in power? At a practical level it may be unnecessary and irrelevant to decide between these alternatives. For if the standards which are in the end held to be justified seem to be equally justified no matter what criteria we employ in judging them, then the argument about the appropriate way of justifying our standards will seem to be of purely theoretical import, matter for sharpening wits in the schools, but irrelevant in the field or the market place.

Social change, however, may bring theory out of the schools and not only into the market place but even onto the battle field. For consider what may happen in a social order where sacred and secular, church and state, king and parliament, or rich and poor fall apart. The criteria that used to return the same answers to the questions, What standards ought I to accept? and, What ought I to do? now provide several answers derived from the new competition between rival criteria. What God commands or is alleged to command, what has the sanctions of power behind it, what is endorsed by legitimate authority, and what appears to lead to the satisfaction of contemporary wants and needs are no longer the same. That the argument is no longer the same as before may be concealed by the fact that the partisans of different criteria will naturally enough attempt to redefine their rivals out of the field by trying to show with Hobbes that legitimate authority just is victorious power, or with the puritans that what God commands is what we would recognize as satisfying our wants and needs if we were not so totally depraved by sin, or with the royalists that obedience to the king's legitimate authority is what God commands. Nonetheless, we can recognize that the criteria have fallen apart; and in recognizing this, we recognize the relevance of a class of question which is at once moral and philosophical.

What kind of backing is logically appropriate to moral rules? What kind of warrant do they require? So far we have encountered in the history of ethics at least three main types of answer. The backing of being part of a form of human life in which our desires and dispositions would be formed and trained toward a recognition and pursuit of certain goods (Plato and Aristotle); the backing of being part of a set of divine commandments, obedience to which will be rewarded and disobedience to which will be punished (Christianity); and the backing of being instructed as to what action will produce for us most of what we now want (the sophists and Hobbes). Each of these answers specifies a different morality; and each of them specifies a different logical form and status for moral judgments. For the first, the key concept is "good," used functionally; and the key judgments are that certain things, sections, or people are good—that is, are well fitted for certain roles or functions in the background picture of social life which this view always has to presuppose. For the second, the key concept is expressed by "Thou shalt," and the key judgments express consequences of reward and punishment. For the third, the key concepts are those of means to a given end, of our desires as they are; and the key judgments are of corresponding form. It is of course obvious, and has already been stressed, that it is possible to combine and vary these three in all sorts of ways: Aquinas' blend of Greek and Christian is the most important. But how do we decide between them? Clearly to lay down some logical form as the form of the moral judgment and to rule out others as illegitimate would itself be an arbitrary and illegitimate procedure. But what we can do is to note the theory of human nature and of the physical universe presupposed by each different view; and if we do so the superiority of the Greek view—at least in its Aristotelian form—to either of its rivals appears plain—on at least two counts in respect of Christianity, and on at least one as regards the "actions whose consequences will be most desirable" view. Begin with the latter: quite clearly our desires as they are stand in need of criticism and correction. Those who speak blandly of moral rules as designed to maximize pleasure and minimize pain have apparently never reflected on such questions as whether the pleasure afforded to medieval Christians or modern Germans by persecuting Jews did not perhaps outweigh the pain caused to Jews and therefore justify the persecution. That they did not weigh the merits of this argument is perhaps to their credit morally; but intellectually it means that they have ignored both the possibility of transforming human nature and the means available for criticizing it in the ideals which are implicit not only in the private heroic dreams of individuals, but in the very way actions may be envisaged in a given society. For we do not have to see Aristotle's ideal life or the ideal of a Christian saint or the ideals of chivalry as private intentions: they are the ideals implicit in the way of life of Greek gentlemen or in that of the early church in its pagan environment or in the institutions of knighthood and war. To detach these ideals from their social environment is to evacuate them of significant content; it was Karl Marx who remarked that what Don Quixote had to learn was that not every economic order is equally compatible with knight errantry. But within their natural social environment these ideals may be used to criticize not only our actions, but our actual aims and desires.

Christianity shares with the Aristotelian view the advantage of not taking our actual desires as given; and it incarnates one moral ideal which is foreign to both the other views, the ideal expressed by saying that somehow or other all men are equal in the sight of God. The dividing line between all moralities which are moralities for a group and all moralities which are moralities for men as such is historically drawn by Christianity. This doctrine in secular form, as a demand for minimum equal rights for all men and hence for a minimum of freedom, is Christianity's chief seventeenth-century achievement, expressed centrally in the manifesto of the Diggers and in some of the claims of some of the Levellers. The left-wing movements in the parliamentary army in the English civil war express for the first time secular concepts of freedom and equality which break with all traditional forms of social hierarchy. But before we examine these new concepts we must look at what happened to Christianity.

Christianity's greatest moral weaknesses are two: first, the sheer extent of its metaphysical commitments; and second, the fact that it has to assert that the point and purpose of this life and this world is in the end to be found in another world. As long as men find this life inherently unsatisfactory, so long are they therefore likely to be interested in the Christian claims; but insofar as they do find adequate projects and purposes, their interest is likely to be weakened. And with the expansion of life which is made possible by economic growth, other-worldly religions are, in fact, universally eroded. But even more importantly, belief in a God of any specific kind becomes increasingly a formality— when it is not actually abandoned. There occur side by side a process of intellectual criticism of religious beliefs and a process of social abandonment.

Intellectually, first deists and then skeptics question the possibility of miracles, the truth of the historical narratives in which Christianity is alleged to rest, the traditional proofs of the existence of God, and the intolerance of ecclesiastical morality. Socially, what was a religious morality becomes increasingly a religious form and frame disguising or merely decorating purely secular ideals and pursuits. As a matter of history, the culmination of this process in the eighteenth century is a victory for the morality whose ancestry includes Hobbes and the sophists.

In both England and New England in the seventeenth and eighteenth centuries puritanism is transformed from a critique of the established order in the name of King Jesus to an endorsement of the new economic activities of the middle classes. At the end of this process economic man emerges fully fledged; throughout, human nature appears as given, and human need or what is useful to supply it as a single, uncomplicated standard for action. Utility and advantage are treated as clear and perspicuous notions which stand in no further need of justification. We can see this process most clearly exemplified in the writings of Defoe, who was unusually self-aware, and unusually aware, too, of the nature of the times. He sees that the Christianity of the Commonwealth period has evaporated: " . . . no such zeal for the Christian religion will be found in our days, or perhaps in any region of the world, till Heaven beats the drums itself, and the glorious legions from above come down on purpose to propagate the work, and reduce the whole world to the obedience of King Jesus—a time which some tell us is not far off, but of which I heard nothing in all my travels and illuminations, no, not one word."[32] Moreover, all Defoe's heroes are moved by the values of double-entry bookkeeping and human feelings are allowed to enter only into the interstices left by profitability. As Moll Flanders puts it, "with money in the pocket one is at home anywhere." The little Moor without whom Crusoe could not have escaped from slavery and whom Crusoe had decided "to love ever after" is sold into slavery himself by Crusoe for sixty pieces of eight (admittedly with a promise from the purchaser to free the slave after ten years; provided, of course, that he has been converted to Christianity). The wives of the colonists in The Farther Adventures of Robinson Crusoe are assessed wholly in economic terms. Of Defoe's characters it is often true that "enjoyment is subordinated to capital; and the individual who enjoys to the individual who capitalizes." Marx, who wrote this about capitalist human nature, would have appreciated Defoe's conclusion that usefulness is "the great pleasure, and justly deemed by all good men the truest and noblest end of life, in which men come nearest to the character of our B. Saviour, who went about doing good."

But the assertion of economic values and the absorption of religious values into them is only one side of the story. I have already noticed the increasing importance in the preceding period of the concept of "the individual." The individual is now on the scene with a vengeance. Robinson Crusoe becomes the bible of a generation which includes both Rousseau and Adam Smith. The novel with its stress on individual experience and its value is about to emerge as the dominant literary form. Social life becomes essentially an arena for the struggles and conflicts of individual wills. The first ancestor of all these individuals is perhaps Milton's Satan, who brought Blake over to the devil's party and has been seen as the first Whig. For Satan's motto, Non Serviam, marks not merely a personal revolt against God, but a revolt against the concept of an ordained and unchangeable hierarchy. The complexity and interest of Satan lies in the fact that he both has to and cannot reject this hierarchy: the only alternative to service is monarchy; but monarchy implies the hierarchy which revolt rejects. Equally, Satan's spiritual descendant, Tom Jones, is caught in the same dilemma. Tom Jones wins his Sophia in the end because a mixture of personal quality and sheer good luck enable him to make his way. But at the end, if he is in fact to have his Sophia, it has to be shown that he is really of good birth, that he, too, really belongs by right to the squirearchy. The values of the traditional social hierarchy are only half challenged.

We thus find a form of social life in which a traditional order is challenged by forms of innovation in which liberty and property are twin sides of the same coin. To make one's way is to make one's way *economically*, at least in the first instance. But the badge of success remains acceptance by those already on top in the established order of things. Yet this very mobility in society and this very encounter of two orders breeds questioning of a radical kind. Perhaps the utopian claims for freedom made by the Diggers and Levellers had declined into the freedom of the puritan and ever less puritan merchant. But they remain a specter to haunt the eighteenth century. Hume is appalled by the suggestion of a law which apportions property to those best able to make use of it or to men as men. "But were mankind to execute such a law; so great is the uncertainty of merit, both from its natural obscurity, and from the self-conceit of each individual, that no determinate rule of conduct would ever result from it; and the total dissolution of society must be the immediate consequence. Fanatics may suppose, *that dominion is founded on grace, and that saints alone inherit the earth*; but the civil magistrate very justly puts these sublime theorists on the same footing with common robbers, and teaches them by the severest discipline, that a rule, which, in speculation, may seem the most advantageous to society, may yet be found, in practice, totally pernicious and destructive. That there were *religious* fanatics of this kind in England, who claimed an equal distribution of property, were a kind of *political* fanatic, which arose from the religious species and more openly answered their pretensions. . . ."[33]

Who then *were* the Levellers and the Diggers? and why do they mark a turning point in the history of morality and produce consequences for philosophical ethics? What is the doctrine of freedom that in the early eighteenth century was temporarily lost or transformed? It is the doctrine that every man has a natural right to certain freedoms simply because he is a man. Diggers and Levellers give different interpretations to this doctrine at the economic level; the Diggers believed in a community of goods, and especially in common ownership of land, the Levellers in private property. The Levellers themselves at different times gave different and inconsistent expressions to this belief at a political level; sometimes they claimed universal manhood suffrage, and some-times they were prepared to exclude servants and beggars (who in the seventeenth century were probably more than half the male population of England). But always behind their specific claims was the doctrine expressed by Colonel Thomas Rainborough in the Putney debates: "For really I think that the poorest he that is in England hath a life to live as the greatest he; and therefore truly, sir, I think it's clear, that every man that is to live under a government ought first by his own consent to put himself under that government."[34] Rainborough said this in a debate between the representatives of the Leveller rank and file in the Cromwellian army and Cromwell, Ireton, and other leading officers on Putney Heath in October 1647. The debate was over the political stand that the army should take in settling affairs after the King's defeat. Ireton and Cromwell wished for a restricted property franchise; to this the reply of Rainborough and others was that in that case the poor men who fought in the parliamentary army were to get nothing for their pains. Instead of exchanging tyranny for liberty they would have exchanged tyranny for tyranny. But had they known this in advance, they would never have fought. The case that Rainborough advanced at Putney in 1647 had a year earlier been expressed in theoretical terms by Richard Overton in his *An Arrow Against All Tyrants*. "To every Individu-all in nature is given an individual property by nature, not to be invaded or usurped by any: for every one as he is himselfe, so he hath a selfe propriety, else could he not be himselfe, and on this no second may presume to deprive any of, without manifest violation and affront to the very principles of nature, and of the Rules of equity and justice between man and man; mine and thine cannot be, except this be; No man hath power over my rights and liberties and I over no mans; I may be but an Individuall, enjoy my selfe, and my selfe propriety, and may write my selfe no more than my selfe, or presume any further; if I doe, I am an encroacher & an invader upon an other mans Right, to which I have no Right."[35]

So came the doctrine of natural rights in its revolutionary form into the modern world. Overton's nature is very different from Hobbes': the principles of nature as much constrain me from invading the domain of others as they entitle me to resist others who invade my domain. What is my domain? my "selfe?" my "selfe propriety?" The latter word is the immediate ancestor of, but not the same word as property. Overton understood, as Locke was to understand, that I am only able to act as a person insofar as I have a minimal control over things. My knife or my hammer or my pen may not be quite as necessary to me as my hand is, but are necessary in a comparable kind of way. But now what entitles this "selfe" to rights? The attack upon the concept of natural rights normally takes the following form.

A right can only be claimed or exercised in virtue of a rule which entitles a certain class of people to claim or exercise the right. Such rules are intelligible when embodied in some system of positive law, enacted by a sovereign legislature. But outside ordinary positive law the notion of a right appears only to make sense if we suppose a divine lawgiver who has enacted a system of law for the universe. Yet the claim that there are natural rights does not rest on an appeal to divine law, and it does not rest, exhypothesi it cannot rest, on any appeal to positive law. For the particular legal system does not concede to some individual or class within the community the rights to which he or they are entitled. So, it is argued, alleged "natural rights" do not satisfy the minimal condition necessary for a right to exist and to be recognized. Critics of this kind therefore conclude either that the doctrine of natural rights is inherently confused or that it is just a way of expressing a moral principle that all men ought to have certain rights recognized and protected by positive law and its sanctions. The latter alternative is certainly mistaken; for when men appeal to the doctrine of natural rights they are never just saying that they ought to enjoy certain rights, they are always attempting to give a reason for holding this. So if this line of criticism is correct, it appears that we ought to conclude that the claim to natural rights is nonsensical. But is it?

If another claims something from me, and does not or cannot invoke positive law to justify his claim, then I can ask him in virtue of what it is that he makes this claim. He might provide such a sufficient justification for his claim if he could establish, first, that I had explicitly or tacitly conceded his right by agreeing to some contract or promise of the form "If you do this, then I will do that," and if he could establish, second, that he had done for his part whatever it was that the contract specified. That is, anyone who wishes to establish that he has a claim against me as of right may do this is if he is able to show that I have acknowledged a certain contractual obligation and that he has performed whatever is laid down by the contract in question. From this general argument we can now move once more to the doctrine of natural rights.

The essence of the claim to natural rights is that no one has a right against me unless he can cite some contract, my consent to it, and his performance of his obligations under it. To say that I have a right on some point is simply to say that no one may legitimately interfere with me unless he can establish a specific right against me in this way. Thus the function of the doctrine of natural right is to lay down conditions to which anyone who wishes to establish a right against me must conform. And "anyone" here includes the state. It follows that any state which claims rights against me, that is, legitimate authority over me— and my property—must establish the existence of a contract whose form we have already specified in outline, my consent to it, and the state's performance of its part under the contract. This apparently trivial conclusion throws much light on seventeenth-century—and later —political theory. It explains why the social contract is necessary for anyone who wishes to defend the legitimacy of state power; Hobbes misplaced the role of the contract. It does not and cannot underlie or explain social life as such, for contracts presuppose, as I have already argued, the existence of social life and indeed of some fairly high degree of civilization. But some doctrine of social contract must underlie any claim to legitimacy. In the seventeenth century this claim becomes crucial for state power. In the Middle Ages the legitimacy of the final authority, the sovereign prince, was bound up with all the other ties of obligation and duty binding superiors and inferiors. These ties are by the seventeenth century fatally loosened. Man and man confront one another in an arena where the cash nexus of the free-market economy and the power of the centralizing state have together helped to destroy the social bonds on which traditional claims to legitimacy were founded. But how to legitimate the new order and especially the sovereign power? Claims to divine right and scriptural authority founder on arbitrariness. So the state must fall back on appeal, implicit or explicit, to social contract. But at once two points. The very claims of the state imply and allow a prepolitical (and such is the force of *natural*) right of the individual over whom authority is asserted to be satisfied that there is a contract, that he has consented to it, and that the state has performed its part. But, of course, normally there is no such contract, for there is no such consent. Individuals have no opportunity for expression of either consent or dissent. Thus the doctrine of natural rights is in this form a key doctrine of liberty. For it shows that most claims of most states to exercise legitimate authority over us are and must be unfounded. That radical consequences for both morals and politics ensue are obvious. It is thus the case that a great step forward in moral and political philosophy was taken by half-forgotten thinkers like Rainborough, Winstanley the Digger, and Overton and other Levellers. That they are forgotten is due to the various ways their doctrine was transmuted in the following generations. Morally, as I have already noticed, the rights of the individual were increasingly connected with the right of freedom in the market economy. Politically, the doctrine of John Locke displaced theirs. But because Locke's doctrine is as important for morals as for politics, to it we must now turn.

# 12

# THE BRITISH EIGHTEENTH-CENTURY ARGUMENT

John Locke's *Two Treatises of Government* was published in England in 1690 with the avowed motive of justifying the Whig rebellion and revolution of 1688, which had put William of Orange on the English throne. Locke wished to defend the new regime by showing that rebellion by Williamites against King James had been legitimate, but that rebellion by Jacobites against King William in 1689 and after would be illegitimate. Thus Locke poses once more the Hobbesian questions, In what does the legitimate authority of a sovereign consist? and, When, if ever, is rebellion justified?

Like Hobbes, Locke begins from a portrait of the state of nature. But the Lockean state of nature is not in fact presocial, nor premoral. Men in it live in families, in a settled social order. They have and enjoy property. They make and acknowledge claims upon one another. But their life has defects. Every rational creature is aware of the law of nature; but the bias of interest and lack of attention cause men to apply it more rigorously in the case of others than of themselves, while crimes that are committed may well go unpunished for lack of a proper authority. Disputes between men have no impartial arbiter to decide them, and every dispute will therefore tend toward a state of war between the parties. All these considerations make desirable the handing over of authority to a civil power in whom trust can be reposed. So the contract. The aim of the contract is to create an authority adequate to safeguard our natural rights, and for Locke the most important of rights is that of property. Locke begins from a position not too dissimilar from that of Overton. A man's person and his property are so closely linked that his natural right to liberty must extend from one to the other. To what property am I entitled? To that which my labor has created. A man may acquire as much property as his labor enables him to make use of. We must remember at this point that what is being spoken of is a man's rights in a state of nature, prior to the laws of civil society. Locke supposes a state of affairs where land is unlimited and transfer of property not yet instituted. Can such a state of things exist? "In the beginning all the world was America, and more so than it is now; for no such thing as money was anywhere known."[36]

What is the effect of the contract? Men hand over to a legislative and executive power the authority to pass and to enforce laws which will protect their natural rights. In so doing, they both transfer that authority and set limits to it; for insofar as the civil authority does not protect natural rights, it ceases to be a legitimate authority. The guarantee that it will protect such rights lies in the provision that the only valid laws are those passed by a majority vote. In this aspect of his thought Locke is the ancestor of liberal democracy. But with just this aspect of his thought a difficulty arises. The laws are designed for the protection of property. Who are the possessors of property? Although Locke believed that a man could not alienate away from himself the right to liberty for his person (the legal expression of which includes such measures as habeas corpus), he does allow that property is alienable. A man's initial right is only to such property as his labor has created; but with the wealth derived therefrom he may acquire the property of others and he may acquire servants. If he does, their labor creates property for him. Therefore, gross inequality in property is consistent with Locke's doctrine of a natural right to property. Not only this, but Locke seems to have been aware of the fact that more than half the population of England was effectively propertyless. How, then, is he able to reconcile his view of the right of the majority to rule with his view of the natural right to property? Is he not involved in the difficulty which has been alleged against the Levellers? That if the kind of franchise which they advocated had been brought in, the majority of the voters would in fact have chosen to abolish even such civil and religious liberty as existed under the Parliament and under Cromwell, and would have voted to restore the monarchy. So, against Locke, might it not be argued that to give the rule to the majority will be to give the rule to the many whose interest lies in the abolition of the right of the few to the property which they have acquired? This problem is raised nowhere explicitly in Locke, and the reason may be that Locke takes it for granted that the answer to this question is No; and he is able to take this for granted, because he is able to assume that what the majority do and will accept is an oligarchical government controlled by the property owners, and especially by the owners of large-scale property. Why is he able to assume this? Perhaps because of his doctrine of tacit consent.

Locke writes that "every Man, that hath any Possession, or Enjoyment, of any part of the Dominions of any Government, doth thereby give his *tacit Consent*, and is as far forth obliged to Obedience to the Laws of that Government, during such Enjoyment, as any one under it; whether this his Possession be of Land, to him and his Heirs for ever, or a Lodging only for a Week; or whether it be barely travelling freely on the Highway; and in Effect, it reaches as far as the very being of any one within the Territories of that Government."[37] Thus it follows that the wandering gypsy on the road has consented to the authority of the government, which may therefore legitimately conscript him into its armed forces. Locke's doctrine is important because it is the doctrine of every modern state which claims to be democratic, but which like every state wishes to coerce its citizens. Even if the citizens are not consulted and have no means of expressing their views on a given topic, they are held to have tacitly consented to the actions of governments. Moreover, we can see why modern democratic states have no alternative but to fall back upon a doctrine of this kind. For, like Locke's Whig oligarchy, they have nothing to ground their legitimacy upon but popular consent; and, as in Locke's Whig oligarchy, the majority of their subjects have no genuine opportunity to participate in the political process except in the most passive way. It follows that either the authority claimed by the government of these states is not genuine, and that their subjects are therefore under no obligation to obey them, or that they are legitimated by some kind of tacit consent on the part of the subjects. But for the latter alternative to hold, the doctrine of tacit consent must, of course, be meaningful. Unfortunately—for the state—it is not. For the minimum conditions for the word *consent* to have meaningful application include at least that the man alleged to have consented shall somehow have signified his consent and that he shall have sometime indicated his understanding of what he has consented to. But neither of these conditions is satisfied by the doctrine of tacit consent.

Locke's own doctrine also stands or falls with his particular version of the argument that natural rights derive from a moral law which we apprehend by reason. In the *Essay concerning Human Understanding* he argues that although our moral ideas derive from sense experience, the relations between these ideas are such that "morality is capable of demonstration, as well as mathematics." The propositions of morals can be apprehended as certain truths merely by a scrutiny of the terms which they contain and the ideas expressed by these terms. What are the key moral terms? *Good* is that which causes pleasure or diminishes pain; *evil* that which causes pain or diminishes pleasure. Moral good is the conformity of our actions to a law the sanctions of which are rewards of pleasure and punishments of pain. There are three kinds of law— divine, civil, and those conventions established tacitly with a quite different criterion of consent from that involved in the *Treatise* (for now consent to "the law of opinion or reputation" is signified by *active* approval of what the law enjoins or prohibits).

In this view of moral judgments as founded upon the rational scrutiny of moral concepts Locke has both English predecessors and English successors. What is distinctive in Locke is the way in which good and evil are defined in terms of pleasure and pain without the abandonment of this semi-Platonic view of moral concepts. The reference to Plato is important; the view of moral judgments as resembling mathematical is found in Locke's immediate predecessors, the Cambridge Platonists, a group of Anglican metaphysicians and moralists who included Benjamin Whichcote and Henry More. More had argued in his *Enchiridion Ethicum* (1668) that the twenty-three fundamental moral principles which he enumerates are self-evident moral truths. If we look at them, we shall perhaps be tempted to conclude that the resemblance between moral truths and mathematical consists in the fact that the alleged moral truths turn out to be mere tautologies, at best definitions of the key moral terms rather than judgments which make use of them. The first of More's truths, for example, is that "Good is that which is pleasing, agreeable and fitting to some perceptive life, or to a degree of this life, and which is conjoined with the conservation of the percipient," which is clearly intended as a definition. But those English philosophers from the Cambridge Platonists onward who held that moral distinctions are derived from reason in a manner similar to that in which mathematical distinctions are derived cannot be adequately characterized solely in terms of a confusion between the role of definitions and that of substantial moral judgments. Of this confusion they were certainly often guilty; but they combined with it a much more plausible contention, whose authentic ancestor is indeed Plato. This is the doctrine that it is a condition of having grasped a moral concept that one should have grasped the criteria for its correct application, and that these criteria are unambiguous and sufficient to determine the truth of any moral judgment. Of this doctrine two things must be said. The first is that it makes moral judgments resemble empirical judgments as much as it makes them resemble mathematical; if I have grasped the concepts expressed by the word *red*, then I have grasped the criteria for correctly calling some object red. This point the Cambridge Platonists themselves might have made; for they were equally anxious to stress the a-priori element in empirical knowledge. The second remark worth making is that if this view is correct, then of two men who judge differently on a moral question it must always be the case that one at least must simply have failed to grasp the relevant concept and so have failed to use the relevant moral expression correctly. But this appears certainly to be a mistake. Any adequate account of moral concepts must include some more plausible account of moral disagreement than this.

This was not, however, the ground on which the ethical rationalists were attacked by their contemporaries. Anthony Ashley, the Earl of Shaftesbury and Locke's pupil, argued that it is not by reason but by a moral sense that moral distinctions are made. "No sooner are actions viewed, no sooner the human affections and passions discerned (and they are most of them as soon discerned as felt) than straight an inward eye distinguishes and sees the fair and shapely, the amiable and admirable, apart from the deformed, the foul, the odious or the despicable. How is it possible therefore not to own that as these distinctions have their foundation in nature, the discernment itself is natural and from nature alone?"[38] A moral judgment is thus the expression of a response of feeling to some property of an action, just as, on Shaftesbury's view, an aesthetic judgment is the expression of just such a response to the properties of shapes and figures. But what are the properties of the actions which evoke a favorable rather than an unfavorable response? The virtuous man is he who had harmonized his own inclinations and affections in a way that renders them also harmonious with the inclinations and affections of his fellow creatures. Harmony is the great moral property. Between what will satisfy me and what will be for the good of others there is no conflict. Man's *natural* bent is toward benevolence. This appears to Shaftesbury to be a simple matter of contingent fact. It is as a simple matter of contingent fact that Bernard de Mandeville questions it.

In *The Grumbling Hive, or Knaves Turned Honest* and in *The Fable of the Bees, or Private Vices Public Benefits* Mandeville attacks Shaftesbury's two central propositions—that man's natural bent is to act in an altruistic way, and that it is altruism and benevolence that procure social benefit. In fact, argues Mandeville, the spring of action is private and egoistical self-interest; and the public good of society is the outcome of the private individual's disregard for any good but his own. It is a happy accident that the pursuit of enjoyment and luxury promotes economic enterprise, and that the promotion of economic enterprise raises the level of general prosperity. Were men in fact virtuous in the way that Shaftesbury supposes, social life would never advance at all. The notion that private virtue is a public good is derived from the claims to private virtue made by those who wish to disguise their self-seeking behind moral professions in order to aggrandize themselves more successfully.

Mandeville thus raises the second great issue for English moral philosophy in the eighteenth century. If moral judgments are expressions of feeling, how can they be more than expressions of self-interest? If moral action is grounded in feeling, what feelings provide the springs of benevolence? From Mandeville onward philosophers divide not only upon the issue of the moral sense versus reason, but also—

although sometimes implicitly rather than explicitly—on the correct way to answer Mandeville. The greatest of the moral-sense theorists between Shaftesbury and Hume, Francis Hutcheson, simply evaded the issue. The moral sense is one which perceives those properties which arouse responses of moral feeling (there is also an aesthetic sense, which stands to beauty as the moral sense does to virtue). The properties which arouse a pleasurable and approving response are those of benevolence. What we approve are not actions in themselves but actions as manifestations of traits of character, and our approval seems to consist simply in the arousal of the required response. But why do we approve of benevolence rather than of self-interest? Hutcheson has no answer to this question. He merely asserts that we do. Equally, when he treats of benevolence as the whole of virtue, he rests his view on mere assertion. It is noteworthy that in his account of choice Hutcheson never puts himself in the place of the agent. He speaks, and anyone who held his views would have had to speak, as a purely external observer. It is in the course of this account that a famous phrase enters the history of ethics for the first time, when Hutcheson asserts that "that nation is best which procures the greatest happiness for the greatest numbers, and that worst which in like manner occasions misery,"[39] and so becomes the father of utilitarianism.

The reason why we could not hope to find any adequate answer to Mandeville in either Shaftesbury or Hutcheson is fairly clear. Both of them assimilate ethics to aesthetics; both are preoccupied with describing the character of our response to virtuous actions rather than with clarifying the way in which moral judgments may provide us with reasons for acting in one way rather than another. Both speak from the standpoint of the critic of action rather than from that of the agent. Neither therefore is under pressure to provide us either with an account of how reasoning can be practical or with an adequate theory of motives. Unfortunately, although these defects are in some ways supplied by the two greatest of English eighteenth-century moralists, Butler and Hume, they, as it were, divided the problems between them and thus solved neither of them. Butler attacks the problem of moral reasoning, but never asks—or rather, asks and answers in the sketchiest and most unsatisfactory fashion—how this kind of argument can weigh with human agents. Hume tries to supply an adequate account of motives, but leaves no proper place for moral reasoning. Nor can we by adding Butler to Hume, supply the deficiencies of each. For what is omitted in each distorts what is supplied.

Joseph Butler (1692–1752), Bishop of Durham, denied at least two of Hutcheson's central positions. He begins, in fact, from a position closer to that of Shaftesbury. We have a variety of "appetites, passions, and affections." Benevolence is merely one affection among others, which deserves its due but no more than its due. To see it, as Hutcheson did, as the whole of virtue is not merely a mistake but a pernicious mistake. For it leads straight to the criterion of the promotion of the future happiness of mankind in general as the criterion by which my present actions should be judged. But the use of this criterion would sanction the commital of every kind of crime or injustice, provided only that such crimes and injustices appeared likely to promote the long-run happiness of the greatest number. This objection of Butler's really falls into two parts. He believes that we cannot in fact be sufficiently certain of what the consequences of our action will be for us to justify present action by future consequences; and he believes that the moral character of actions is and must be independent of their consequences. To the former of these contentions a utilitarian might well reply that the criterion of the greatest happiness only has application insofar as consequences are genuinely predictable; the argument between him and Butler then becomes a factual one as to how far consequences can reliably be predicted. The crux of the argument therefore lies in Butler's latter contention. Are there classes of actions which ought to be done, and which ought to be prohibited, independently of and irrespective of their possible consequences?

Butler's positive answer to this question is part of his total doctrine. The mistake made by philosophers as different as Mandeville and Hutcheson is that they suppose benevolence and self-love to be opposed. Self-love is the desire for our own happiness, but our natures are so constituted that part of our happiness derives from gratifying our desire to be benevolent toward others. An excessive indulgence of those appetites which are inconsistent with benevolence would in fact lead to our unhappiness and thus would be a denial of self-love. Nonetheless, men do give themselves up to such passions and affections "to their known prejudice and ruin, and in direct contradition to manifest and real interest and the loudest calls of self-love." How do we avoid such prejudice and ruin? By rational reflection. It is "cool" or "reasonable" self-love that we need to guide us. But how does reasonable self-love reason?

"There is a superior principle of reflection or conscience in every man, which distinguishes between the internal principles of his heart, as well as his external actions."[40] Reasonable self-love consists in governing our actions in conformity with a hierarchy of principles which define human nature and what its good consists in. There is no clash between duty and interest, for to perform the actions that we ought and to refrain from prohibited actions will ensure our happiness. But how do we know which actions are enjoined and which proscribed? Here the argument becomes entirely obscure because it is circular. I ought to perform those actions which will satisfy my nature as a rational and moral being; my nature as a rational and moral being is defined by reference to my adherence to certain principles; and those principles demand obedience because the actions which they enjoin will as a matter of fact satisfy my nature as a rational and moral being. Suppose I do not perform these actions, what then? Is Butler arguing that as a matter of fact if I am immoral, I will always be unhappy? Certainly I shall be unhappy if I have a well-instructed moral reason. But I may in fact fail to recognize the authority of genuine conscience and so not be disquieted. Moreover I may, although Butler judges this to be the exception rather than the rule, find that duty and interest do not precisely coincide, so far as life in this present world is concerned. The providence of God insures such a coincidence in the world to come, but even though this is so, so far as the present is concerned, my duty and my happiness are not necessarily coincident. Thus the satisfaction of my nature as a reasonable and moral being is not precisely coincident with my happiness in any empirical sense. How then does the criterion of duty manifest itself? At this point Butler only fails to notice the circularity of his argument because he exchanges argument for rhetoric. The rhetoric is magnificent, but it remains rhetoric. "Had it strength," he says of conscience, "as it has right; had it power, as it has manifest authority, it would absolutely govern the world."[41]

What is valuable in Butler is his revival of the Greek notion of moral reasoning as determined by premises about what will or will not satisfy our nature as rational animals. What is defective is the omission of any justification for construing our nature in the way that he does. We can trace this defect to at least two sources, Butler's theology and his individualism. The theology is pernicious because it enables him to bring in the eternal world to redress the balance of duty and interest in the temporal world. The individualism is apparent in his account of human nature, which is expressed in terms of the self-awareness of the single individual. Contrast Aristotle, whose account of human nature and what will satisfy it presupposes a social framework of a certain kind. Or if we remember Plato, whose account of justice as an inner state in which rational principle governs appetite appears to be the same type of account as Butler gives, we ought to remember that the justice of the inner state is connected with a form of life in a given type of society. Indeed, the comparison with Plato and Aristotle suggests a general diagnosis of the difficulties of eighteenth-century English moral philosophy.

Traditional European society inherited from the Greeks and from Christianity a moral vocabulary in which to judge an action good was to judge it to be the action of a good man, and to judge a man good was to judge him as manifesting dispositions (virtues) which enabled him to play a certain kind of role in a certain kind of social life. The acceptance of this kind of social life as the norm by which actions are judged is not something asserted within the moral system. It is the presupposition of there being moral judgments at all. Actual social life did in fact always diverge widely from the norms; but not so widely that it could not be seen as an imperfect reflection of the norms. But that breakup of the traditional forms of social life which was produced by the rise of individualism, begotten partly by Protestantism and capitalism, made the reality of social life so divergent from the norms implied in the traditional vocabulary that all the links between duty and happiness were gradually broken. The consequence was a redefinition of the moral terms. Happiness is no longer defined in terms of satisfactions which are understood in the light of the criteria governing a form of social life; it is defined in terms of individual psychology. Since such a psychology does not yet exist, it has to be invented. Hence the whole apparatus of appetites, passions, inclinations, principles, which is found in every eighteenth-century moral philosopher. Yet in spite of all this psychological construction, *happiness* remains a difficult key term for moral philosophy, if only because all too often what would in an obvious sense make us happy is what in an obvious sense we ought *not* to do. Consequently there is an instability in the history of the moral argument, exhibited in an oscillation between attempts to define morality in terms of consequences leading to happiness and attempts to define morality in terms that have nothing to do with consequences or happiness at all. So long as theology survives as a socially influential force it can be called in to connect virtue with happiness in a world other than this. But theology itself became more and more the victim of its environment.

In a writer like Butler the appeal to divine providence is reasonably sophisticated. In lesser figures such as Abraham Tucker or Archdeacon William Paley, God has clearly been turned from an object of awe and veneration into a device for bridging otherwise unbridgable gaps in philosophical argument. But the very crudity of their views helps to make the issue clearer. Tucker, in *The Light of Nature Pursued*, argued, first, that men only and always pursue their private satisfactions, and second, that the basic moral rule is that we should all work for the good of all men, to increase the amount of satisfaction in the universe, whether it is our own or that of others. His fundamental task, therefore, is to show how men constituted in accordance with his first conclusion could possibly accept his second conclusion as their rule of life. Tucker's answer is that if I so work as to increase the happiness of all men, then God has in fact insured that all the happiness there was, is, and shall be is deposited, as Tucker puts it, in the "bank of the universe." This happiness God has divided into equal shares—equal because our original corruption makes us all equally undeserving—to be allotted one per person. I become entitled to my share by working to increase the common stock. By so working I increase that stock and thus my own share. I am, in fact, a partner in a cosmic joint stock enterprise of which God is the unremunerated managing director.

Tucker's treatment of happiness as though it were quantitative in the way that money is, is important. So is his treatment of theology as merely providing additional information that the prudent investor in his own happiness will take into account in calculating his actions. In both he was followed by Paley, who believes that the rule of morality is provided by the divine will, and that the motive for morality is our own happiness, and more especially, our everlasting happiness. What is crucial about Paley and Tucker is that they are logically committed to the view that if God did not exist, then there would be no good reason for being other than entirely selfish. Indeed they do not so much mark the distinction between vice and virtue as obliterate it. For what we normally call vice or selfishness turns out to be merely imprudent, miscalculated short-term selfishness rather than prudent long-term selfishness.

It is so often asserted by religious apologists that religion is a necessary foundation for morality that it is worth insisting upon the relief that one must feel in turning away from the narrow, niggardly self-interested writings of clergymen such as Paley and Tucker (though not of course Butler) to the generous and acute observations of the irreligious and skeptical writer who would have to be accounted the greatest of all English moralists, were he not a Scotsman. David Hume had an unusually attractive character for a moral philosopher. "Upon the whole," wrote Adam Smith after his death in 1776, "I have always considered him both in his lifetime and since his death, as approaching as nearly to the idea of a perfectly wise and virtuous man, as perhaps the nature of human frailty will admit." He said of himself that he was "a man of Mild Disposition, of Government of Temper, of an open social and cheerful Humour, capable of Attachment, but little susceptible of Enmity, and of great Moderation in all my Passions. Even my love of literary fame, my ruling Passion, never soured my humour, not withstanding my frequent Disappointments." His two chief disappointments were the cold reception of the two works which contain his moral philosophy. In 1738 the *Treatise of Human Nature* "fell dead-born from the Press;" in 1752 the *Enquiry Concerning the Principles of Morals* "came unnoticed and unobserved into the world."

Hume began under Hutcheson's influence, but while he follows Hutcheson in his rejection of rationalist ethics, the arguments with which he develops his own position are original and far more powerful than anything in Hutcheson. Moral judgments, so Hume argues, cannot be judgments of reason because reason can never move us to action, while the whole point and purpose of the use of moral judgments is to guide our actions. Reason is concerned either with relations of ideas, as in mathematics, or with matters of fact. Neither of these can move us to act. We are moved to act not by this or that being the case, but by the prospect of pleasure or pain from what is or will be the case. It is the passions and not reason which are aroused by the prospect of pleasure and pain. Reason can inform the passions as to whether the object they seek exists and as to what the most economical and effective means of seeking it may be. But reason cannot judge or criticize the passions. It follows without paradox that "'Tis not contrary to reason to prefer the destruction of the whole world to the scratching of my finger." For reason cannot in any sense adjudicate between the passions. "Reason is, and ought only to be the slave of the passions, and can never pretend to any other office than to serve and obey them."[42]

We cannot discover the ground for moral approval or disapproval in any distinctions or relations of the kind that reason can grasp. Consider incest in animals, or the effect of a sapling which destroys the parent oak. We do not judge these as we judge incest in human beings, or parricide. Why not? Not because the animals or the tree lack reason to discern that what they do is wrong. For if reason's function is to discern that what is done is wrong, what is done must be wrong independently of discerning it to be so. But we do not judge trees or animals capable of virtue or vice at all. Hence, since our rational apprehension of relations among trees and animals does not differ from our rational apprehension of relations among humans, moral judgment cannot be founded upon rational apprehension. "Morality, therefore, is more properly felt than judged of."[43] "Take any action allowed to be vicious: wilful murder, for instance. Examine it in all lights and see if you can find that matter of fact or real existence, which you call vice. In whichever way you take it, you find only certain passions, motives, volitions and thoughts. There is no other matter of fact in the case. The vice entirely escapes you, as long as you consider the object. You never can find it, till you turn your reflection into your own breast and find a sentiment of disapprobation which arises in you towards this action. Here is a matter of fact; but it is the object of feeling, not of reason. It lies in yourself, not in the object."[44] "To have the sense of virtue is nothing but to feel a satisfaction of a particular kind from the contemplation of a character. The very feeling constitutes our praise or admiration."[45]

Who are Hume's targets here? Not only rationalist philosophers, such as Malebranche, Montesquieu, and Wollaston, although these are not neglected. In a famous footnote William Wollaston, the deistic author of *The Religion of Nature Delineated* (1722), is singled out for attention. Wollaston was the author of the perverse but ingenious theory that the distinction between vice and virtue which reason apprehends is simply the distinction between the true and the false. All wrongdoing is a species of lying, and lying is saying or representing what is false. To call something wrong is simply to say that it is a lie. Stealing is wrong because it is representing what belongs to someone else as belonging to oneself by treating it as if it belonged to oneself. Adultery is wrong because by treating someone else's wife as if she were your own you represent her to be your own wife. Hume demolishes this theory splendidly, first, by pointing out that it makes the wrongness of adultery to consist in the false impression it gives of one's marital relationships, and so has the consequence of making adultery to be not wrong provided that I commit it entirely unobserved; and second, by pointing out that if true, it prevents me from explaining why lying is wrong. For the notion of wrongness has been explained in terms of the notion of lying. Wollaston, in any case, confused lying (which involves an intention to deceive) with simply saying what is in fact false. But Hume is concerned to produce a form of argument which will have a more general application. He wishes to show that moral conclusions cannot be based on anything that reason could establish; that it is logically impossible that any genuine or alleged factual truth could provide a basis for morality. In so doing he is out to refute theologically based ethics quite as much as rationalism.

When Hume was dying he was called upon by his friend the pious and lecherous Boswell, who was anxious to see the great skeptic's deathbed repentance. Hume disappointed Boswell by remaining immune to the consolations of either theism or immortality, but Boswell has left a splendid record of their conversation. "I asked him if he was not religious when he was young. He said he was, and he used to read the *Whole Duty of Man*; that he made an abstract from the Catalogue of vices at the end of it, and examined himself by this, leaving out Murder and Theft and such vices as he had no choice of committing, having no inclination to commit them."

The *Whole Duty of Man* was a seventeenth-century work of popular devotion, probably by the royalist divine Allestree. It is full of arguments in which the premises are factual, to the effect that God has done something or given us something, and the conclusions are moral, to the effect that we ought therefore to perform some particular duty. So it is argued that "whoever is in distress for any thing, wherewith I can supply him, that distress of his makes it a duty on me to supply him and this in all kinds of events. Now the ground of its being a duty is that God hath given me abilities not only for their own use, but for the advantage and benefit of others."[46] Hume summarizes his case against such arguments in a famous passage: "I cannot forbear adding to these reasonings an observation, which may, perhaps, be found of some importance. In every system of morality, which I have hitherto met with, I have always remark'd, that the author proceeds for some time in the ordinary way of reasoning, and establishes the being of a God, or makes observations concerning human affairs; when of a sudden I am surpriz'd to find, that instead of the usual copulations of propositions, *is*, and *is not*, I meet with no proposition that is not connected with an *ought*, or an *ought not*. This change is imperceptible; but is, however, of the last consequence. For as this *ought*, or *ought not*, expresses some new relation or affirmation, 'tis necessary that it shou'd be observ'd and explain'd; and at the same time that a reason should be given for what seems altogether inconceivable, how this new relation can be a deduction from others which are entirely different from it. But as authors do not commonly use this precaution, I shall presume to recommend it to the readers and am persuaded, that this small attention cou'd subvert all the vulgar systems of morality, and let us see, that the distinction of vice and virtue is founded not merely on the relations of objects, nor is perceiv'd by reason."[47]

How did Hume intend this passage to be taken? He has been almost universally read as asserting that there are two classes of assertion, factual and moral, whose relationship is such that no set of factual premises can entail a moral conclusion. This has been held to be a special case of the more general logical truth that no set of factual premises can entail an evaluative conclusion. How are *moral* and *evaluative* defined by writers who not only suppose this to have been Hume's point but also suppose this to be a crucial discovery about the logic of moral discourse? They cannot *define* either *moral* or *evaluative* by means of the notion of not being entailed by factual premises; for if they did, they could not treat the alleged discovery that moral conclusions cannot be entailed by factual premises as more than a tautology of the most insignificant kind. Nor is it plausible to define *moral*, or even *evaluative*, in terms of its function in guiding action or not guiding action, if the definition is to enable us to contrast these terms with *factual*; for, clearly, purely factual assertions such as "This house is on fire" or "That fungus which you are about to eat is poisonous" are capable of guiding action. How then are we to understand their contention? Perhaps in the following way.

The expression "You ought" has a complex background. It differs from the imperative mood of the verbs to which it is attached in at least two connected ways. The first and fundamental one is that the use of *ought* originally implied the ability of the speaker to back up his *ought* with a reason, whereas the use of the simple imperative does not and did not carry any such implication. The reasons which can be employed to back up an *ought* are of different kinds. "You ought to do that—if you want to achieve such and such." Or "You ought—because you are a chief [tutor, night watchman] to. . . ." And so on. Because the *ought* of "You ought" has this backing of reasons, it always has a range of application beyond the person to whom it is immediately addressed—namely, the whole class of persons for whom the reason implied or stated holds good (the class of those who want to achieve such-and-such and the class of chiefs in the two examples). This is the second difference between *ought* and imperatives.

In this original situation what distinguished the moral *ought* from other uses was the kind of reason implied or given for the injunction. Within the relevant class of reason there were various species; "You ought to do this if you want to live up to this ideal" (to be a magnanimous man, a perfect knight, one of the saints) and "You ought to do this if you want to discharge your function as a . . ." are samples. But as shared ideals and accepted functions drop away in the age of individualism, the injunctions have less and less backing. The end of this process is the appearance of a "You ought . . ." unbacked by reasons, announcing traditional moral rules in a vacuum so far as ends are concerned, and addressed to an unlimited class of persons. For this *ought* the title of the moral *ought* is claimed, and it has two properties. It tells us what to do as an imperative does, and it is addressed to anyone who happens to be in the relevant circumstances. When to this use of "You ought" the response is, But why ought I? the only ultimate answer is "You just ought," although there may be an immediate form of reply in which some particular injunction is deduced from a general principle containing the same *ought*.

Of this *ought* it is clear that it cannot be deducted from any *is*; and since it is probably in the eighteenth century that this *ought* first appears, perhaps it is of this *ought* that Hume is speaking. But a careful reading of the passage leaves it ambiguous as to whether Hume is asserting that the transition from *is* to *ought* needs great care, or that it is in fact logically impossible; whether he is deducing that most transitions from *is* to *ought* have in fact been of a fallacious kind, or that any such transition must necessarily be fallacious. Some very limited support for preferring the former to the latter interpretation might be drawn from the fact that in Hume's own moral philosophy the transition from *is* to *ought* is made and made clearly. But too much must not be made of this, for Hume is a notoriously inconsistent author. Yet how does Hume make this transition?

Hume, as we have already seen, argues that when we call an action virtuous or vicious we are saying that it arouses in us a certain feeling, that it pleases us in a certain way. In what way? This question Hume leaves unanswered. He passes on to give an account of why we have the moral rules we do have, why it is *this* rather than *that* which we judge virtuous. The basic terms of this account are utility and sympathy. Consider for example the account of justice which Hume gives in the *Treatise*. He begins by asking why we accept and obey rules which it would often be in our interest to break. He denies that we are by nature so constituted that we have a natural regard for public rather than private interest. "In general, it may be affirm'd that there is no such passion in human minds as the love of mankind, merely as such, independent of personal qualities, of services, or of relation to oneself."[48] If private interest would lead us to flout the rules, and we have no natural regard for public interest, how then do the rules come about? Because it is a fact that without rules of justice there would be no stability of property, and indeed no property, an *artificial* virtue has been created, that of abiding by the rules of justice, and we exhibit this virtue not perhaps so much because we are aware of the benefit that flows from our observing the rules as because we are conscious of how much we are harmed by others infringing them. Our long-term benefit from insisting on strict observance of the rules will always outweigh our short-term benefit from breaking them on this occasion.

In the *Enquiry* human nature is exhibited as less self-interested. "It appears also, that, in our general approbation of character and manners, the useful tendency of the social interests moves us not by any regards to self-interest, but has an influence much more universal and extensive. It appears that a tendency to public good, and to the promoting of peace, harmony, and order in society does always, by affecting the benevolent principles of our frame, engage us on the side of the social virtues."[49] But what is clear is that Hume's altered picture of human nature is made to provide the same type of explanation and justification of moral rules. We are so constituted that we have certain desires and needs; these desires and needs are served by maintaining the moral rules. Hence their explanation and justification. In such an account we certainly begin with an *is* and end with an *ought*.

On most topics Hume is a moral conservative. His skeptical views on religion led him to attack the prohibition of suicide, but he is generally the spokesman for the moral *status quo*. Unchastity in women is more immoral than unchastity in men, for it may lead to confusion over heirs and endangering of property rights. The natural obligation to behave justly is not so strong between princes in their political transactions as it is between private individuals in their social transactions, for the advantage to be gained from abiding by the rules is much greater among individuals within a state than it is among sovereign heads of state. Indeed, Hume is for the most part avowedly engaged in explaining why we have the rules that we do and not in any work of criticism. Just here lies his weakness.

Hume treats moral rules as given, partly because he treats human nature as given. Even though a historian, he was an essentially unhistorical thinker. Feelings, sentiments, passions, are unproblematic and uncriticizable. We just do have the feelings which we have. "A passion is an original existence." But desires, emotions, and the like do not just happen; they are not sensations. They can, to varying degrees, be modified, criticized, rejected, developed, and so on. But this point is not taken with full seriousness either by Hume or by his successors.

Richard Price, a Unitarian minister, was perhaps the most important of Hume's immediate successors. Price argues in his *Review of the Principal Questions and Difficulties of Morals* (1757) that moral distinctions are intellectually grounded just as the rationalists said that they were, and that the apprehension of first principles in morals is not a matter of argument but of grasping their self-evidence. *Ought*, and other moral terms likewise, cannot be explained in terms of any state of feeling, partly because I can always ask, Ought I to feel like this? If asked to justify my judgments, I can only avoid infinite and vicious regress if I allow that there are some actions that are ultimately approved, and for justifying which no reason can be assigned. If asked to explain the concept of duty or obligation, I can only reply that its meaning is evident to any rational being. The basic concepts of right and wrong are "simple ideas," not susceptible of further analysis.

The only other post-Humean moralist worthy of note is Hume's friend the economist Adam Smith. Smith, like Hume, appeals to sympathy as the basis of morals. He makes use of a figure who also appears in Hume—the imaginary impartial spectator of our actions, who provides the standard by which they are to be judged. Smith disagrees with Hume on the question of utility; when we morally approve of a man's conduct we approve of it primarily as fitting or proper, and not as useful. The discernment of propriety in our own actions is the guide to right conduct; or rather, we must ask whether the imaginary spectator would judge our actions to be proper. By so doing, we overcome the bias of self-love. The detail of Smith's account is full of interest; his central thesis leaves us with the difficulty we discovered in earlier writers. Why, given the psychological account of human nature that has been proposed, should we take the attitude we do to moral precepts? If we need moral precepts to correct self-love, what is the character of this need in us? The whole difficulty is engendered by the way the discussion is carried on in two stages. First, human nature is characterized; and the moral rules are introduced as an addendum, to be explained as expressions of or means to the satisfaction of the already specified nature. Yet the human nature specified is individualist human nature, unamenable to moral rules. And are we not, in any case, back again with a new form of the error committed by the sophists and by Hobbes? Can we actually characterize individuals apart from and prior to their adherence to certain rules?

The successors of Hume and Adam Smith in Scottish philosophy have little to say to us. Thomas Reid was a rationalist in the spirit of Price. James Beattie, Dugald Stewart, and Thomas Brown belong to the class of Hume's critics whom Kant castigated for their epistemological misunderstandings of Hume. It is, in fact, elsewhere that we shall find the highest achievements of the eighteenth century in ethics. But the barrenness of Hume's successors is not accidental. They had inherited a set of insoluble problems. Small wonder that they either assert the existence of self-evident moral perceptions, as Stewart does, or assert that God has constructed our emotions so that we approve of what it is most expedient for us to approve of, as Brown does. Appeals to self-evidence of this kind, which are involved in all their arguments, are at best defensive strategies for whatever moral positions are taken to be part of common sense. And because common sense is never more than an inherited amalgam of past clarities and past confusions, the defenders of common sense are unlikely to enlighten us.

# 13

## THE FRENCH EIGHTEENTH-CENTURY ARGUMENT

No greater contrast can be envisaged than that between Hume and Montesquieu. Hume breathes the spirit of his own age, while that Montesquieu was much read but little influential is scarcely surprising. For apart from Vico, whom he almost certainly had not read, the writers whom he most resembles are Durkheim and Weber. Charles-Louis de Secondat, Baron de la Brède et de Montesquieu (1689–1755) was an Anglophile French aristocrat who grasped in a moment of illumination, not dissimilar to that in which Descartes founded modern philosophy, the great truths that societies are not mere collections of individuals, and that social institutions are not means to the psychological ends of such individuals. In so doing, he broke both with the utilitarianism and with the individualism of his century. His consequent motive was a practical one; he wished to understand society in order to create an applied science of government by means of which the human condition might be improved.

What creates different forms of social life? "Men are governed by many factors: climate, religion, law, the precepts of government, the examples of the past, customs, manners; and from the combination of such influences there arises a general spirit." The lawgiver must study the particular society for which he is legislating, because societies greatly differ. The totality of relationships which the lawgiver must take into account compose "the spirit of the laws," the phrase which Montesquieu used as a title for his major book.

Montesquieu takes the isolated Hobbesian individual to be not only a myth, but a gratuitously misleading myth. If we look at the societies to which individuals belong, we discover that they exemplify quite different types of system. What ends an individual has, what needs, what values, will depend upon the nature of the social system to which he belongs. But social institutions and the whole framework of legal, customary, and moral rules are devices not to secure ends external to themselves, but native to the psychology of the individual—rather, such institutions and rules supply the necessary background against which alone the ends and needs of the individual can be intelligible. This contention is close to that of Aristotle; and Montesquieu is in many ways an Aristotelian thinker. But he stresses explicitly, in a way that Aristotle never does, the social milieu in which politics and morals have to be placed. He is the first moralist with a sociological perspective. (Vico precedes him as a sociologist, but is not in the same sense a moralist.)

The types of society enumerated by Montesquieu are three: despotic, monarchical, and republican. Each type has its own kind of health and its own characteristic ailments. Each is marked by a dominant ethos: despotisms by fear, monarchies by honor, republics by virtue. Montesquieu's own moral preferences emerge in two ways: implicitly in his tone of voice, which betrays a modified admiration for republics, an approval of monarchy, and a genuine dislike of despotism; and explicitly in his repudiation of the attempt to state true moral precepts for all times and places. "When Montezuma insisted that the religion of the Spaniards was good for their country and the Mexican for his own, what he said was not absurd."[50] Each society has its own standards and its own forms of justification. But from this it does follow that every form of justification which attempts to provide norms of a supracultural kind is bound to fail; hence Montesquieu without inconsistency could attack a variety of moral views as ill-founded.

More than this, Montesquieu combined with his relativism a belief in certain eternal norms, and it perhaps seems more difficult at this point in the argument to acquit him of inconsistency. We have, according to Montesquieu, a concept of justice at least which we can formulate independently of any existing legal system and in the light of which we can criticize all such systems. We can judge positive laws to be more or less just. How can Montesquieu believe both that every society has its own standards and that, nonetheless, there are eternal norms by means of which such standards can be criticized?

If we read Montesquieu as merely asserting that there are certain necessary conditions which any positive code of laws or rules must satisfy if it is to be called just, then he is not inconsistent in also asserting that what is held to be just must vary from society to society. For although the same necessary conditions must be satisfied in all societies, the satisfaction of these conditions may in no society be sufficient to characterize an action, policy, or rule as just. Thus Montesquieu might mean, for example, that in all societies it is necessary for the law to specify the same punishment for the same offense if it is to be characterized as just, but that what offenses are punished may vary indefinitely from society to society. But while perhaps this is part of what Montesquieu meant, he does in fact seem to go further than this; for he is willing to speak of a state of nature where human conduct would be governed simply by the rules of natural justice. And if the rules of natural justice are to be sufficient to govern conduct, then they must in fact have all the characteristics of a positive code—except that they are divinely enacted. But in that case, what becomes of relativism? What becomes of the thesis that every society must be judged in its own terms?

There is no clear answer in Montesquieu. He just is inconsistent. Sometimes he seems committed to the view that there is no standpoint outside or beyond that of a given society. Sometimes—more interestingly still—he seems to make political liberty his criterion for judging a society. His three basic types of society are despotism, republicanism, and monarchy. In a despotic state the only law is the fiat of the ruler; hence there is no legal tradition and no established framework. The principle of government is fear, fear of the consequences of disobedience. The part that an established legal framework might play in guiding conduct is taken by religion or custom. In a republican state the motive for obedience to the law is the sense of civic virtue. A republican government has to take positive steps to educate its citizens into such a sense, and the demands made upon the citizens will be high. Less so in a monarchy, where the appeal is to the sense of honor and to the rewards of position. A monarchy is a hierarchical society, and the values of its subjects are the values of rank and status. It is clear that this part of Montesquieu's theory is relativistic. The questions, Which is the most honorable course of action? and, Which is the most expedient and least dangerous course of action? appear as rival inter-pretations of the question, Which is the *best* course of action? and there is no room for the question, Which is the best motive, fear, virtue, or honor? Each is best adapted to its own type of society.

Montesquieu's relativism stands in sharp contrast to the absolutist ethics of most writers of the French Enlightenment. But these did not, of course, agree among themselves. Helvétius perhaps stands at one extreme, Diderot at another. Claude-Adrien Helvétius (1715–71) caused such scandal with his psychological materialism that he was forced to retire from the French royal service. Reasoning, as well as perception, according to Helvétius, consists solely in a chain of sensa-tions. Of sensations, some are painful, some pleasant, some neutral. Everyone desires his own pleasure and nothing else. Everything else which men appear to desire they desire only as a means to their pleas-ure. Some men are pained by the pain of others and pleased by the pleasure of others. They exhibit what we call benevolence. Moral words are used to pick out types of sensibility which are universally approved as useful and pleasing. Apparent disputes and disagreements over moral questions would all be removed if confusion over the definition of moral words were removed. Such confusions can only be removed by free discussion. Where is free discussion possible? Only in England; scarcely at all in France.

At this point in the argument we encounter one of the most charac-teristic paradoxes of the Enlightenment. On the one hand, Helvétius espouses a completely determinist psychology. On the other, he believes in almost limitless possibilities of transforming human nature, if only political despotism and ecclesiastical obscurantism did not pre-vent a radical reform of the educational system. For by conditioning the child at a sufficiently early age we can bring him to take pleasure in benevolence and altruism. When Helvétius first describes benevolence he makes it appear as if it is just a fact that some men do take pleasure in pleasing others; now he writes as if everyone *ought* to take such pleasure. Covertly, the agent's own pleasure has ceased to be the sole criterion of right action.

The complexity of the thought of Denis Diderot (1713–84), coeditor with d'Alembert of the *Encyclopédie*, is alone enough to put him at the opposite pole of the Enlightenment from Helvétius. Diderot, like Montesquieu, believes in eternal moral laws; like Montesquieu, he is also well aware of moral variations between societies. In his *Supplement to Bougainville's "Voyage"* he compares Polynesian institutions with European, and the comparison is greatly to the advantage of the former. But his conclusion is not that we should straightaway replace Catholicism and monogamy by their Polynesian alternatives, for this kind of drastic innovation would disrupt society and multiply unhappiness. What he does insist upon is the gradual replacement of institutions in which impulse and desire are frustrated by institutions which allow them expression. But almost alone among the writers of the Enlightenment, Diderot can always see numerous sides to every question. In *Rameau's Nephew* he presents a dialogue with the nephew of the composer, who represents all those impulses upon which respectable society necessarily frowns, but by which in more or less disguised forms it is then victimized. In so doing, Diderot takes an enormous step forward. Both Plato and the Christians put certain basic human desires under a ban as evil; but what happens to them then? If they are not allowed a legitimate outlet, is not this equivalent to prescribing an illegitimate outlet for them? And if this is so, isn't the evil created by the would-be good? Diderot's argument is inconclusive. But it challenges the Christian, and especially the Protestant, view of man at its most vulnerable point.

If the evil in human nature can be traced to specific causes, what becomes of the dogma of original sin? If the specific causes of evil include the propagation of dogmas such as the dogma of original sin, what becomes of the whole theological enterprise? This is the question posed most systematically by Rousseau. Rousseau however cannot be discussed simply as one among others with the writers of the Enlightenment, partly because he deliberately set himself against the whole trend of the Enlightenment, and partly because he exists as a moral philosopher on an incomparably higher level than any other writer of the eighteenth century except for Hume and Kant. We can bring out Rousseau's importance best by considering the different attitude to liberty taken by the typical writers of the Enlightenment and by Rousseau. For Montesquieu, Voltaire, and Helvétius alike the ideals of political liberty are incarnated in the English Revolution of 1688. Freedom means freedom for Whig lords and also for intellectuals like themselves. But for those whom Voltaire called "the rabble" obedience is still the order of the day. Thus on the only point on which the writers of the Enlightenment were predisposed to be moral innovators they adopted a position which was essentially arbitrary, which accepted the *status quo* as a whole, while questioning it in part, especially where it affected their own interests. No wonder that these would-be radicals so eagerly sought and accepted relationships with royal patrons, Diderot with Catherine of Russia, Voltaire with Frederick of Prussia. On moral questions in general, the Enlightenment critique of society is simply that men behave irrationally; and the recipe for social improvement is that henceforward men should behave rationally. But to the questions of why men are irrational, and what they would have to do to become rational, few answers are given beyond the panaceas of free discussion and education. It is with relief that one turns from this mediocrity to the passion of Rousseau.

Jean-Jacques Rousseau has been variously credited with the rise of romanticism, the decline of the West, and more plausibly, the French Revolution. Thomas Carlyle is said—possibly apocryphally—to have once been dining with a businessman who tired of Carlyle's loquacity and turned to him with the reproach, "Ideas, Mr. Carlyle, ideas, nothing but ideas!" Carlyle replied, "There was once a man called Rousseau who wrote a book containing nothing but ideas. The second edition was bound in the skins of those who laughed at the first." What then was so influential in what Rousseau had to say?

The simple, central, powerful concept in Rousseau is that of a human nature which is overlaid and distorted by existing social and political institutions, but whose authentic wants and needs provide us with a basis for morals and a measure of the corruption of social institutions. His concept of human nature is far more sophisticated than that of other writers who have appealed to an original human nature; for Rousseau does not deny that human nature has a history, that it can be and is often transformed, so that new desires and motives appear. The history of man begins in the state of nature, but Rousseau's view of the state of nature is quite unlike that of Hobbes. First, it is not presocial. Man's natural, unreflective impulses are not those of self-aggrandizement; natural man is moved by self-love, but self-love is not inconsistent with feelings of sympathy and compassion. Even some animals, Rousseau noted, go to the aid of others. Second, human wants are limited by the natural environment. Rousseau is well aware of what Hobbes seems not to know, that human desires are elicited by being presented with objects of desire; and natural man is presented with few desirable objects. "The only goods he acknowledges in the world are food, a woman, and sleep; the only ills he fears are pain and hunger." Third, like Hobbes, Rousseau believes that in a state of nature certain moral distinctions are not yet made; since there is as yet no property, there is no use for the concepts of justice and injustice. But it does not follow from this for Rousseau that *no* moral predicates as yet have application. Natural man, following his impulses of need and occasional sympathy, is good and not evil. The Christian doctrine of original sin is as false as the Hobbesian doctrine of nature.

After the state of nature comes social life. Experience of the advantages of cooperative enterprise, the institution of property, skills in agriculture and working metals—all these lead into complex forms of social organization, although there are as yet no political institutions. The institution of property and the growth of wealth lead to inequality, oppression, enslavement, and consequent theft and other crimes. Because it is now possible to speak of what is rightly mine or thine, the concepts of justice and injustice come to have application. But the development of moral distinctions parallels a growth in moral depravity. The ills born of this depravity lead to a strong desire for political and legal institutions. These institutions are born of a social contract.

As with some earlier contract theorists, Rousseau did not believe that he was recounting history. He says explicitly that he is concerned with an area of inquiry where facts are not available; he is therefore contructing a hypothesis to explain the present state of man and society, but this hypothesis cannot rise to the level of historical fact. His account is, in fact, in the form of a functional explanation which exhibits certain features of social life as serving certain ends. In the case of political institutions he wishes to draw a contrast between the ends which they might serve (and which in the narrative of the contract they were originally introduced to serve) and the ends which they actually do serve. The state, according to Rousseau was originally introduced as a law-making and law-enforcing agency which by providing impartial justice would rectify the disorders arising from social inequality. It might be made to serve these ends again, but it has in fact been made into an instrument of despotism and inequality. In the state of society before the contract, the need was for leaders who would undertake to prevent the abuse of power; in fact those leaders have established, and used laws to establish, a state of affairs where the powerful and the propertied were able not only to oppress the poor but to invoke legitimate authority to back up their oppression.

This is the account of the origin of inequality which Rousseau gave in an essay in a prize competition run by the Académie de Dijon, which did not win the prize but was published in 1758. He was at that time already forty-six years old; four years later he published *Du contrat social* and *Emile*, and as a result had to leave France. While in exile he took refuge with Hume, who behaved with generosity toward a guest of impossible temperament. Rousseau was the worst kind of paranoid and hypochondriac, the type who does in fact suffer persecution and is in fact constantly ill, and who therefore is able to justify to himself the irrationalities with which he alienates his friends. But his tortured sensibility and his labored introspection bore fruit not only in a better description of human emotion than any other eighteenth-century writer offers us but also in a subtler analysis.

From Hobbes onward the psychological problem had been posed, Why should men do other than act to their own immediate advantage? The solutions in both French and English writers tend to fall into two groups. Either it is suggested that there is an independent source of altruism in human nature, or it is suggested that altruism is merely disguised self-love. The first type of solution depends upon an a-priori psychology tailored to fit the problem; the second, as we have already seen in discussing Hobbes, is palpably false.

It is Rousseau who sees his way to a dissolution rather than a solution of the problem by discerning that the notions of self-interest and selfishness have not the elementary and simple character that both

Hobbes and his successors assigned to them. This is for two reasons, both of which are found in Rousseau. The first is that the man who is able to consider the alternatives of consulting his own interest or of consulting that of others must (even though he chooses to consult his own interests) be already involved sympathetically with others to at least some extent in order for their interest to appear to present him with an alternative. The newborn baby is not selfish, for it confronts no alternatives of altruism and selfishness. Even the psychopath is not selfish. Neither psychopath nor infant has developed to the point at which selfishness is possible. The second reason is that in the pursuit of most characteristically human goals it is impossible to separate out a part that is the consulting of my own interest and a part that is devoted to the needs of others. Hobbes pictures men as social beings only contingently, through the accident of social contact. Hume, in the Enquiry at least, pictures them as having a spring of sympathy for others independent of their aims for themselves. Rousseau sees that what men aim at for themselves is a certain kind of life lived in a certain type of relationship with others. True self-love, our primitive passion, provides the notion of a reciprocal relationship of the self to others and so a basis for an appreciation of justice. Gradually the more complex virtues are evolved as the simpler moral feelings are educated. The moral simplicities of the heart are a safe guide.

When, however, we consult these simplicities we discover a sharp contrast between what they enjoin and what is enjoined by the morality which existing institutions have produced. The reform of those institutions is therefore the precondition of systematic moral reform. Civilization continually produces new desires and needs, and these new goals are above all acquisitive, concerned with property and with power. Men become selfish through the multiplication of private interests in an acquisitive society. The task of the social reformer, therefore, is to construct institutions in which the primitive regard for the needs of others will be restored in the form of a regard for the common good. Men have to learn how in advanced communities they can act not as private individuals, as men, but rather as citizens.

The detail of the political arrangements which Rousseau proposes is scarcely germane; what does matter is his conception of politics as the expression through institutions of a genuine common will, "the general will," which he contrasts with "the will of all," the sum, as it were, of individual wills. This is not, however, a matter of politics as distinct from morals. "Society has to be studied in the individual, and the individual in society; those who wish to separate politics from morals will never understand either." What does this mean? Rousseau understood, as Kant was later to observe, that I cannot answer the question, What ought I to do? until I have answered the question, Who am I? But any answer to this question will specify, as Kant did not understand, my place is a nexus of social relationships, and it is within these and the possibilities which they make available that ends in the light of which actions may be criticized are discovered. But if I judge, as Rousseau did, that the social order to which I actually belong is corrupted and corrupting, I shall have to discover the ends for moral action not implicit in the forms of social activity which I already share with my fellow men, but in a form of social life which does not yet exist but which might be brought into existence. What authority has this not-yet-existent form of social life over me to provide me with norms? Rousseau's answer is that it will be seen to be a just order by the uncorrupted heart. If, as he sometimes seems about to do, Rousseau went on to say that the heart is only uncorrupted in a just social order, then he would be involved in a logically vicious circularity. But in fact Rousseau, especially in the *Vicaire savoyard*, seems to insist that a true conscience is always accessible. If we consult it, we may still go astray intellectually, but not morally. That is why, when conscience is institutionalized in the form of deliberative assemblies whose regard for the common good and for the norms of justice render them voices of the general will, it remains true that "the general will is always right and promotes the public advantage; but it does not follow that the deliberations of the people are always equally right. Our will is always for our own good, but we do not always see what that good is; the people is never corrupted, but it is often deceived, and on such occasions only does it seem to will what is bad."[51]

What is clearest in this passage is that Rousseau takes it for granted that there is a single common good, that the wants and needs of all the citizens do coincide in this good, that there are not irreconcilable social groupings within society. As to the nature of this common good we can at worst miscalculate. But why, then, do private interests multiply?

Why is the common good disregarded? Rousseau's brilliant, if primitive, sociological insight into the divisive nature of modern society is scarcely coherent with his assertions on other occasions of the power and universality of moral feeling. This dilemma of Rousseau's is not peculiar to him. If I can purge society of corruption by appeal to universally valid moral principles to which either every heart or every mind or both must give testimony, then how can society ever have become corrupted in the first place? I avoid this dilemma only either by denying the possibility of abolishing the corruption of society, or by insisting that society is not homogeneous, that the moral principles to which I appeal express the wants and ends of some but not others, and that in appealing to those principles I can expect concurrence only from those whose wants and needs are of the relevant kind.

The latter way out was to be taken by Marx, who spoke approvingly of "Rousseau's simple moral sense;" the former way, by the conservatives who reacted to the French Revolution. All human hearts, so their argument runs, are at once corrupted and yet aware of a law which judges them. The pure heart cannot be contrasted with the impure social order, for the impurity is in the social order only because it is in the heart first, and it is in all hearts. The doctrine of original sin, muted in Burke, loud in de Maistre, is conservatism's reply to Rousseau. There is a recurring pattern in the history of the West from the eighteenth century onward in which every major failure in the human struggle for self-improvement and liberation is greeted as new evidence for the dogma of original sin. The tone changes: a Reinhold Niebuhr on the failure of the Russion Revolution is very different from a de Maistre on the failure of the French. But the dogmatic stock in trade is the same. It is one of Rousseau's cardinal virtues to have asked for an explanation of specific evils in human life, and in so doing, to have opened the way for sociological hope to replace theological despair. Yet it remains true that Rousseau himself was a pessimist; the discovery of what conditions are an empirical prerequisite for social reform can itself lead to pessimism. And where Rousseau had specified the climatic, economic, and social preconditions of democracy he was forced to conclude that only one people in Europe were capable of it: the Corsicans.

# 14

## KANT

Kant stands at one of the great dividing points in the history of ethics. For perhaps the majority of later philosophical writers, including many who are self-consciously anti-Kantian, ethics is defined as a subject in Kantian terms. For many who have never heard of philosophy, let alone of Kant, morality is roughly what Kant said it was. Why this is so can only be suggested when what Kant said has been understood. But at the outset we have to note one very general point about Kant. He was in one sense both a typical and supreme representative of the Enlightenment; typical because of his belief in the power of courageous reasoning and in the effectiveness of the reform of institutions (when all states are republics there will be no more war); supreme because in what he thought he either solved the recurrent problems of the Enlightenment or reformulated them in a much more fruitful way. The greatest example of this is his synthesis of those two idols of the Enlightenment, Newton's physics and the empiricism of Helvétius and Hume, in the *Critique of Pure Reason*. The empiricists had argued that we have rational grounds for belief in nothing beyond what our senses have already encountered; Newton's physics offered us laws applicable to all events in space and time. How to reconcile them? We can, Kant argues, be assured a priori that all our experience will turn out to be law governed and to be law governed after the manner of Newtonian causality, not because of the character of the external world, but because of the character of the concepts through which we grasp that world. Experience is not a mere passive reception of impressions; it is the active grasping and comprehension of perceptions, and without the concepts and categories by means of which we order and understand perceptions, it would be formless and meaningless. "Concepts without perceptions are empty; perceptions without concepts are blind."

Kant's theory of knowledge, even as so very briefly adumbrated, is important for his theory of morals in at least two ways. Because causal relations are discovered only when we apply the categories to experience, we have no way of inferring causal relationships beyond and outside experience; we cannot, therefore, validly infer from the causal order of nature to a God who is the author of nature. Nature is entirely impersonal and nonmoral; it may be viewed *as if* it were the product of a great and benevolent designer, but we cannot affirm that it is such. We have, therefore, to look for the realm of morals outside the realm of nature. Morals must be independent of how the world goes, for how the world goes is nonmoral. Moreover, Kant never proceeds, as Descartes and some of the empiricists did, by looking for a basis for knowledge, for some set of first principles or hard data, in order to vindicate our claims to knowledge against some hypothetical skeptic. Kant takes the existence of arithmetic and that of Newtonian mechanics for granted and inquires what must be the case with our concepts for these sciences to be possible. So also with morals. Kant takes the existence of an ordinary moral consiousness for granted; his own parents, whose sacrifices had made his education possible, and whose intellectual gifts were notably less than his own, seemed to him models of simple goodness. When Kant read Rousseau, Rousseau's remarks on the dignity of ordinary human nature struck home at once. It is the moral consciousness of this ordinary human nature which provides the philosopher with an object for analysis; as in the theory of knowledge, the philosopher's task is not to seek for a basis or a vindication, but to ask what character our moral concepts and precepts must have to make morality as it is possible.

Kant therefore is among those philosophers who see their task as one of *post eventum* analysis; science is what it is, morality is what it is, and there's an end on't. This essentially conservative view is all the more surprising when we recall that Kant's lifetime (1724–1804) was a period of rapid social change. Part of the explanation of Kant's attitudes is perhaps biographical; Königsberg, near Prussia's eastern limits, was no metropolis, and Kant led an isolated academic existence. But much more important is the fact that Kant conceived his task as the isolation of the a priori, and therefore unchanging, elements of morality. In different societies there might be different moral schemes; Kant insisted on his own students coming to terms with the empirical study of human nature. But what is it that makes these schemes *moral*? What form must a precept have if it is to be recognized as a *moral* precept?

Kant approaches this question from an initial assertion that nothing is unconditionally good—except a good will. Health, wealth, intellect, are good only insofar as they are used well. But the good will is good; it "shines forth like a precious jewel," even if "through the niggardly provision of a stepmotherly nature," the agent is insufficiently strong, rich, or clever to bring about desirable states of affairs. Attention is thus focused from the outset on the agent's will, on his motives and intentions, rather than upon what he actually does. What motives or intentions make the good will good?

The good will's only motive is to do its duty for the sake of doing its duty. Whatever it intends to do, it intends because it is its duty. A man may do what is, in fact, his duty from quite other motives. A shopkeeper giving the correct change may be honest not because it is his duty to be honest but because honesty pays off by bringing him custom and increasing his profits. But it is important to note here that a will can fail to be good not only because duty may be done from self-interested motives but also because duty may be done from altruistic motives which nonetheless spring from inclination. If I am a friendly, cheerful, kind person by nature, who enjoys helping others, my altruistic acts, which may be what duty in fact demands from me, may be done not because duty demands them but just because I have an inclination to behave in this way—I enjoy it. If so, my will fails to be decisively good, just as if I had acted from self-interest. Kant rarely mentions and never dwells upon the difference between inclinations to act in one way rather than another; the whole contrast is between duty upon the one hand and inclination of every kind upon the other. For inclination belongs to our determined physical and psychological nature; we cannot in Kant's view choose our inclinations. What we can do is to choose between our inclination and our duty. How, then, does duty present itself to me? It presents itself as obedience to a law that is universally binding on all rational beings. What is the content of this law? and how do I become aware of it?

I become aware of it as a set of precepts which, in prescribing to myself I can consistently will, should be obeyed by all rational beings. The test of a genuine moral imperative is that I can universalize it— that is, that I can will that it should be a universal law, or, as Kant puts it in another formulation, that I can will that it should be a law of nature. The point of this latter formulation is to stress that not only must I be able to will that the precept in question should be recognized as a law universally, but I must also be able to will that it should be acted on universally—in the appropriate circumstances. The sense of "be able to" and "can" in these formulations is equivalent to "can without inconsistency," the demand for consistency being part of the demand for rationality in a law that men prescribe to themselves as rational beings. Kant's most helpful example is that of promise keeping. Suppose that I am tempted to break a promise. The precept upon which I am considering acting may be formulated as: "I may always break a promise when it is in my interest to do so." Can I consistently will that this precept should be universally acknowledged and acted upon? If all men acted upon this precept, and broke their promises whenever it suited them, clearly the practices of making and of relying upon promises would break down, for nobody would be able to trust the promises of others, and consequently, utterances of the form "I promise to . . ." would cease to have point. Hence to will that this precept should be universalized is to will that promise keeping should no longer be possible. But to will that I should be able to act on this precept (which I must will as part of willing that the precept should be universalized) is to will that I should be able to make promises and break them, and this is to will that the practice of promise keeping should continue, so that I can take advantage of it. Hence to will that this precept should be universalized is to will both that promise keeping as a practice should continue and also that it should not. So I cannot universalize this precept consistently, and thus it cannot be a true moral imperative, or as Kant calls it, a categorical imperative.

In calling moral imperatives categorical Kant contrasts them with hypothetical imperatives. A hypothetical imperative is of the form "You ought to do such and such if . . ." The if may introduce either of two types of condition. There are hypothetical imperatives of skill—"You ought to do such and such [or, Do such and such] if you wish to produce this sort of result" (e.g., "Press the switch if you wish to ring the bell"); and hypothetical imperatives of prudence—"You ought to do such and such if you wish to be happy [or, for your advantage]." The categorical imperative is limited by no conditions. It is simply of the form "You ought to do such and such." A version of Kant's categorical imperative certainly appears in ordinary moral utterance in our society. "You ought to do it." "Why?" "There's no reason. You just ought." The force of "There's no reason" is to draw a contrast with the cases where you ought to do something because it will be to your pleasure or advantage or will bring about some result you want. Thus, the distinction between categorical and hypothetical imperatives is at this level a familiar one. What is unfamiliar is the Kantian test of ability to universalize the precept consistently. For what is not present in our everyday moral discourse is the concept of a rational—and because rational, objective—criterion for deciding which are the authentic moral imperatives. The historical importance of Kant is partly that his criterion is designed to replace two alternative criteria.

According to Kant, the rational being utters the commands of morality to himself. He obeys no one but himself. Obedience is not automatic because we are not wholly rational beings but are compounded of reason and of what Kant calls sensibility, in which is included all our physiological and psychological makeup. Kant contrasts what he calls "pathological love," by which he means not morbid or unnatural love but natural affection, the love that springs up in us spontaneously, with "the love that can be commanded," which is obedience to the categorical imperative, and which he equates with the love for our neighbor that Jesus commanded. But Jesus cannot be for us a moral authority; or rather, he is only insofar as our rational nature recognizes him as such and accords him authority; and if that is the authority which we accept, it is in fact our own reason, and not Jesus, which we are taking to be ultimately authoritative. We can put the same point in another way. Suppose that a divine being, real or alleged, commands me to do something. I only ought to do what he commands if what he commands is right. But if I am in a position to judge for myself whether what he commands is right or not, then I have no need of the divine being to instruct me in what I ought to do. Inescapably, each of us is his own moral authority. To recognize this, which Kant calls the autonomy of the moral agent, is to recognize also that external authority, even if divine, can provide no criterion for morality. To suppose that it could would be to be guilty of heteronomy, of the attempt to subject the agent to a law outside himself, alien to his nature as a rational being. But belief in a divine law as the source of morality is not the only kind of heteronomy. If we attempt to find a criterion for assessing moral precepts in the concept of happiness or of what would satisfy human wants and needs, we shall be equally wrongheaded. The realm of inclination is as alien to our rational natures as any divine commandments are. Hence Aristotle's εὐδαιμονία is as useless for morality as Christ's law.

It is useless, in any case, because it can provide no fixed guide. The notion of happiness is indefinitely variable, depending upon variations in psychological make-up. But the moral law must be entirely unvarying. When I have discerned a categorical imperative I have discerned a rule which has no exceptions. In a short essay called "On the Supposed Right of Telling a Lie from Benevolent Motives," Kant replied to Benjamin Constant, who had criticized him on this point. Suppose that a would-be murderer inquires from me the whereabouts of his intended victim. And suppose that I lie in order to save the victim. The murderer then proceeds to follow my directions, but, unknown to me, the victim has in fact removed himself to precisely the place to which I have directed the murderer. Consequently, the murder is effected as a consequence of my lie, and I am responsible precisely because I lied. But had I told the truth, I could not have been held responsible, no matter what happened. For it is my duty to obey the imperative and not to look to the consequences. The resemblance of Kant's view to that of Butler is striking; and it is no accident that for Kant, as for Butler, the insistence upon the irrelevant consequences is balanced by an invocation of theology. Kant argues that my duty is my duty irrespective of the consequences, whether in this world or the next. He has none of the crudity and insensitivity of the theological utilitarians. But he still argues, or rather asserts, that it would be intolerable if in fact duty were not in the end crowned with happiness. The odd thing is that if happiness is as indeterminate a notion as he suggests elsewhere—and as he suggests rightly elsewhere, for the Kantian notion of happiness has been detached from any notion of socially established ends and the satisfaction to be gained from achieving them—he can scarcely be consistent here in introducing happiness as the reward of virtue which though unsought, being indeed the reward of virtue only if it is unsought, is that without which the whole enterprise of morality would scarcely make sense. What this amounts to is a tacit admission that without some such notion, not morality itself, but the Kantian interpretation of it scarcely makes sense.

Practical reason presupposes on Kant's view a belief in God, freedom, and immortality. God is required as a power capable of realizing the *summum bonum*, of crowning virtue with happiness; immortality is required because virtue and happiness manifestly do not coincide in this life; and freedom is the presupposition of the categorical imperative. For it is only in acts of obedience to the categorical imperative that we are delivered from the bondage of our own inclinations. The *ought* of the categorical imperative can only have application to an agent capable of obedience. In this sense *ought* implies *can*. And to be capable of obedience implies that one has evaded the determination of one's actions by one's inclinations, simply because the imperative which guides action determined by inclination is always a hypothetical one. This is the content of moral freedom.

The power of this Kantian picture is undeniable, and its power is increased rather than diminished when the doctrine of the categorical imperative is detached from the dubious support offered by the Kantian forms of belief in God and immortality. Whence does this power derive? In the course of the discussion of Hume I described the emergence of the moral *ought* in the modern sense. Although we can discuss the first signs of philosophical recognition for this *ought* in a writer like Hume, his utilitarianism does not allow him to give it a central place. But with Kant this *ought* is not only central but all absorbing. The word *duty* is detached altogether from its root connection with the fulfillment of a particular role or the carrying out of the functions of a particular office. It becomes singular rather than plural, and it is defined in terms of obedience to categorical moral imperatives—that is, in terms of injunctions containing the new *ought*. The very detachment of the categorical imperative from contingent events and needs and from social circumstances makes it in at least two ways an acceptable form of moral precept for emerging liberal individualist society.

It makes the individual morally sovereign; it enables him to reject all external authorities. And it leaves the individual free to pursue whatever it is that he does, without suggesting that he ought to do something else. This latter point is perhaps less obvious than the first. The typical examples of alleged categorical imperatives given by Kant tell us what *not* to do; not to break promises, tell lies, commit suicide, and so on. But as to what activities we ought to engage in, what ends we should pursue, the categorical imperative seems to be silent. Morality sets limits to the ways in which and the means by which we conduct our lives; it does not give them direction. Thus morality apparently sanctions any way of life which is compatible with keeping our promises, telling the truth, and so on.

A closely related point moves nearer to matters of directly philosophical interest. The doctrine of the categorical imperative provides me with a test for rejecting proposed maxims; it does not tell me whence I am to derive the maxims which first provide the need for a test. Thus the Kantian doctrine is parasitic upon some already existing morality, within which it allows us to sift—or rather, within which it would allow us to sift if the test it provided were a reliable test. But in fact it is not, even on its own terms. For the Kantian test of a true moral precept is that it is one that I can consistently universalize. In fact, however, with sufficient ingenuity almost every precept can be consistently universalized. For all that I need to do is to characterize the proposed action in such a way that the maxim will permit me to do what I want while prohibiting others from doing what would nullify the maxim if universalized. Kant asks if I can consistently universalize the maxim that I may break my promises whenever it suits me. Suppose, however, that he had inquired whether I can consistently universalize the maxim "I may break my promises only when. . . ." The gap is filled by a description devised so that it will apply to my present circumstances but to very few others, and to none such that if someone else obeyed the maxim, it would inconvenience me, let alone show the maxim incapable of consistent universality. It follows that in practice the test of the categorical imperative imposes restrictions only on those insufficiently equipped with ingenuity. And this surely is scarcely what Kant intended.

The logical emptiness of the test of the categorical imperative is itself of social importance. Because the Kantian notion of duty is so formal that it can be given almost any content, it becomes available to provide a sanction and a motive for the specific duties which any particular social and moral tradition may propose. Because it detaches the notion of duty from the notions of ends, purposes, wants, and needs it suggests that, given a proposed course of action, I may only ask whether, in doing it, I can consistently will that it shall be universally done, and not ask what ends or purposes it serves. Anyone educated into the Kantian notion of duty will, so far, have been educated into easy conformism with authority.

Nothing, of course, could be further from the intentions or from the spirit of Kant himself. His wish is to exhibit the moral individual as being a standpoint and a criterion superior to and outside any actual social order. He sympathizes with the French Revolution. He hated servility and valued independence of mind. Paternalism, so he held, was the grossest form of despotism.[52] But the consequences of his doctrines, in German history at least, suggest that the attempt to find a moral standpoint completely independent of the social order may be a quest for an illusion, a quest that renders one a mere conformist servant of the social order much more than does the morality of those who recognize the impossibility of a code which does not to some extent as least express the wants and needs of men in particular social circumstances.

# 15

## HEGEL AND MARX

It would be satisfying in some ways to make Hegel the culmination of the history of ethics: partly because Hegel himself saw the history of philosophy as ending with himself; more importantly because by Hegel's time all the fundamental positions have been taken up. After Hegel they reappear in new guises and with new variations, but their reappearance is a testimony to the impossibility of fundamental innovation. The young Hegel set himself a problem which has already appeared in the argument: why are modern Germans (or Europeans in general) not like ancient Greeks? His answer is that through the rise of Christianity the individual and the state have become divided, so that the individual looks to transcendent criteria rather than to those implicit in the practice of his own political community. (Christianity separates the man whose destiny is eternal from the citizen; its God is the ruler of the world, not the deity of hearth and city.) Greek ethics presupposed the shared structure of the πόλις, and the consequent shared goals and desires. Modern (eighteenth-century) communities are collections of individuals. Hegel usually writes as if the Greek πόλις were more harmonious than in fact it was; he often ignores the existence of slaves. But then, so did Plato and Aristotle. Yet if Hegel's vision of Greek harmony is exaggerated it provides him with clues for the diagnosis of individualism, and with clues of a historical kind. For

Hegel is the first author to understand that there is not a single permanent moral question. His whole philosophy is an attempt to show that the history of philosophy is at the core of philosophy. And he believes this because he believes that philosophy clarifies and articulates the same concepts which are implicit in ordinary thought and practice. Since these have a history, philosophy too must be a historical discipline. It is true that Hegel, especially in his later writings, often treats concepts as if they are timeless entities somehow independent of the flux of the changing world. But even here there is usually some saving clause to make it clear that this is only a *façon de parler*.

If, then, for Hegel the clue to ethics is in the history of ethics, the Hegelian philosophy must cover the ground already traversed in these essays—and more. So it does, and in a variety of ways. The accounts of morality and its history given in the *Phenomenology of Mind* and in the *Philosophy of Right* are by no means identical. Moreover, in the *Phenomenology* at least, Hegel covers the same ground more than once in different ways. What I shall do, therefore, is to try to outline Hegel's general view of the history of morality and of the role of moral philosophy in that history; then look at what is illuminating in Hegel's changes of mind; and finally, criticize Hegel's own solution.

Hegel envisages the most elementary forms of human life as essentially unreflective. The individual is absorbed into a closed society in which he acts out his customary role. In such a society the questions, What shall I do? How shall I live? cannot arise. It is as I become conscious through my relationships with other people of my status as a person, apart from the roles which I fill, that room is made for these questions. As society becomes more complex, as possibilities of alternative ways of life grow, so choices multiply. But in choosing I cannot discount the criteria of contemporary social practice. Seventeenth- and eighteenth-century writers, like Greek sophists before them, write as if the individual with his psychologically determined passions approaches social life with ends and aims already given; for Hegel this is a profound illusion. What passions and what ends the individual has and can have are a matter of the kind of social structure in which the individual finds himself. Desires are elicited and specified by the objects presented to them; the objects of desire, and especially of desires to live in one way rather than another, cannot be the same in all societies. But it is not necessarily the case that the desires elicited by a particular form of social life will find satisfaction within that form. The working out of the ends of contemporary practice may, in fact, destroy the very form of life which brought the desire for those ends into being. The reflective criticism of both ends and means may have unintended consequences.

In the light of these considerations Hegel pictures developed society in terms of a succession of forms of life, each of which, by a natural transition, is transformed into its successor. In the *Phenomenology* there is no suggestion—there is, indeed, a denial—that actual historical periods must rigorously follow out this pattern. Rather, the suggestion is that insofar as they do follow out this pattern, their history exhibits the logic of these Hegelian transitions. There are two particular sequences which any interpretation of Hegel must take seriously. The first of these is not specifically concerned with morality, but it is concerned with the nature of the framework within which moral questions arise. It is also an excellent introduction to Hegel's own fundamental attitudes.

When the self-consciousness of individuals realizes itself in social roles, a central part is played by the relationship of Master and Serf. In this relationship the Master at the outset envisages himself alone as a fully self-conscious person; his Serf he seeks to reduce to the level of a thing, a mere instrument. But as the relationship develops the Master, too, is deformed, and more radically than the Serf is. For the relationship is defined in terms of their relationship to material things. These provide work for the Serf, but merely transient enjoyments for the Master. The Serf is indeed deformed, for his aims are so limited by the aims and the commands of the Master, that he can do little more than assert himself in the barest possible way; but the Master, insofar as he sees himself as Master, cannot find in the Serf any response through which in turn he could find himself as a fully developed person. He has cut himself off from the kind of relationship in which self-consciousness grows through being an object of regard by others, through finding itself "mirrored" in others. Whereas the Serf can see in the Master something at least that he wants to become. But for both it is true that growth in self-consciousness is fatally limited by the Master–Serf relationship.

Hegel then looks at three false solutions to the problem posed by that relationship. And in doing this he is thinking back to imperial Rome and to the attitudes engendered in a society actually dominated by the Master–Serf theme, not only in the institution of slavery itself, but in the relation of Caesar to his subjects and in the whole ranking of superiors and inferiors. The first false solution is stoicism: the acceptance of necessity, the identification of oneself with the universal reason of the cosmos, whatever one's rank or relationship. Emperor and slave equally envisage themselves as citizens of the world. But this is to mask their real relationship, rather than to transform it. This is to try to think away the reality of serfdom by invoking the idea of freedom. So equally with skepticism, a frame of mind which casts doubt on all received beliefs and distinctions enforced by those who are Masters, but which has to exist in an individual who continues to live in that same world of received beliefs and distinctions. So the skeptic always has two attitudes of mind, one reserved for his academic reflections, in which he defies the ruling ideology, one for his daily commerce with social reality, in which he conforms to it. The dilemma of being unable to extract oneself from a social world which deforms at one and the same time both one's relations with others and one's own personality is finally given social expression in the form of life which Hegel calls that of the Unhappy Consciousness.

This is the epoch of Catholic Christianity. In it, the essential distress of the deformed, because unfree, character of human life and the consciousness of the possibility, indeed the necessity, of overcoming this, are represented in the form of the contrast between the fallen world of humanity and the perfection of the divine. The ideal is seen as something transcendent, existing outside and apart from human life. In the doctrine of the atonement the reconciliation of man as he is, with the ideal is portrayed in symbolic form. But those who remain within the symbolism and take it for a reality are thereby denied the reality which is symbolized. The crusaders try to find the ideal in militant action; instead of the ideal they find—a grave. The monastic orders try to find the ideal in asceticism; in so doing, they become prey to that very preoccupation with the flesh, with finitude, which they sought to escape. The way out is to see that Christianity symbolizes the human condition aptly enough, but that Christianity understood as literal truth is not the cure, but part of the disease. What condition? What cure? What disease?

One might begin from the Master–Serf relation again; but it is important to see that this for Hegel only provides a special case of a more general feature of human life and thought. This feature is what Hegel calls "the negative." This concept can be explained as follows. If we wish to understand any concept or explain any belief, we must first locate it in the system of which it is a part; this system will manifest itself both in a characteristic mode of life and in characteristic forms of theorizing. The relation between the mode of life and the theorizing will not always be the same, but to some degree the theorizing will make articulate the concepts and beliefs implicit in the mode of life. (Hegel here anticipates the later treatment of religion in simpler societies by social anthropologists; and also Weber's treatment of Protestantism and capitalism.) Yet in so doing, the more conscious the agent becomes of the form of life in which he is involved as a whole, as a form of life, the more he will acquire goods which lie outside and beyond that form of life, the achieving of which demand that it be transcended. The form of life now appears as setting limits to the agent, limitations against which he must struggle and which he must overcome. What were horizons become barriers. But in so doing, they play a positive role; they define the obstacles the transcending of which is the contemporary achievement of freedom. For freedom is the core of characteristically human life. Hegel is not here quarreling with Aristotle or with Kant, who see man as essentially rational. What he believes is that human rationality has a history, and that its history is the criticism both in life and in thought of the limitations of each of its own specific historical forms. "The negative," the limiting factors, the role of the horizon and the obstacle, these are what is original in Hegel. So the Hegelian methodological injunction about any epoch is, "Understand its life and thought in terms of its aims and goals, and understand its aims and goals by means of identifying what men saw as the obstacles in their path." You will then have identified their concept of freedom, even if they did not use the word *freedom* in that connection.

By *freedom* Hegel meant neither some property either possessed by (Kant) or available to (the Stoics) all men, no matter what they did, nor some specific state of social life (J. S. Mill). What freedom is in each time and place is defined by the specific limitations of that time and place and by the characteristic goals of that time and place. So it is correct to say in the Hegelian sense that the Levellers, the American colonists, John Brown at Harpers Ferry, and the South African Bantu today are all claiming their freedom, even though what they claim is substantially different in each case. To put it in another way, when we speak of men as being unfree, what we mean is always relative to an implicit normative picture of human life, by means of which we identify what human bondage is. And this is true not only of societies but also of individuals. The Hegelian concept of freedom is equally relevant to the problem of political freedom and to the traditional philosophical free-will problem.

We have already encountered fragments of this problem in Aristotle and the Stoics, in Hobbes and in Kant. For Hobbes and Hume, to be free is to be unconstrained by external factors, by bonds or threats; the actions of both free and unfree are equally susceptible of causal explanation in terms of factors sufficient to produce their actions. So Hobbes and Hume insist that all human actions are determined, but that some are nonetheless free. Doubt about this account springs not so much from any belief that to be free is to be uncaused, as from the fact that in certain cases the discovery of a causal explanation for actions leads us to cease to blame the agent, to treat him as not responsible for his actions. There does, therefore, seem to be some connection between actions being free and their not having certain sorts of cause. What is needed here is an extension of the kind of investigation of words like *voluntary* and *deliberate* which we find in Aristotle to other expressions involved, and to provide this has been part of the original contribution of analytical philosophy in the twentieth century. What Hegel does usefully point out is that the norms of voluntariness are not necessarily the same in all societies; the factors which we can demand of an agent that they should be under his control vary. With individuals this is clear: whether we blame someone for something often depends upon how much he does know of the factors involved and upon how much he could be expected to know. Thus the extension of reason is always an extension of the area in which we can exercise responsibility; and freedom cannot be extended without increasing understanding. It is on these grounds that Hegel links freedom and reason.

It is often difficult in reading Hegel to be sure how far he thinks he is offering us a-priori conceptual truths, how far he is offering us large-scale empirical generalizations, and how far he is pointing out what are characteristics rather than universal connections between concepts. Hegel's dialectical logic is specifically concerned with the last, but the obscurity of his language can leave the reader very unclear on large issues. So Hegel was perhaps trapped by his own obscurity when he increasingly concluded that history is an inevitable progress of freedom to higher and higher forms, the Prussian state and Hegel's own philosophy providing the culmination of this progress. But this later equation has unhappily discredited two key points that Hegel makes about freedom.

The first is that the concept of freedom is such that once it is presented no one can deny its claims. The testimony to this is the way in which conservative theorists insist that they are not enemies of freedom, they merely offer a different understanding of it. Illuminatingly, the differences between conservative and radical theorists usually turn out to be rooted in different and rival claims about the goals and desires of some social group. (This is the source of the conservative myth about agitators, men who pretend to be spokesmen for what would otherwise be, and is in their heart of hearts, a thoroughly contented group.) According to Hegel the reason why no one can deny the claims of freedom is that everyone seeks it for himself, and seeks it for himself as a good—that is, the merits he claims for freedom are such that it must be a good for everyone and not just for himself.

Moreover, the connection between freedom and the other virtues is emphasized by Hegel as by no other author. In the *Philosophy of History* the Master–Serf relationship is exemplified in different types of kingdom, the Oriental, the Greek, and the Roman; and in the account of the struggle between patricians and plebs in ancient Rome we are shown how the virtues of both parties degenerate, so that power and ambition dominate the scene. More generally, Hegel's attitude to the qualities which we take to be virtuous is a much more complex one than that of, say, Aristotle. Hegel shares many of Aristotle's valuations; he allows certain dispositions to be virtues in any society. He is certainly not a complete relativist. But, unlike Aristotle, he is keenly aware that circumstances alter virtues; a precept or a quality which is admirable in

one society may be used to oppress in another. Courage may be transformed into senseless desperation—compare the last stands of the
heroes of the Icelandic sagas, of Gisli the Soursop, for example, with
the last stands of the Hitler Youth in 1945. Generosity may become
weakness. Benevolence can be an instrument of tyranny. To this a number of replies may be made. An Aristotelian may insist that by definition this cannot be so; what is not done in the right time and place, to
or by the right person, cannot be benevolence, or generosity, or
courage. The doctrine of the mean shows it to be so. But this is too easy.
Certainly the critic may use the Aristotelian criteria after the event; but
the agent who is acting with the only criterion he has is exhibiting
courage, or benevolence, as he knows it. Then the reply will be that he
does not know enough. But although this may be so, it would be odd
therefore to say that what young Nazis exhibited was not courage or
loyalty, but a mere counterfeit. The lesson is rather that virtues themselves may for some people in some circumstances be weaknesses and
not strengths. To this a Kantian will reply that we are served by our
motives and intentions. To which the Hegelian answer is that motives
and intentions, too, are transformed in different settings. Even the
Kantian "good will" may be corrupted. Again the Kantian may seek a
definitional defense. If corrupt, not the good will. But once again this
will not do. For by all the criteria available to the agent his motives may
exemplify the good will, and yet be instruments of corruption.

How this is so comes out very clearly in Hegel's sketches of various
moral forms of "false consciousness." By a false consciousness Hegel
means a conceptual scheme which both illuminates and misrepresents;
so the conceptual schemes of individualist society are genuinely
illuminating in that they bring out authentic features of that society
and of its characteristic modes of theorizing, but misrepresent in that
they conceal the limitations of individualism, partly by representing as
universal and necessary features of the moral life what are only features
of individualism.

The first of these individualist doctrines is the kind of hedonism in
which the dominant principle is the pursuit of one's own happiness.
The trouble with this is that, as each person pursues his own satisfaction, he finds himself assessed by others in terms of his role in their
pursuit of their happiness. He assists in creating a general situation in

which the intersection of the various pursuits of private ends produces a series of dramatic crises; each person becomes "the fate" of another. Impersonal forces of disharmony seem to rule. This leads to disillusionment, to the acceptance of the fact that life is ruled by impersonal necessities. This acceptance is then turned into a kind of inner nobility. The individual is one brand of romantic hero. He follows his way through a world he disdains. He is, in fact, a kind of high-minded hedonist whose doctrine equally with its predecessor leads to anarchic clashes. He does not seek pleasure now, but to follow the dictates of a noble heart. But in so doing, he finds others impersonal and heartless. In the next stage of individualism's self-development the individual opposes himself to the external social reality which has proved his enemy. In the name of Virtue he takes up arms against the World. The World must be defeated by Virtue so thoroughly that it scarcely exists as an adversary. And once the World is no longer the enemy, Virtue becomes Virtue in the world, Virtue that does the worldly duty which lies to hand. This is the phase of the individualist dialectic which Hegel calls "the spiritual zoo and humbug, or the affair-on-hand itself."

In this phase the agent does his duty in his immediate sphere without asking about the context within which he acts or the wider effects of his actions. He accepts deliberately a limited vision both of his actions and of his responsibilities. His is not to reason why. (He lives in a spiritual zoo; the animals are all in separate cages.) He boasts of minding his own business. He is the outcome of all good bureaucrats, of those technical specialists such as Eichmann who boasted that they merely discharged their function in arranging for so much transport to be provided between point X and point Y. Whether the cargo was sheep or Jews, whether points X and Y were farm and butcher's slaughterhouse or ghetto and gas chamber, was no concern of theirs. But, of course, Hegel's characterization applies also in every other sphere where the matter-in-hand is absolutized. Professor J. N. Findlay[53] has pointed out how it illuminates the cult of "pure" scholarship, where a care for the truth alone is used to diguise the kind of self-seeking and competitive rivalry which pervade academic life.

The worst of it is that in its devotion to the affair-on-hand the individual reason now presents itself as a moral legislator: the task before you is your duty. First uttering imperatives to us and then offering us a test of self-consistent universalizibility, as we have already noticed in discussing Kant, lets in almost any action. It is not irrelevant to note here that the moral basis on which Eichmann himself claimed to have been educated was that of the categorical imperative.

What is common to all these doctrines is that they are attempts by the individual to supply his own morality, and at one and the same time, to claim for it a genuine universality. As such they are all self-defeating. For what gives a sanction to our moral choices is in part the fact that the criteria which govern our choices are not chosen. Therefore, if I make up my mind for myself, if I set myself my goals, I can at best provide a countefeit of morality. Where, then, do I find criteria? In the established social practice of a well-ordered community. Here I find criteria proposed to me which I can make my own in the sense that I can frame my choices and my actions in accordance with them, but their authority is derived not from my choice but from the way in which in such a community they cannot fail to be regarded as normative. Thus Hegel's final standpoint is that the moral life can only be led within a certain type of community, and that in such a community certain values will prove indispensable. He thus adopts a position different from both the subjectiveness and the objectiveness of the eighteenth century—and of their later heirs. From the standpoint of the isolated individual, choice between values is open; but for the individual integrated into his society it is not. Seen from within such a society certain values impose themselves as authoritative upon the individual; seen from without, they appear a matter of arbitrary choice. Plato and Aristotle saw the good as objective and authoritative because they wrote from within the society of the πόλις. The eighteenth-century individualist sees the good as the expression of his feelings or the mandate of his individual reason because he writes as it were from outside the social framework. Society appears to him an aggregate of individuals. But what for modern man can take the place of the πόλις? It is in his answer to this question that Hegel is at his least convincing.

The Hegelian notions of reason and freedom are essentially critical; their use is to point to the inadequacy of any given social and conceptual order. But Hegel in the culmination of his systems speaks as if they represent ideals that can in fact be achieved, as if they are specifications of an ideal, and finally true and rational, philosophy and of an ideal, and finally satisfactory, social order. With them the Absolute will have come upon the scene. The final reconciliation of God and man symbolized in the Christian doctrine of the Last Things will have been achieved. And this Hegel after the *Phenomenology* seems to believe. In the *Logic* he can write that the thoughts he is uttering are the thoughts of God. Indeed, his mature philosophy entails that he and King Frederick William are parts of the contemporary incarnation of the Absolute.

The arguments by which Hegel reaches his conclusion are exceptionally bad ones. But his conclusion is not quite so entirely absurd and despicable as it is sometimes represented to be. Those to whom it is said that Hegel exalted the state—and the Prussian state at that—often conclude that Hegel was therefore an early totalitarian. In fact the form of state which Hegel exalts is a moderate constitutional monarchy, and his praise of the Prussian state is based on his (not entirely correct) belief that the Prussian state of his own day was such a monarchy. Hegel can rightly be called a conservative; but insofar as he praises the state, it is because the state incarnates in fact—so he believes—certain social and moral values.

Suppose, however, that one dispensed with the Hegelian Absolute but otherwise remained a Hegelian. What conclusion would one reach about morals then? In the first instance, perhaps the conclusion of the Young or Left Hegelians that the free and rational community which will be the modern version of the $\pi\delta\lambda\iota\varsigma$ is not yet; that it has to be brought into existence. But how? Hegel's own mature belief was that the whole of human history exemplified the self-development of the Absolute Idea in its progress through self-estrangement to a final reconciliation with itself. This cosmic pageant is a drama which gives meaning to each separate historical episode. The Absolute, not to be identified with any finite part of the historical process, achieves its own realization in the development of the whole. The older Hegel treats the Absolute and its progress in history more and more as Christians have treated notions of God and his providence; less and less does he note his own earlier warnings against the danger of construing Christianity literally, of confusing symbol and concept. He thus treats the whole of history as exemplifying some kind of logical necessity, as exhibiting a development in which one stage cannot but give way to its successor. And, as the connections between stages are logical, as they are exemplifications of the movement of the Idea, it is natural to construe Hegel as believing that the rational progress of man in history is essentially a progress in thought. One epoch replaces another by thinking more thoroughly and more rationally. It follows that historical progress depends on progress in thinking. This conclusion was retained by the Young Hegelians long after they had abandoned belief in the Absolute. They took it in fact that their task was to cleanse Hegelianism of its religious and metaphysical elements, and to do this by philosophizing better than Hegel himself; so also in the political sphere what counted was the success of their theorizing. They therefore embarked upon the criticism of religion and of political institutions. Of their works, D. F. Strauss's rationalistic *Life of Jesus* achieved lasting note in the history of New Testament criticism. But their most lasting memorial was the recruitment of the young Karl Marx.

Marx's starting point is that of the earlier Hegel. His own wish to criticize Hegel's heirs, whether Left or Right, led him later on to emphasize the contrasts between himself and Hegel, and subsequent Marxists have had other reasons for suppressing the Hegelian aspects of Marx. But this has led to a falsification of Marx, whose central concept is that of freedom, and of freedom in the Hegelian sense. Hegel had written of the idea of freedom that "this very idea itself is the actuality of men—not something which they have, as men, but which they are." Marx wrote that "Freedom is so much the essence of man that even its opponents realize it . . . No man fights freedom; he fights at most the freedom of others."[54]

Like Hegel, Marx envisages freedom in terms of the overcoming of the limitations and constraints of one social order by bringing another, less limited social order into being. Unlike Hegel, he does not see those limitations and constraints as primarily the limitations and constraints of a given conceptual scheme. What constitutes a social order, what constitutes both its possibilities and its limitations, is the dominant form of work by which its material sustenance is produced. The forms of work vary with the forms of technology; and both the division of labor and the consequent division of masters and laborers are divisive of human society, producing classes and conflicts between them. The conceptual schemes through which men grasp their own society have a dual role; they both partly reveal the nature of that activity and partly conceal its true character. So the critique of concepts and the struggle to transform society necessarily go hand in hand, although in different periods the relation between these two tasks will be different.

This replacement of the Hegelian self-development of the Absolute Idea by the economic and social history of classes leads to a transformation of the Hegelian view of individualism. For Hegel the various individualist conceptual schemes were both an achievement and a barrier to further achievement, stages in the development of human consciousness about morality which in turn reveal their particular limitations. So, too, they are for Marx. But they can only be understood by being interpreted in the context of bourgeois society.

The essence of bourgeois society is technical innovation in the interests of capital accumulation. The bonds of feudal society are destroyed, a spirit of enterprise is unleashed, and the power of man over nature is indefinitely extended. Hence in bourgeois social life the concept of the freedom of the individual, liberated into a free-market economy, is central. But the freedoms which the individual enjoys in what Hegel called civil, Marx bourgeois, society are partly illusory; for the social and economic forms of that same society imprison the free individual in a set of relationships which nullify his civil and legal freedom and stunt his growth. In all societies the nature of human labor and of social organization has resulted in an inability of man to understand himself and his possibilities except in distorted forms. Men see themselves in the grip of impersonal powers and forces, which are in fact their own forms of social life, the fruits of their own actions falsely objectified and endowed with independent existence. Equally, they see themselves as free agents in areas of their life where the economic and social forms are in fact dictating the roles they live out. These twin and inescapable illusions constitute the alienation of man; his loss of the grasp of his own nature. In bourgeois society alienation exemplifies itself in the institutions of private property, which in turn exacerbate alienations. Individualist moral philosophers share in both the liberating and the constricting characteristics of bourgeois society. They represent both the genuine advance in human liberation which it represents and its specific form of human alienation.

For Marx in his early systematic writings the key contrast in bourgeois society is between what bourgeois philosophy and political economy reveal about human possibility and what the empirical study of bourgeois society reveals about the contemporary human activity. The freedom destroyed by bourgeois economy and the human needs which bourgeois industry fails to meet stand in judgment on that economy and industry; but this is not merely an appeal to the ideal against the real. For the goals of freedom and of human need are the goals implicit in the struggle of the working class in bourgeois society. But the goals have to be specified in terms of the achievement of a new form of society in which class division—and with it, bourgeois society—would be abolished. That is, within bourgeois society there are two social groups and at least, constituted by the dominant and the dominated class. Each of these has its own fundamental goals and form of life. It follows that moral precepts may find a role within the social life of each class. But there are no independent, transcendent norms which are above those issues which divide the classes. Certainly, many of the same precepts will occur in the moralities of each class, simply in virtue of each class being a human group. But these will not serve to determine the relations between classes.

When this background has been filled in, one can, I think, understand Marx's attitudes on various occasions to the passing of moral judgments as entirely self-consistent. Marx on the one hand believed that in matters of conflict between social classes the appeal to moral judgments was not only pointless but positively misleading. So he tried to excise from documents of the First International appeals for justice for the working class. For to whom are these appeals being made? Presumably to those responsible for exploitation; but they are acting in accordance with the norms of their class, and although individual philanthropic moralists may be found among the bourgeoisie, philanthropy cannot alter class structure. But one may nonetheless use morally evaluative language in at least two ways. One may use it simply in the course of describing actions and institutions; no language adequately descriptive of slavery could fail to be condemnatory to anyone with certain attitudes and aims. Or one may use it explicitly to condemn, appealing not to some independent classless tribunal, but to the terms in which one's opponents have themselves chosen to be judged. So in the *Manifesto* Marx throws back the charges leveled against communism by bourgeois critics, arguing that they stand condemned not on his premises but on their own.

We can express Marx's attitude to morality in another way. The use of moral vocabulary always presupposes a shared form of social order. Appeal to moral principles against some existing state of affairs is always an appeal within the limits of that form of society; to appeal against that form of society we must find a vocabulary which does not presuppose its existence. Such a vocabulary one finds in the form of expression of wants and needs which are unsatisfiable within the existing society, wants and needs which demand a new social order.

So Marx appeals to the wants and needs of the working class against the social order of bourgeois society. But he never raises two questions which are crucial for his own doctrine. The first concerns the role of morality within the working-class movement. Because he sees the creation of the working class as economically determined by the development of capitalism, and because he believes that the necessities of capitalism will force the working class into self-conscious antagonism to capitalism, he never discusses the question of what principles of action are to inform the working-class movement. This omission is part of a more general lacuna in his argument. About the nature of the decline of capitalist economy Marx is sufficiently specific; about the details of a socialist economy, although what he says is sparse, we may take him to be adequate from his own point of view. But about the nature of the transition from capitalism to socialism he is unclear. Hence we remain uncertain as to how Marx conceives it possible that a society prey to the errors of moral individualism may come to recognize and transcend them.

Marx's second great omission concerns the morality of socialist and communist society. He does indeed speak in at least one passage as though communism will be an embodiment of the Kantian kingdom of ends. But he is at best allusive on this topic. The consequence of these two related omissions is that Marx left later Marxists room for interpolation at this point. What he could not have foreseen is what would be interpolated. Bernstein, the revisionist Marxist, who did not believe that socialism would arrive in the predictable future, tried to find a Kantian basis for the labor movement's activities; Kautsky saw that in Bernstein's hands the appeal to the categorical imperative became exactly the kind of appeal to a morality above class and above society which Marx condemned. What he offered in its place, however, was simply a crude utilitarianism. The weakness to which this exposed latter-day Marxism can only be made clear when we have examined utilitarianism itself.

# 16

## KIERKEGAARD TO NIETZSCHE

The Kantian individual finds the test for his maxims in the objective test of the categorical imperative; the Hegelian individual finds his criteria in the norms of the free and rational society. The fundamental doctrine of Søren Kierkegaard is that not only are there no genuine objective tests in morality; but that doctrines which assert that there are function as devices to disguise the fact that our moral standards are, and can only be, chosen. The individual utters his moral precepts to himself in a far stronger sense than the Kantian individual did; for their only sanction and authority is that he has chosen to utter them.

Kierkegaard was born in Copenhagen in 1813. The radical form of Protestant Christianity which he embraced and his rejection of Hegel's doctrines both spring from the same source; the fundamental role which he allots to the act of choice. It is not just in morals, but in every sphere which touches on human existence that the relevant criteria lack objective justification. Such justification may be in place in mathematics and in the natural sciences; but elsewhere rational argument can do no more than to present us with alternatives between which we must make our own choices. Some of Kierkegaard's own writings take the form of such a presentation, various literary devices such as the use of pseudonyms being employed to conceal the fact that it is one and the same man who is advancing the rival claims of contrasting and conflicting positions. But this is not mere irrationalism, an arbitrary exaltation of arbitrary choice. For Kierkegaard believes that rational argument itself shows us that in the end the choice of the individual must be sovereign.

Suppose that one believes that one's moral position can be rationally justified, that it is a conclusion which can be validly derived from certain premises. Then these premises in turn must be vindicated, and if their vindication consists in deriving them from conclusions based on more fundamental premises, the same problem will arise. But the chain of reasons must have an ending, and we must reach a point where we simply choose to stand by certain premises. At this point decision has replaced argument; and in all arguments on human existence there will be some such point. This argument is applied to moral questions in Kierkegaard's early work Either/Or.

Here Kierkegaard contrasts two ways of life which he calls "the ethical" and "the aesthetic." The aesthetic life is that of the man whose only goal is his own satisfaction. What he must avoid are pain and boredom. Romantic love, which exists only to satisfy the passion of the moment and is ever flying to new satisfactions, is his characteristic sexual relationship. Marriage, with its lifelong and inescapable duties, is characteristic of the ethical, which is the sphere of obligations, of rules which admit of no exception. The arguments in favor of the ethical mode of life are put into the mouth of Judge Wilhelm; those in favor of the aesthetic are taken ostensibly from the papers of a younger, anonymous figure, "A." The two arguments cannot meet, for Judge Wilhelm uses ethical criteria to judge between the ethical and the aesthetic, while "A" uses aesthetic criteria. The argument of each depends upon a prior choice, and the prior choice settles what the conclusion of each's argument will be. And the reader, too, must choose. But the careful reader may well begin to have doubts here of at least two kinds.

The first is drawn from the nature of Kierkegaard's own presentation. For while Kierkegaard claims to be neutral between the two positions, one can have no doubt which he favors. He describes the aesthetic state of mind as one of permanent and ever renewed dissatisfaction, of traveling hopefully so as not to arrive. The ethical by contrast appears as a realm of quiet satisfaction in the obligation fulfilled, the limited task well done. The very disclaimer of partisanship by Kierkegaard itself has a partisan effect—in favor of the ethical. But is this just perhaps a flaw in the literary achievement? Could not Kierkegaard have presented a genuinely neutral account of the two standpoints?

Only if we suppose it possible to address an individual who is devoid of desires, goals, and needs prior to the presentation of the two cases. As such, the individual would be almost a man without characteristics. He acquires them only through his choices. But who is this "I" who chooses? And for such a being what can hang in any case upon choosing in one way rather than in another? These questions never receive an answer in Kierkegaard, partly because he treats "the individual" as an ultimate category and partly because he understands the real existence of the individual as being what the individual is "before God." For Kierkegaard the ethical is only a prologue to the religious, and the religious is necessarily offensive to human reason. One of Hegel's key faults in Kierkegaard's eyes was that he tried to present religion in rational terms. But from an authentically Christian point of view Christianity must be seen as bringing the truth to a human reason which does not possess it, which prior to the Christian revelation is alien to the truth. So it is that from the standpoint of a self-sufficient human reason, Christianity necessarily appears as paradoxical and irrational. Christian faith depends not on argument, but on choice, both for the more general reasons cited by Kierkegaard, which I have already mentioned, and for these special reasons. Skeptical objections to Christianity are not in reality grounded on intellectual doubt; they arise from "insubordination, unwillingness to obey, rebellion against all authority." Hence the important decision is either to do or not to do what God commands in his self-revelation.

The example Kierkegaard invokes is that of Abraham and Isaac. Abraham is commanded by God to sacrifice his son. This command is contrary, not merely to inclination but also to duty. What God commands is, from the standpoint of the ethical, simple murder. There is thus a break between the highest merely human consciousness and the divine intrusion of the apparently scandalous and absurd. It is important to note that there is not a hint in Kierkegaard of the view taken by some Old Testament critics that the function of this story was to preach the abolition of human sacrifice and to educate the Hebrews into a belief that such a killing was in fact, not what God willed, but murder. The notion of revelation as progressive, as always suited to—but always slightly above the moral level of—those to whom it is addressed, is alien to Kierkegaard.

Kierkegaard, then, stands at an extreme point, both in the development of Christianity and in the development of individualism. So far as Christianity is concerned, he poses one horn of a dilemma which had been arising for Christianity ever since the revival of Aristotle in the Middle Ages. Either Christianity accepts the terms of secular reason and argues on these, or it insists on being judged by no criteria but its own. The first alternative leads, as Kierkegaard saw it lead in Hegel's writings, to the reduction of Christianity to something other than itself; the second leads to Christianity becoming self-enclosed and unintelligible. Theologians who recognize this have sometimes been dismayed by Kierkegaard's candor. But Kierkegaard's type of Christianity is in some ways a natural counterpart to his individualism. For it is only when writing from within a Christian position that Kierkegaard can find any reasons for answering the question, How shall I live? in one way rather than another. One may suspect that the need to be able to answer this question is one of the unavowed sources of his Christianity. The choices made by the individual confronting the alternatives of the ethical and the aesthetic, or the ethical and the religious, are according to Kierkegaard criterionless. But if this were genuinely so, how could it be right to choose one rather than the other? Yet the whole point of such choices, and of the pain that the making of them involves, is that one may choose wrongly. Kierkegaard's conceptual framework makes it impossible to say this, although sometimes Kierkegaard himself is inconsistent enough to use this kind of language. He moves uneasily between speaking from within an order in which God's will provides criteria for action and speaking as the lonely individual outside all criteria.

Of Kierkegaard's themes, at least one, that of the irrationality of Christianity, reappears in the strange, ironical pages of Heinrich Heine's *History of Philosophy and Religion in Germany*. But here the unintelligibility and unacceptability of Christianity are taken seriously: "Can you hear the ringing of the bell? Kneel down—they are bringing the sacraments to a dying God." Writing in 1832, Heine connects the intellectual past of Germany with prophecies of a coming catastrophe. The argument is two-sided. On the one hand, there has been a continuous secularization of German life. Catholicism overcomes Nordic heathenism, but at the cost of taking a good deal of it into herself; Luther creates a new German consciousness, partly through the German Bible, but leaves Germany a prey to Protestant spirituality; Spinoza, Wolff, Kant, and Hegel secularize religion finally and replace the supernatural by the natural. But all this took place only in the realm of ideas. Heine says sardonically, "It seems to me that a methodical people, such as we are, must begin with the reformation, must then occupy itself with systems of philosophy, and that only after their completion could it pass to the political revolution. I find this sequence quite rational. The heads that have first served for the speculations of philosophy can afterwards be struck off by the revolution for whatever object it pleases; but philosophy would not have been able to utilize the heads struck off by the revolution that preceded it."[55] But what in fact has happened is that only the surface of life has been touched by these intellectual changes. Christianity is the only bar to the old paganism of the Germans; and critical philosophy, especially Kantian philosophy, has destroyed it. "Christianity—and this is its fairest merit—subdued to a certain extent the brutal warrior ardor of the Germans, but it could not entirely quench it; and when the cross, that remaining talisman, falls to pieces, then will break forth again the ferocity of the old combatants. . . . There will be played in Germany a drama compared to which the French Revolution will seem but an innocent idyll."[56]

The prophecy came true one hundred years later. What is its relevance to the history of philosophy? British moral philosophers of the nineteenth century, as we shall see in the next chapter, essentially found themselves at home in their society. This is not to say that they were passive conformists. Both utilitarians and idealists found themselves among at least the moderate reformers. But the criteria for reform which they proposed were such as they could expect to find echoed by their fellow countrymen. Not so with German philosophers. As with Hegel in his old age, or with his right-wing followers, the German philosophers provided a justification of the *status quo*—or else they found themselves outside the academic establishment, shunned as critics. Thus German nineteenth-century moral philosophers cannot hope to represent themselves as merely analyzing what is already present in ordering moral consciousness; they see the moral as something they are bound to condemn. Equally, from the other side, ordinary morality finds its sources in romantic rationalism or in the ideals of the Prussian bureaucracy and requires a hostility to the purely critical intellect. Hence the great moral philosophers of the nineteenth century are all anti-German Germans, constructing systems against the moral *status quo*. Heine is their forerunner, but the great names among them are Schopenhauer and Nietzsche.

Schopenhauer stands in sharp contrast to both Hegel and Kierkegaard. Against Hegel's view of every part of the universe having meaning insofar as it stands in relation to a systematic rational whole, and Kierkegaard's stress on the value of the individual, Schopenhauer sees the universe as meaningless and the individual as having no value. He admired Plato and Kant because they did not attempt to find a rational order in the merely phenomenal; he hated and despised Hegel, whom he thought of as a timeserver. And professional academic philosophers in general he thought committed to supplying metaphysical consolation in return for payment. "By the Greeks they were called sophists, by the moderns they are called professors of philosophy." But his dislike of Hegel has to be set beside the fact that he attempted to rival Hegel as a lecturer in Berlin by putting on his lectures at the same hour as Hegel's; Hegel's lectures remained crowded, Schopenhauer's were empty.

What is Schopenhauer's message? The world is the expression of blind striving or Will. We know our own inner nature as Will in direct experience; thought is but one of the outward forms or disguises taken by Will. Life is blind, cruel, meaningless; but we disguise this fact in our theorizing, and in our actions we cling to life through extremes of pain and suffering. The natural world bears witness to the continuous reproduction of the species, and the continuous destruction of the individual. The forms remain the same; the individuals who exemplify them continually perish. (In this we get a hint of Schopenhauer's relation to Plato and Kant.) Thus experience testifies to the way in which the world is pervaded by pain and destruction, while religion and philosophy try to construct justifications for the universe which will show that pain and destruction have not the last word, and in so doing, they themselves testify to the force of Cosmic Will, which has as its aim the continuing of existence on any terms. Schopenhauer explains religion as the human expression of this desire for continued existence. Were we totally certain of our survival after death, or of our extinction at death, religion would be functionless. Moreover, it is not only in our anxiety to continue existing that we exhibit ourselves as manifestations of Will. We also do so in the way that we devote ourselves to continuing the species; sexual passion overrides all our impulses to avoid suffering and responsibility. Yet the pleasures of passionate love are momentary and vanishing compared with the troubles it brings upon us. We may rationalize our pursuit of various ends and claim to find good in achieving them; the truth is, we are what we are constituted by the blind strivings of Will, and our thinking cannot alter anything about us.

So seriously does Schopenhauer take this that he treats our entire personality as given from the outset. What we are essentially is Will, and unalterable Will. No experience, no reflection, no learning, can alter what we are. Our character is fixed, our motives are determined. It follows that traditional morality and traditional moral philosophy are founded on a mistake, the mistake of supposing that moral precepts can alter conduct, whether our own or that of others. What, then, can moral philosophy do? It can explain the moral valuations which we do in fact make by an analysis of human nature.

If we carry through such an analysis, we discover three basic motives in human nature. The first is our old friend self-interest. On this Schopenhauer has little original to say. The second, however, is the fruit of acute observation. It is malice. Schopenhauer observed, as perhaps no previous philosopher or psychologist had done, the gratuitous character of malice. We do not harm others only when and in order that we may benefit ourselves. And when others undergo misfortunes our pleasure in their misfortunes is unconnected with any thought of our own self-interest. It is pure pleasure: "For man is the only animal which causes pain to others without any further purpose than just to cause it. Other animals never do it except to satisfy their hunger, or in the rage of combat." The appalling record of human life, of the suffering and infliction of pain, is relieved only when the third motive, sympathy or compassion, appears. To feel compassion is to put oneself imaginatively in the place of the sufferer and to alter one's actions appropriately either by desisting from what would have caused pain or by devoting oneself to its relief. But the exhibiting of compassion has yet a further significance.

In a moment of compassion we extinguish self-will. We cease to strive for our own existence; we are relieved from the burden of individuality and we cease to be the plaything of Will. The same relief is granted to us in the contemplation of works of art. And in the life of a Christ or of a Buddha we find a systematic disciplining of self and exercising of compassion in which selfhood and striving approach the goal of final extinction. Thus Schopenhauer's message is in the end an injunction to return to the sources of Buddhist teaching.

A first reaction to Schopenhauer must always be perhaps to note the contrast between the brilliance of his observations of human nature (which go far beyond anything I have suggested) and the arbitrary system-building in which those observations are embedded. He stands out among philosophers by his insistence upon the all-pervasive character of pain and suffering in human life to date. But his general pessimism is as unilluminating as it is striking. Because for him these evils arise from existence as such, he is unable to give any accurate account of them in their historical context; all epochs and states of affairs, all societies, and all projects are equally infected by evil. But he provides an important corrective to the easy liberal optimism of so much of nineteenth-century life; and those who reacted against that optimism find Schopenhauer a seminal influence. Certainly he was this upon Nietzsche.

Nietzsche in fact stands at the point at which all the contradictory influences of the nineteenth century are brought to bear. He was himself only too conscious of this and sought isolation; part of what he admired in Schopenhauer was his ability to cast off academic and conformist ambitions. His loneliness as a character is matched by his resistance to the spirit of the age. He intensely disliked the crude imperialist politics of the German Empire of 1871. He hated Pan-Germanism in all forms and especially in its racialist, anti-Semitic ones. But he equally disliked modern socialism, which he saw as a new incarnation of the Christian values he most despised. Christianity is for Nietzsche at the core of the modern sickness. Why? Because

Christianity has led to a systematic devaluation of this world in favor of the next, and thus to a false spirituality. Above all, because Christianity has embodied values that were destructive of all moral values, including its own. Nietzsche sees himself as writing in an age of moral vacuum. He has three tasks: to exhibit the historical and psychological causes of the vacuum; to unmask false candidates for the role of the new morality; and finally, to transcend the limitations of all hitherto existing systems of morality, and by a "transvaluation of values," to prophetically introduce a new way of life.

The historical background to the present malaise is rooted in Christianity's victory over the Greeks. Nietzsche in the *Genealogy of Morals* begins by attacking "English psychologists" who have argued that the word *good* was first applied to altruistic actions because these were socially useful. (Nietzsche seems to be referring to the whole utilitarian tradition and to Herbert Spencer: "People tell me," he writes "that those men are simply dull old frogs.") In fact, he replies, the egoistic-altruistic contrast is not primitive; for in the earliest uses of *good* it does not arise. *Good* was the word used by "the noble, mighty, highly-placed and high-minded;" its earliest uses were "in contradistinction to all that was base, low-minded and plebeian." As we saw in discussing the history of ‘$\dot{\alpha}\gamma\alpha\theta o\varsigma$’ in Greek, Nietzsche is fundamentally in the right. He is right too when he relates how the word *good* is in due time used in conjunction with altered criteria; but in *place* of the actual complexities of Greek and Hebrew history *he puts* a sharp contrast between the original Greek aristocrat and "the" Jew. The Jew substitutes for the aristocratic morality of self-affirmation the slave morality of envy. The Christian finally exalts the virtues of the weak, the humble, the poor, the oppressed; not in fact because of love of these, but because of a hidden rancor and hate of strength, of pride in life, of self-affirmation. About Jesus, Nietzsche seems to have been ambivalent; on Paul or Luther he feels free to unleash his rage. "Faith was at all times, for example in Luther, only a cloak, a pretext, a *screen* behind which the instincts played their game—a shrewed *blindness* about the dominance of certain instincts."[57]

Yet now God is dead. The sanction of traditional slave morality has gone. And all the contemporary attempts to replace Christianity are forms of self-deception in one way or another. Kantian ethics pretends to give the endorsement of universal law to the individualist's moral attitudes. "Kant wanted to prove in a way that would dumbfound the 'common man' that the 'common man' was right." But Nietzsche's accusation is that in fact Kant assumes what he sets out to prove. He takes it for granted that we are entitled to make moral judgments and inquires what must be the case if that is so; he never asks, as Nietzsche does, whether we are so entitled. Nietzsche's reply is that we, in trying to bind others by universal moral judgments, pretend to be speaking in the name of pure practical reason, but are in fact using these judgments as a weapon against those of whom we are jealous. The utilitarians are also attacked on grounds drawn from psychology. "Man does not seek happiness; only the Englishman does that."[58] Not happiness but power is the fundamental human goal. Sympathetic interpreters of the Nietzschean "will to power" have insisted that by power Nietzsche does not mean power over others; he saw the ideal expression of power in the type of personality in which the limitations of self-love have been overcome, but which nonetheless affirms itself. It is when the will to power is not allowed expression, but is hidden and repressed, that it turns into a drive against others, summoning up ideals in the name of which such oppression can be carried out. But Nietzsche's examples of the type of personality of which he thought well are highly dubious; in what he is condemning he is far more clearly justified. The emasculated asceticism of Wagner's romantic-Christian Parsifal he abhors; even Cesare Borgia is far healthier than that. (*Health* and *sickness* are key words in Nietzsche.) Napoleon is a synthesis of the human and the brutish. Julius Caesar and Spinoza are greatly admired. And in a most vivid and telling phrase Nietzsche speaks of his ideal as "the Roman Caesar with Christ's soul." Yet, from all this, does one get a clear picture of the Superman (a bad, but by now unavoidable, translation of *Ubermensch*—"the man who transcends")?

The conventional charge against Nietzsche has been that he was the forerunner of Nazism, the prophet of "the blond beast" of later anti-Semitic glorification. The conventional answer has fallen into two parts. The first, which is unassailable, is that while he was the critic of Judaism as religion and as morality, he was equally the critic of Christianity; and that racialism, most of all German racialism (he thought Slavs on the whole superior to Germans, and preferred Poles most of all), was condemned by him in the frankest terms. The second is that the Superman is a morally unambiguous and praiseworthy character. But the difficulty here is to know just what content the notion of the Superman had for Nietzsche. The multiplication of reservations renders everything more obscure. What worries us in Nietzsche is perhaps like what worries us in Kant.

We have already noticed Hegel's criticism of Kant, that the conscientious moral agent dominated by the form of the categorical imperative is in fact licensed to do anything at all—provided he does it conscientiously. What looked like a restrictive guide to conduct is in fact empty of restriction. So likewise, and more crudely, with the notion of the Superman. In the name of the Will to Power what might one not do? In what does the superiority of the superior type of human being manifest itself in late nineteenth-century terms? Nietzsche was flagrantly misrepresented by his nationalist, anti-Semitic, and finally Nazi sister. But what one must insist upon is that both the violence of Nietzsche's language and the emptiness of the Nietzschean ideal provided an excellent scaffolding for Frau Förster-Nietzsche to build around. There is a deep historical irresponsibility in Nietzsche. The explanation of it is in part that he believed the mass of men to be beyond redemption anyway. "Not to the people let Zarathustra speak. . . . To lure many away from the herd, therefore I came."

We thus end the nineteenth century with the most perceptive of German moralists turning his back upon his own society. It would not be absurd to try to understand this attitude in the light of a society which was about to turn its back upon the whole human tradition of morality. Thomas Mann once spoke of the artist as a seismograph in whose work tremors as yet unobserved are registered. The German philosophers of the nineteenth century signal tremors far beneath the surface of their society; they signal catastrophe to come.

# 17

## REFORMERS, UTILITARIANS, IDEALISTS

A striking feature of moral and political argument in the modern world is the extent to which it is innovators, radicals, and revolutionaries who revive old doctrines, while their conservative and reactionary opponents are the inventors of new ones. So the contract theorists and the believers in natural rights in the seventeenth century were reviving features of medieval doctrines, while the doctrine of the divine right of kings was essentially a sixteenth- and seventeenth-century invention. So also, at the time of the French Revolution, it is Tom Paine who revives Locke, and it is Burke who invents a quite new form of the appeal to tradition. Paine is not a source of philosophical argument in himself; his importance lies in the way in which he, and more especially, his French associates helped to force the moral traditions of the English ruling oligarchy away from the doctrine of natural rights. How did they do this?

The danger of all appeals to general principles on one's own behalf on a particular occasion is that one renders oneself liable to have the same principles invoked against one on some subsequent occasion. Precisely this is what happened to the English ruling class; the principles of 1688 were invoked against them by the Americans in 1776 and by the revolutionaries against their French colleagues in 1789. It was this fact which underpinned Tom Paine's appeal to the rights of man; and it was this fact that Richard Price, whom we have already noticed in his role as a believer in the rational intuition of moral first principles, emphasized in his sermon at the dissenting meetinghouse in Old Jewry in November, 1789. Price emphasized the assertion in 1689 of the right to choose and to dismiss sovereigns, and above all, of the right to frame anew the constitution, and reiterated the correctness of this assertion. In so doing, he played his part in goading both to fury and to reply Edmund Burke. Burke's attitude to the mass of men is well conveyed by his phrase "a swinish multitude;" his attitude to the rights of man is entirely coherent with this. He denies, first as a matter of history, that the Whig Revolution of 1688 did involve the kind of assertion of rights that Price claimed. The displacement of James II was due to a fear lest his critics should weaken the throne and the hereditary principle; hence the preference for the next line in succession, even though it was the German line of Hanover, in order that that principle might not be discredited. But Burke was not merely concerned with history. Not only was 1689 not an appeal to natural rights, there are no such rights. They are metaphysical fictions.

Burke says of the writers of the French Revolution that they are "so taken up with their theories about the rights of man, that they have totally forgotten his nature." By *nature* Burke does not mean a state prior to a social contract, but *society* as it is, and above all, as it has grown to be. Theoretically based plans for the reform of society are violations of a divinely ordained history of social growth, so that Burke can speak of social development as "the known march of the ordinary Providence of God." Established institutions are thus rated as high by Burke as they are low by Rousseau. Both invoke "nature," but while for Rousseau nature is contrasted with society, for Burke nature includes society. Burke however does not view nature simply as all that is; for if nature were all-inclusive, one could not war against it, as revolutionaries do. Nature is in fact equated by Burke with certain established norms and procedures, including the procedure of relying on prevailing habit rather than on argument. "Politics ought to be adjusted, not to human reasonings, but to human nature, of which the reason is but a part, and by no means the greatest part."[59] This is not just a doctrine about politics, but about the moral life in general. Hence Burke's defense of what he calls "prejudice." "Prejudice is of ready application in the emergency; it previously engages the mind in a steady course of wisdom and virtue, and does not leave the man hesitating in the moment of decision, skeptical, puzzled, and unresolved. Prejudice renders a man's virtue his habit, and not a series of unconnected acts."[60]

Burke's positions are of importance, if only because of their subsequent influence. The assessment of them confronts one initial difficulty, namely that if Burke is right, rational argument upon these topics is misplaced. Hence by even venturing to argue with him we appear to presuppose the truth of what we are trying to establish. But this difficulty is not in fact ours, but Burke's. For to deny the possibility of rational argument playing the role of arbiter means that in advancing one's views one cannot be appealing to any criterion by which they may be established. But if this is so, then not only can one not argue in one's own favor, but one has made it difficult to understand what it could mean to call one's views "true" or "false." For the application of these predicates always involves an appeal to some criterion. Suppose, however, that at this point we look to Burke's practice of arguing rather than to his principle of condemning argument. We shall then find in his arguments two mistakes, both diagnosed by William Godwin, the anarchist, in what is in effect a reply to Burke's *Reflections on the Revolution in France, Political Justice*.

First of all, Burke confuses society and the state. He assimilates particular forms of political institution to institutions in general. From premises which assert merely the need for stable and established social arrangements he tries to derive the conclusion that Louis XVI's head should not be cut off. The roots of this confusion are more interesting than the confusion itself. Burke understands that appeal to moral and other norms presupposes an established form of social life. He tries to picture the revolutionary theorist as a man who wishes to destroy the very social life which is necessary to give meaning to the norms in the name of which he intends to carry out his act of destruction. But in so doing, he equates the notion of an established form of social life with the notion of an established set of institutional arrangements. In fact, the institutions of a society may well be at odds with its norms. To maintain these institutions may be fatally destructive. Burke never noticed the fact that revolutions are extremely difficult to make. Theorists become revolutionaries only when their theories are able to articulate a deep dissatisfaction which the theorists did not invent. And at this point it is the refusal to destroy and recreate social institutions which is destructive of social life itself. The true nihilists in history were all kings: Charles I, Louis XVI, and Tsar Nicholas. The revolutionaries in their societies had to save social life from their rulers' destructive maintenance of the existing order.

Secondly, Burke's defense of prejudice and habit against reflective criticism rests on an inadequate analysis of the notion of following a rule. I may in my conduct follow and abide by rules which I have never made explicit; breaches of such rules may shame or shock me without my articulating any formula adequately expressive of the rule. But such unreflective behavior is as much rule governed as is the behaviour of the man who consciously invokes an expressly formulated maxim. And it is clearly the kind of behavior which Burke wants to exalt; we use words like *habit* and *prejudice* to bring out not that such conduct is not governed by rules, but that our attitude to the rules is unreflective. Burke is right to suppose that the moral life would be destroyed by our reflecting upon our rules of conduct prior to each and every action. Action must for the most part rely on our habitual dispositions to do this rather than that. But if for this reason, reflection can only be occasional, the importance of such occasions is heightened, not lessened. Because we are right not to be continually re-scrutinizing our principles, it does not follow that we are wrong ever to scrutinize them. So Godwin speaks rightly of a need to articulate and examine them, "to cast away the coat of prejudice and to leave nothing but the naked reason."

Godwin, who was married to the mother of female emancipation, Mary Wollstonecraft, and who was the father of Shelley's second wife, was the prototype of the innovating moralist in the modern world. The kind of abuse which was later to be hurled at a Bertrand Russell or a Wilhelm Reich was showered on Godwin. De Quincey recalled in his reminiscences that "most people felt of Mr. Godwin with the same alienation and horror as of a ghoul, or a bloodless vampyre, or the monster created by Frankenstein." Godwin in fact was a humane and sensitive man who applied himself to the classical problem of eighteenth-century moral theory. He accepted from Hume the view that we are moved to action by feelings not by reason and from Locke the view that it is reason which discerns moral distinctions. He thus has a more complex position than most eighteenth-century writers. Our feelings move us to action, but they will only move us to right action if we have a clear and rational view of the facts. Such a view includes taking into account the consequences of our actions; it must also include the application to them of principles such as that of impartiality, of not making exceptions to general rules in our own or in anyone else's favor. Godwin's view that there are rational moral principles of an inescapable kind is never developed with sufficient clarity. But he is as much as anyone since Aristotle the father of the notion that at the foundation of morals lies the principle that if morality is to be argued about at all, then the onus of justification lies upon those who propose to treat men differently. The very process of moral argument presupposes the principle that everyone is to be treated the same until reason to the contrary is shown. This principle is formal in the sense that it does not prescribe how in fact anyone is to be treated. But it has important practical consequences. For it forces into the open the justification of treating people differently because of their age, sex, intelligence, or color. Equality in its most minimal form is embodied in a society in which this is the case.

Godwin himself extended the scope of principles of reason far beyond this. He thought that reason showed me that there is more value in the happiness of a number of men than in that of one, and that this is true irrespective of whether that one is myself, my friend or relative, or a total stranger. Hence I ought to prefer the general happiness to my own. To the rejoinder that if I do so, it is only because I am so psychologically constituted that I will feel unhappier if I disregard the general happiness of others than if I disregard my own, Godwin's reply is that the pain which I feel at disregarding the unhappiness of others is felt only because I recognize that I ought to be benevolent. The pain cannot be the reason for my action, for it is only because I have quite a different sort of reason for it that I am liable to feel the characteristic pain. It is only in the light of my rational principles, for example, that my own actions will inspire in me satisfaction or guilt.

If men have within themselves rational principles prescribing the general good, why do men disregard that good? Godwin's answer is that we are corrupted by the social environment, and above all, by the influence of government. For government claims an authority which belongs only to right reason. And right reason is only grasped by individuals, assisted by the rational persuasion of other individuals. The hope for man lies in the perfectability of human nature. Godwin's belief is that the influences of social and governmental forms can be overcome and replaced by a free community of rational beings in which it is the opinions of those who are informed and objective that will carry weight.

Godwin is a figure curiously akin to and curiously at odds with Bentham. Where Godwin is utopian in his political proposals, Bentham is the careful reformer, anxious to escape accusations of utopianism by being prepared to suggest the exact size of the beds to be used in prisons or the precise reforms needed in the laws of evidence. Where Godwin believes human nature to be committed *au fond* to disinterestedness, Bentham believes that private interest always needs to be weighted and guided if it is to serve public interest. Yet Bentham's criterion of the greatest happiness of the greatest number is essentially the same as Godwin's; both were in limited sympathy with the French Revolution; both represent the future rather than the past. It can be put like this: if one takes the stock of characteristically modern liberal clichés and banalities, one is in a world of which both Godwin and Bentham are ancestors. For both, society is nothing but a collection of individuals; for both, the good of individuals is a matter of their happiness; for both, that happiness can be summed and calculated. In Godwin the notions of good and evil still retain some of their traditional force; in Bentham they are to be redefined in terms of pleasure and pain.

Bentham's thesis was not of course that words such as *good* and *right* were or had been used by most people to mean "productive of the greatest happiness of the greatest number" or some equivalent phrase. It is not even the case that Bentham always propounded the same thesis. Sometimes he seems to be concerned not with the meaning of terms in the moral vocabulary, but only with the statement of a moral—and political—criterion. Sometimes he does indeed offer us a definition, but in the form of a proposal rather than of an elucidation. He says in effect that we may define *good* and *right* in terms of the concept of the greatest happiness of the greatest number or we may not; but that unless we do, shall talk nonsense. And sometimes he seems not to distinguish these tasks. Nor for his purposes does he need to distinguish them. For his central proposal amounts to the contention that the only rational and consistent criterion available for the guidance of action is the assessment of the pleasurable and painful consequences of any particular action, and that the meaning of evaluative expressions can only be understood in this context. There is no alternative rational criterion for at least two kinds of reason.

The first is that theories, such as those based on a belief in natural law or natural rights, which suppose that there are rights, duties, and obligations apart from and prior to those embodied in positive law are thought by Bentham to rest on a basis of logical error. For they are, on his view, the product of a belief that words like *duty* and *obligation* are names which have a sense and a reference quite independent of their use in any particular context. Bentham's own logical views on this point are a mixture of truth and error. On the one hand, he grasped correctly that only in the context of a sentence, does a naming, describing, or referring expression have meaning—a point that was to be made a commonplace only by Frege and Wittgenstein. On the other hand, it is in no way clear that adherents of natural-law and natural-rights theories are necessarily committed to the logical error of supposing otherwise. A more serious criticism of such theories is intimately connected with one of Bentham's most important motives in attacking them. Suppose that anyone asserts that men possess natural rights or are bound by natural laws: invite him, then, to make a list of such rights or laws. It is notorious that adherents of such theories offer lists which differ in substance from each other. Is there, then, any criterion for the correct inclusion of an item on such a test? Bentham's conviction that there is not was directed in the first instance at the reactionary sanctification of the legal and penal *status quo* that Blackstone, in his *Commentaries on the Law of England*, accomplished by the use of the theory of natural law. But Bentham was completely impartial in the application of his skeptical doubts, and in spite of his sympathy for the American Revolution and for at least the initial phases of the French Revolution, he is trenchant in his criticism of the revolutionary doctrine of the rights of man, a doctrine which he declares to be nonsense, and in his criticism of the doctrine of imprescriptible natural rights—"nonsense on stilts."

If, then, a first reason for holding that only the principle of utility, the principle of the greatest happiness of the greatest number, furnishes us with a criterion for action is the alleged logical impossibility of any metaphysical theory of morals, a second is the foundation laid for the principle in human psychology. Men are made so that they are placed under the dominion of "two sovereign masters," pain and pleasure. Bentham's psychology, whose source is in Hartley, is mechanical and associationist. We cannot but pursue pleasure and flee pain, and the association of the prospect of either with something else will draw us to or repel us from whatever pleasure or pain is associated with. Bentham takes it for granted that *pleasure* and *pain* are correlative terms, and that both are equally simple and unitary concepts. He gives fifty-eight synonyms for *pleasure*, and his logical sophistication about naming on other occasions does not prevent him from behaving as if *happiness*, *enjoyment*, and *pleasure* all name or characterize the same sensation. Different sources of pleasure can be measured and compared in respect of the intensity and duration of the sensation derived from them, the certainty or otherwise of having the sensation, and the propinquity or remoteness of the pleasure. In choosing between alternatives, quantity of pleasure is the only criterion: "Quantity of pleasure being equal, pushpin is as good as poetry."[61] Moreover, in summing up the pleasures of a number of people everybody is to count for one and nobody as more than one.

If each individual is in fact moved by the prospects of his own pleasure or pain, what becomes of altruism? Bentham's thought is not entirely coherent here: on the one hand, in his political and legislative proposals he recognizes the conflict between public and private interest and the need for molding human nature. His wish to construct a society in which a man's pursuit of his private pleasure and his pursuit of the greatest happiness of the greatest number will coincide clearly rests on the assumption that society is not at present so organized. But elsewhere, and especially in the *Deontology*, Bentham implicitly identifies the greatest happiness of the individual with that to be found in the pursuit of the greatest happiness of the greatest number. The only motive for obeying the rules necessary to social life is the pleasure to be found in obedience or the pain resulting from disobeying them.

There is no problem which Benthamite utilitarianism raises which was not raised within the utilitarian tradition itself, and the burden of these problems fell upon John Stuart Mill. His father, James Mill, was an enthusiastic collaborator of Bentham's, himself a psychologist in the tradition of Hartley, who once wrote that he aspired to make the human mind as plain as the road from St. Paul's to Charing Cross. This spirit of self-confidence was scarcely inherited by his son. In late adolescence, after an education which had laid adult burdens upon him from the earliest possible age, he turned from his absorption in schemes of social reform to inquire whether, if all such projects were to be accomplished, this would render him happy. The sinking heart with which he answered "No" presaged a nervous breakdown from which he was rescued to an important extent by the poetry of Wordsworth and Coleridge. But it was to be significant for more than Mill's personal life that the coincidence between private happiness and that of the greatest number should have failed the utilitarians themselves so early. Mill's whole tenor of thought is that of a utilitarian who cannot avoid any of the difficulties which this doctrine raises, but who cannot conceive of abandoning his doctrine either. What are the difficulties?

First, Mill abandons the view that the comparison between pleasures is or can be purely quantitative. He introduces a qualitative distinction between "higher" and "lower" pleasures. The higher pleasures are to be preferred: better Socrates dissatisfied than a fool satisfied. How can we be sure of this? Only he who has experienced both is qualified to judge, and only the wise man who prefers the Socratic classification has this experience. Yet here doubt necessarily arises: how could a Mill know what it was like to be a satisfied fool, any more than the fool could know what it was like to be Mill? The point of this question extends further than to cast doubt upon a single contention of Mill's. For what it brings out is that Mill is still engaged, as Bentham was, in trying to bring all the objects and goals of human desire under a single concept, that of pleasure, and trying to show them as all commensurable with each other in a single scale of evaluation. Moreover, he, like Bentham, treats pleasure as a unitary concept.

He is able to do so because the concept of pleasure has tended to degenerate, just as the concept of duty has. I have already suggested that in the case of duty, a highly specific concept associated with the notion of the duties of an office holder evaporates into a generalized notion of "what a man ought to do." So pleasure as the concept of one specific kind of goal is transformed into the concept of any goal at all. Both hedonists and puritans contribute to the history of this degeneration. Hedonists, who begin by commending pleasure, against other goals, then become defensive and insist that they are not merely commending wine, women, and song, but also the higher pleasures, such as reading the *Critique of Pure Reason*. Puritans insist that they are not against pleasure as such, but only low or false pleasures. They, too, are for true and lasting pleasures, such as only Zion's children know. So concepts like "pleasure" and "happiness" are stretched and extended in all directions until they are used simply to name whatever men aim at. By this extension they become useless for evaluative and moral purposes. For in evaluation, and especially in moral evaluation, we are not only engaged in grading and in choosing between alternative objects which we already desire; we are also engaged in grading and choosing between the cultivation of alternative dispositions and desires. The injunction "Pursue happiness!" when *happiness* has been given the broad, undifferentiated sense which Bentham and Mill give to it is merely the injunction "Try to achieve what you desire." But as to any question about rival objects of desire, or about alternative and competing desires, this injunction is silent and empty. And this is equally true whether the happiness which I am to cultivate is to be my own or that of the greatest number.

Mill, faced with the objection that there are many cases in which one cannot assess which out of the alternative possible courses of action will produce the greatest happiness of the greatest number, asserts that utilitarianism enjoins no more than that in cases where one can so assess the consequences of action one ought to use the principle of utility as a criterion. But this concession is more deadly than he perceives: for he is forced to allow implicitly that there are other evaluative criteria. What they are and what their relationship to the principle of utility may be he never makes clear. But we may accept Mill's concession in the spirit in which it is offered, if we recognize that when utilitarians speak of the greatest happiness they are often in practice speaking of a quite specific goal for action rather than of the generalized concept of their theoretical appetites. This goal is that of the public welfare, and it is a goal peculiarly relevant to those areas of life in which Bentham was especially interested. Prisons and hospitals, penal codes and constitutional processes—in these areas it is possible to ask and to answer adequately, even if only crudely, the question of how many people's lot will be bettered, how many people's lot will be worsened, by such and such a measure. For we have obvious and established criteria for faring well or ill in these areas. Will ill-health be increased or diminished? Will the attaching of this rather than that penalty to this crime diminish or increase the frequency of its occurrence? Even in these cases there are choices to be made on which no version of the principle of utility can guide us: an example is the choice between devoting resources to health services or devoting them to penal reform. But it is necessary to emphasize that the utilitarian advocacy of the criterion of public happiness is not only a mistake. That it seems so obviously the criterion to be considered in certain areas of life is something we owe to Bentham and Mill.

The concept of happiness is, however, morally dangerous in another way; for we are by now well aware of the malleability of human beings, of the fact that they can be conditioned in a variety of ways into the acceptance of, and satisfaction with, almost anything. That men are happy with their lot never entails that their lot is what it ought to be. For the question can always be raised of how great the price is that is being paid for the happiness. So the concept of the greatest happiness of the greatest number could be used to defend any paternalistic or totalitarian society in which the price paid for happiness is the freedom of the individuals in that society to make their own choices. Freedom and happiness can in certain circumstances be radically incompatible values. We can trace one legitimate offspring of utilitarianism for whom freedom was sacrificed to happiness in the history of Fabian socialism. For Fabianism socialism was a matter of schemes of reform initiated from above by the enlightened few for the welfare of the unenlightened many. Fabianism stands at the opposite pole in the history of socialism from the revolutionary democracy of Rosa Luxemburg or the I.W.W., for whom socialism consisted in workers becoming free from the domination of others, and owners and directors of their work and their lives.

Moreover, the concept of the greatest happiness of the greatest number is only applicable with any kind of moral legitimacy in a society in which it is assumed that nonutilitarian norms of decent behavior are upheld. The concept of the public happiness has obviously legitimate application in a society where the consensus is that the public happiness consists in more and better hospitals and schools; but what application has it in a society where the public happiness is found by the public itself to consist in the mass murder of Jews? If in a society of twelve people, ten are sadists who will get great pleasure from torturing the remaining two, does the principle of utility enjoin that the two should be tortured? Nothing could have been further from the thought of Bentham and Mill. But this only makes it clearer that they are not consistent utilitarians, that they rely on an implicit appeal to other norms, which they covertly use to define the greatest happiness.

It is this sieve-like nature of the utilitarian concept of pleasure or happiness which makes Mill's proof of the principle of utility so unimpressive. Mill's proof runs as follows. He begins by allowing that in any strict sense, proof on matters concerning ultimate ends is not to be obtained. But, nonetheless, we may adduce considerations capable of influencing the intellect. The argument then proceeds from the assertion that just as the only way to show that something is visible is to show that men can see it, so the only way to show that something is desirable is to show that men desire it. But all men desire pleasure. So pleasure is universally desirable. Mill has no problem about the transition from the desire for my own pleasure to that for the greatest happiness of the greatest number, which he makes by means of the bald assertion that the pleasure of another is naturally pleasurable to me. When Mill comes to show that only pleasure is desired his method is to take apparent alternative goals and show that originally they are desired for the pleasure which accompanies them, and only secondarily do they become desired for their own sake. This method of argument is of course necessarily ineffective. If anything, it shows that there *are* goals other than pleasure. But criticism of Mill has centered on that part of his argument where he passes from the assertion that pleasure is desired to the assertion that it is desirable. What Mill's critics, beginning with G. E. Moore, have in effect said is that Mill illegitimately tries to deduce the conclusion that pleasure ought to be desired from the premise that it is in fact desired. But this, so it is alleged, is necessarily a fallacious inference. For an *is* cannot by itself entail an *ought*. One does not have to enter on any general discussion of fact and value to deal with such critics. They are of course right that the inference in question is fallacious if it is intended as an entailment. But they are simply mistaken in their reading of Mill.

For what Mill says about proof makes it clear that he does not intend to use the assertion that all men do in fact desire pleasure as a premise which entails the conclusion that they ought to desire it. What the form of his argument is, is not perhaps entirely clear. But one way of reading him, more consonant with the text of *Utilitarianism*, would be this. He treats that all men desire pleasure as a factual assertion which guarantees the success of an *ad hominem* appeal to anyone who denies his conclusion. If anyone denies that pleasure is desirable, then we can ask him, But don't you desire it? and we know in advance that he must answer yes, and consequently must admit that pleasure is desirable. But this reading of Mill, and indeed any reading, has to interpret him as treating the assertion that all men desire pleasure as a contingent factual assertion. Now it can only be such if *pleasure* is being treated as the name of one possible object of desire among others; for if it is simply an expression equivalent to "whatever men desire," then the assertion is a vacuous tautology and will not serve Mill's argumentative purposes. Yet if *pleasure* is the name of one specific object of desire (the wine, women, and song sense)—as it often is—then it is certainly false that all men desire it (puritans do not) or that it is the only desired goal. It is thus on the haziness of his central concept that Mill founders and not on the transition from *is* to *ought*.

In the course of the previous discussion another difficulty has come into view. Clearly, even on the best and most charitable interpretation of the concept of the greatest happiness of the greatest number, there are occasions where its use as a criterion would lead us to recommend courses of action which conflict sharply with what ordinarily we think we ought to do. A typical case was propounded by a later critic of utiliarianism, E. F. Carritt. The hanging of an innocent man may well redound to the public happiness if certain conditions are satisfied: that he is publicly believed, although not by us, his would-be executioners, to be guilty of murder, let us say, and that his execution will act as a deterrent, preventing the deaths of sundry innocent people in the future. Surely on a utilitarian view, we ought therefore to hang him. There are two possible types of utilitarian response to this criticism. The first is simply to deny that there is anything abhorrent in the situation. Certainly, a tough-minded utilitarian might say that this is the sort of thing that we ought sometimes to do. There is nothing philosophically criticizable in this response when it is taken in isolation from the rest of the case against utilitarianism. But when this response is combined with the protean utilitarian concept of pleasure one understands its danger. For by allowing the principle of utility to override our existing principles—such as that a man ought not to be hanged for a crime which he has not committed—we remove one more barrier to using the concept of the general happiness to license any enormity. That it can be so used has been amply demonstrated in this century; in particular the high-minded are apt to use totalitarianism as a justification to excuse their responsibility for involvement in the large-scale crimes of their societies, such as Auschwitz or Hiroshima. But, it may be objected, this is surely a moral and not a philosophical objection to utilitarianism. To which the reply is plain: utilitarianism which appears under the pretext of offering a criterion, among other things, for distinguishing good and evil, is in fact offering us a revision of those concepts, such that if we accepted it, we could allow that no action, however vile, was evil in itself or prohibited as such. For all actions are to be assessed in terms of their consequences, and if the consequences of an action are going to be productive of the general happiness, then that action, whether it is the execution of the innocent or the murder or rape of children, would be justified. Thus utilitarianism is a revisionary analysis of our attitudes and concepts; and it is relevant to ask whether it would preserve what we value in those attitudes and concepts.

A second type of response, that of Mill himself, is to argue that utilitarianism, rightly understood, does not license actions which we would ordinarily abhor. So Mill argues that only the maintenance of an impartial system of justice, in which innocent and guilty receive their deserts, could serve the general happiness; and more generally, he argues that to allow exceptions to generally beneficial rules is to weaken their authority and so is always to have harmful consequences. Later utilitarians have also argued that the principle of utility is not in all cases a criterion for judging of particular actions; rather, it is often a criterion for judging of principles. This contention has been argued in its most sophisticated form in terms of a distinction between two logically distinct types of rule: summary rules, which are logically subsequent to the actions which they prescribe or prohibit; and rules of practice, which define classes of action and are logically prior to the actions in question. An example of the first type of rule would be one forbidding walking on the grass. The actions, walking or not walking on the grass, are logically prior to any rule about so walking. An example of the second type of rule would be that which specifies the ways in which a batsman may be out at cricket. The concept of "being out" and the associated actions are specifiable only in terms of the rules defining the practices which constitute the game of cricket. The first type of rule may be represented as a summary or generalization about what is enjoined or prohibited in terms of some general criterion on many particular occasions. The second type of rule cannot be so understood. Its application on particular occasions must—logically must— be subsequent to its general formulation. It has been argued that if we apply this distinction to the problem posed for utilitarianism, we see that it is only in the case of the former type of rule that the problem can arise, but that in this case it is easily soluble. If on many particular occasions we find that doing or refraining from doing some particular action is productive of the greatest happiness, then we may summarize our discovery in a general rule prescribing or prohibiting that action. If subsequently we find a case where to do what the rule enjoins would not be productive of the greatest happiness, then we need have no hesitation about abandoning the rule for this occasion, because the rule has no force or authority except that which derives from the greatest happiness principle. But this only applies to the first type of rule.

The second type of rule constitutes or partly constitutes a practice which *as a whole* and in the long run may be justified by appeal to the greatest happiness principle; but one cannot ask for a particular rule to be set aside because on a particular occasion its application violates that principle. For the rule is adhered to because of its connection with the practice, not because directly and in itself it promotes the greatest happiness principle. Thus it is logically inappropriate to ask whether a particular rule in a game should be waived on a particular occasion because its application violates the greatest happiness principle; and it is logically inappropriate to ask for the waiving of a particular rule of justice on a particular occasion because the application of that rule violates the greatest happiness principle. It is a whole system of justice which stands or falls at the bar of the principle of utility, and not the detail of particular cases. So the hanging of the innocent man on a particular occasion to secure a particular deterrent is not sanctioned by a utilitarian justification of justice after all. It is the whole practice of justice with its systematic protection of innocence, and nothing less than that, which receives a utilitarian justification.

Will this defense suffice? Does it succeed in showing that utilitarianism is compatible with our ordinary belief in justice? What it ignores is the fact that we often do waive, and regard ourselves as justified in waiving, principles of justice in the interests of human happiness. So someone may fail to report a crime or fail to punish a criminal because of the effects on his family. The fact that justice is a systematic body of practices, justifiable as a whole in utilitarian terms, is not incompatible with there being clashes between particular applications of the principles of justice and the application of the greatest happiness principle. We then have to decide what weight to give to the principles of justice, and we should not have to make such a decision if it were entirely a matter of applying a single ultimate principle. The value we set upon justice is not, therefore, entirely derived from our adherence to the principle of utility.

Thus the attempt to shore up utilitarianism in this way is itself a misconceived attempt to give a false unity to our values. That such an attempt should be made is easily understood. The individualism of modern society and the increasingly rapid and disruptive rate of social change brings about a situation in which for increasing numbers there is no over-all shape to the moral life but only a set of apparently arbitrary principles inherited from a variety of sources. In such circumstances the need for a public criterion for use in settling moral and evaluative disagreements and conflicts becomes ever more urgent and ever more difficult to meet. The utilitarian criterion, which appears to embody the liberal ideal of happiness, is apparently without rivals, and the fact that the concept of happiness which it embodies is so amorphous and so adaptable makes it not less but more welcome to those who look for a court of appeal on evaluative questions which they can be assured will decide in their own favor.

No philosopher expressed the moral situation of nineteenth-century England—and to some extent we are all still in the nineteenth century—better than Henry Sidgwick. Sidgwick is a touching figure whose defects are usually the defects of his age. He was preoccupied with the loss of his own Christian faith in a way that is foreign to us. His moral psychology is crude because the psychology of his time was crude. And in his moral philosophy he mirrors his age also. For Sidgwick the history of moral philosophy in the preceding century had centered on the clash between utilitarianism and what he called intuitionism. By this he meant the doctrine that moral first principles are intuitively known, the doctrine of Price, and earlier, of Locke. Within utilitarianism further there is the argument about the relationship between the pursuit of my own happiness and the pursuit of the greatest happiness of the greatest number. Sidgwick painstakingly examined all the possible ways of assimilating intuitionism to utilitarianism, or of bridging the gap between the goals of private and public happiness. But in the end there remain three distinct sources of morality. Sidgwick's account of the methods of ethics misses questions beyond those which he explicitly discusses. The background to his account is the moral consciousness of his day, taken as given. Philosophy appears as essentially a clarifying rather than a critical activity. In this respect Sidgwick's is a ghost that haunts much recent writing. In his acceptance of the utilitarian consciousness of his own age he contrasts sharply with his contemporaries T. H. Green and F. H. Bradley.

Green and Bradley are often classed together as Oxford idealists; it is important however to remember that the classing of them together in this way is the work of their later critics. They themselves worked independently, and the similarities in their writings are the result of the similarity of their self-set tasks. Both were keen students of Kant and Hegel; both wish to find materials in Kant and Hegel with which to carry through a criticism of Hume and Mill. Both draw on Greek philosophy as well as on German. But Green was perhaps influenced by

Rousseau as much as by any other author, while there is little trace of Rousseau in Bradley. And Green's philosophical preoccupations were intimately related to his commitments to social and educational reform whereas Bradley was a philosophical recluse.

Both Green and Bradley break with the individualism of utilitarianism. The utilitarian picture of society is of a collection of individuals, each with his own determinate desires and his consequent goals. The shared aims and norms of society are a product of the compromises and agreements of individuals: the public good is a sum total of private goods. Both Green and Bradley break with this picture, whether in its utilitarian or its social contract forms. Both recognize that the individual discovers his aims and his desires from within a set of rule-governed relationships to others. He finds himself through, he identifies himself by means of, a set of relationships through which goals are partly specified for him. The individual then has his choices to make; he can appraise his own desires in a variety of ways. But his nature, including his desires, is not presocial.

If this argument were pursued, it would have to press the question of the relationship of morality to the social framework more seriously and in detail. Both Green and Bradley, however, place the individual not merely in a social, but in a metaphysical context. Or rather, they appear to perform social analysis in a highly metaphysical style. To make clear what this means, it is necessary to follow through the key themes of each in turn. Bradley, for example, poses the question, Why should I be moral?, a question which he uses as the title of one of his *Ethical Studies*, only to reply that, as it stands, the question is improper. For it suggests that there is an end beyond morality, to which the exercise of moral virtue is only a means. But from within the moral consciousness we can discern that morality does have an end, an end not beyond morality but constituted by morality itself in its highest achievement, the realization of the self as a whole. I realize my self as a whole through actions which express the stirring of the self to be something better and higher than it is already, so that the principles to which I aspire to conform come to be the principles expressed in my actual behavior. In any situation of choice between alternatives, I realize my self, first, insofar as I am aware of myself independently of the two alternatives and confronting them; and second, in self-consciously choosing one alternative and identifying myself with it, whereby I bring the whole self into being in concrete form. This Bradley calls "the concrete universal," the judgment of universal import made concrete in the realized activity of the concrete individual.

The self develops to the point at which it realizes itself completely by identifying itself as a part in an infinite whole and so transcending its own finite bounds. "The difficulty is being limited and so not a whole, how to extend myself so as to be a whole? The answer is, be a member in a whole. Here your private self, your finitude ceases as such to exist; it becomes the function of an organism. You must be, not a mere piece of, but a member in, a whole; and as this, must know and will yourself."

What is the whole in which the individual self must realize itself? We get, not a completely coherent answer to this question, but at least part of an answer in a later chapter of *Ethical Studies*, "My Station and Its Duties." Bradley had already, in previous essays, attacked the view that the end which the moral consciousness places before us can be either pleasure or duty for its own sake. His grounds for breaking with Benthamite utilitarianism and with Kantianism are partly different and partly the same. He argues, for example, that pleasure supervenes upon a desired end, and so cannot be the end; and he argues that on the Kantian view duty is proposed as an end for a self which is constituted by desires and inclinations such that duty can have no interest for it, cannot be an end for it. But in both cases he argues that the end proposed is too general and abstract; the formulas of Kant and Bentham alike try to bring the multifarious ends which men in different circumstances and at different times pursue under a single characterization, and in so doing, they present a formula which is in effect contentless. Because it includes anything which a man *might* pursue, it identifies nothing which he *must* pursue, if he is to be true to the deliverances of his moral consciousness.

The end which Bradley lays down is that of finding my station and carrying out its duties. These duties will be specific and concrete. Bradley allows that I may have some choice of what station in life to fill; but once I have chosen some station, the question of what duties attach to it is not a matter of choice. That this is so is of some importance, for it is only insofar as the end is an objective end, and not one chosen by me, that I can hope to realize my individuality through it. What Bradley means by this is not entirely clear, but he is partly making the substantial point that any criteria by which I am to judge of my own moral progress must be criteria whose authority derives from something other than my own choices. For if my own choices is all that is authoritative, I am in the end playing an arbitrary self-enclosed game, a variety of spiritual patience in which if the cards will not come out the first time, I can, if I choose, allow myself a indefinitely large number of reshufflings. Moreover, to fill my station in life, I can utilize every part of my nature; the Kantian divide between duty and inclination is overcome.

What Bradley is presupposing rather than asserting here is that the moral vocabulary can only be given a coherent sense in the context of a form of social life with well-defined roles and functions, and one, moreover, in which men live out the substance of their lives in terms of those roles and functions. But is there such a society any more? Sociologists have often emphasized the difference between a modern individualist society in which a man's life and status can be distinct from his various roles and functions and earlier more integrated forms of society in which a man might fill his station in life in much the way that Bradley envisages. That Bradley is able not to raise this type of question is perhaps due to his ability to pass into a metaphysical style of speech in which it is the nature of reality as such, and nothing less, that guarantees his thesis about morality.

This is less true, but it is still true, of T. H. Green. Green is more self-consciously aware that his moral views require a certain kind of society. But his metaphysical mode enables him to pass from the view that society ought to be the locus of a rational general will of a Rousseauesque kind to the view that at bottom this is what society really is. Green is more socially aware than Bradley because of his own political involvement. He came on the philosophical scene as an educator in a period when liberal young men of the ruling class, morally earnest as a result of their training in evangelical homes and by Arnoldian schoolmasters, who could not imbibe the romantic Toryism of Disraeli, were looking for a frame that would lend meaning to their lives. Green's Balliol pupils carried into the civil service, the church, politics, into the cabinet itself—one of them was a Liberal prime minister—a belief that liberal individualism could be overcome within a liberal framework. Green was the apostle of state intervention in matters of social welfare and of education; he was able to be so because he could see in the state an embodiment of that higher self the realization of which is our moral aim.

Green's *Prolegomena to Ethics* rests its argument on an extended analysis of human nature, designed to show that human existence is not wholly explicable in terms of the laws of nature. Reflection on the purposive and self-conscious character of human existence reveals to us the awareness of ourselves as intelligent beings, and members of a society of intelligent beings, whose final satisfaction cannot be anything merely physical or perishable. What, then, is the human good? We know it only in part, because our faculties for realizing it are themselves only partly realized. But the contemporary moral consciousness is a record of our highest achievement of it to date. Kant was right in thinking that the one unconditional good is the good will; but wrong in his too abstract characterization of it. The good will is manifested in the desire to transcend the existing moral consciousness in the creation of a greater good; and every expression of the good will is the creation of a form of life specifiable along the lines of "the Greek classification on the virtues." The good will is defined as "the will to know what is true, to make what is beautiful, to endure pain and fear, to resist the allurements of pleasure, in the interest of some form of human society."

Green's specification of the good in terms of a form of social life, even if his own specification is a highly abstract one, enables him at least to avoid the individualist puzzles over egoism and altruism. "The idea of a true good does not admit of the distinction between good for self and good for others," precisely because it consists of a form of social life in which different individuals play out their parts. The individual finds his good through a form of life which exists prior to himself.

Yet is Green describing at this point what actually happens? Clearly not. Is he specifying an ideal state of affairs which ought to be brought into existence? Only partly, for he believes the ideal to be implicit in the actual. Like Bradley, he makes it clear that the moral vocabulary cannot be understood except against the background of a certain kind of social life; like Bradley, his metaphysical style enables him to evade the question of the relation between that form of social life and social life as it actually is lived out in nineteenth-century western Europe. But at least Bradley and Green force these questions upon us. Their immediate twentieth-century successors were to write as if morality, and with it, moral philosophy existed apart from all specific social forms.

# 18

## MODERN MORAL PHILOSOPHY

Modern moral philosophy opens on a quietly apocalyptic note. Moral philosophers, it is explained, have hitherto failed to answer the questions which they posed satisfactorily, because they have failed to be clear about the questions themselves. In particular they have failed to distinguish between the questions, What kind of actions ought we to perform? and, What kind of things ought to exist for their own sake? The distinction is made at last, or so it is proclaimed, in the preface to G. E. Moore's *Principia Ethica*. The implication is that the problems will now be solved. The date is 1903.

The answer to the question, What kind of actions ought we to perform? is those "which will cause more good to exist in the universe than any possible kind of alternative." We are thus brought to ask what states of affairs are good, what kind of things ought to exist for their own sake. Moore takes it that the things which ought to exist for their own sake are those which we call intrinsically good. How do we know what is intrinsically good? The answer is that we cannot fail to recognize the property of intrinsic goodness when confronted with it. Propositions concerning what is intrinsically good—as contrasted with what is good only because it is a means to something intrinsically good—are susceptible neither of proof nor of disproof. This is because *good* is the name of a simple, unanalyzable property, which Moore calls "non-natural" because it cannot be identified with any natural property. Moore holds that *good* is indefinable, partly in virtue of an analogy which he propounds between *good* and *yellow*, and partly by reason of an argument about the consequences of holding *good* to be definable. But both the analogy and the argument depend in part on the curious sense which he assigns to *definition*. To define, he holds, is to break up a complex whole into its constituent parts. So the definition of *horse* will be a statement to the effect that it has four legs, a head, a heart, a liver, etc., all of them arranged in definite relations to one another. (Moore recognizes other senses of *definition*, but deliberately puts them on one side.) Now if this is what is meant by *definition*, it is not difficult to agree that *good* is indefinable, but this sense of *definition* is so idiosyncratic that nothing has been gained. Moore also tries to reinforce his case by an appeal to what we allegedly must recognize when we hold a given notion "before" our minds. He says that if we consider *good* and, let us say, *pleasant*, or any other notion with which we might be tempted to confuse *good*, we can see that we "have two different notions before our minds." This technique of holding one's concepts up to the light, as it were, is reinforced by Moore's method of calm assertion. More unwarranted and unwarrantable assertions are perhaps made in *Principia Ethica* than in any other single book of moral philosophy, but they are made with such well-mannered, although slightly browbeating certitude, that it seems almost gross to disagree. But what, then, *is* Moore's case?

Moore originally rests his analogy between *yellow* and *good* on his notion of definition. "Yellow and good, we say, are not complex: they are nations out of which definitions are composed and with which the power of further defining comes." Moreover, just as we cannot identify the meaning of *yellow* with the physical properties of the light which produces the effect of seeing yellow, so we cannot identify the meaning of *good* with the particular natural properties which are associated with good. It might be the case that anything "good" was pleasant, just as all yellow light is of a certain wavelength, but it does not follow that *good* means what *pleasant* means, any more than it follows that *yellow* means the same as "light of a certain wave length."

Moore's one genuine argument is used to show that *good* cannot be the name of any complex whole. Of any such whole, however defined, we can always significantly ask whether it is itself good. This argument can be deployed not only against the attempt to define *good* as the name of a complex, but also against the attempt to define it at all. Suppose that I do identify *good* with *pleasant*. My mistake can be exhibited by showing that I can always significantly ask of pleasure or of anything pleasant, Is it good? But if *good* named the same property that *pleasant* names, to ask, Is what is pleasant good? would be equivalent to asking, Is what is pleasant pleasant?—that is, it would be vacuously tautologous.

Moore frames this argument in order to refute hedonists, whom he conceives to hold two incompatible positions: they hold that pleasure is good, indeed *the* good, in a significant, nontautological sense; and they claim to demonstrate this by urging that *good* means nothing other than what *pleasant* means. But the first position requires that "pleasure is good" be taken to be analytic. Yet it cannot be both. So the hedonist position collapses. But, of course, it only collapses for those hedonists unwise enough to attempt to hold both these positions.

The philosophers whom Moore chiefly criticizes are J. S. Mill and Herbert Spencer. In the case of Mill, Moore's criticisms are misdirected, if only because he reads into Mill a definition of *good* as meaning *pleasant*, whereas all that Mill at the most says is that pleasure provides us with our only criterion of goodness. It is by now almost a commonplace to recognize that Moore misrepresented Mill; it is a measure of the extent to which contemporary philosophers read Mill, but do not read Spencer, that it goes unrecognized that Moore also misrepresented Spencer. Moore accuses Spencer of having thought that *good* meant the same as "more evolved." Spencer's however was a far more complex, if quite implausible, position. Spencer held, first, that human society has evolved, just as the human species evolved, and indeed that the evolution of species and of society can be placed on a single continuous scale. Secondly, he believed that the higher a society is upon this scale the more ideal its morality; and thirdly, that conduct tends more and more toward the end of preserving life, it being assumed that in life there is, especially as one ascends toward the ideal, more pleasure than pain. As with Mill, Spencer may in unguarded moments have given the impression that he was defining the moral vocabulary. But the real

Herbert Spencer is as far from being Moore's straw man as is the real J. S. Mill.[62]

To the doctrine that *good* was the name of a natural property Moore gave the name "the naturalistic fallacy." For Moore this fallacy is committed in the course of any attempt to treat *good* as the name of a property identifiable under any other description. *Good* cannot mean "commanded by God," any more than it can mean *pleasant*, and for the same reasons the expression "the naturalistic fallacy" has since been adopted by the adherents of the view that one cannot logically derive an *ought* from an *is*; but although this latter doctrine is a consequence of Moore's, it is not identical with it.

Is *good*, then, the name of a simple, unanalyzable property? To the doctrine that it is, there are at least two conclusive objections. The first is that we can only use the name of a simple property intelligibly where we are acquainted with some standard example of the property by reference to which we are to recognize whether it is present or absent in other cases. In the case of a simple property like yellow we can use standard examples of the color to recognize other cases of yellow. But how could having learned to recognize a good friend help us to recognize a good watch? Yet if Moore is right, the same simple property is present in both cases. To this, a disciple of Moore might reply that we are confusing the question by our example. A good watch is not "intrinsically" good. But how, then, do we recognize the intrinsically good? The only answer Moore offers is that we just do. Or put this point another way: Moore's account could only reach the level of intelligibility if it were supplemented by an account of how the meaning of *good* is learned, and an account of the relation between learning it in connection with some cases, and knowing how to apply it in others.

The second objection is that Moore's account leaves it entirely unexplained and inexplicable why something's being good should ever furnish us with a reason for action. The analogy with yellow is as much a difficulty for his thesis at this point as it is an aid to him elsewhere. One can imagine a connoisseur with a special taste for yellow objects to whom something's being yellow would furnish him with a reason for acquiring it; but something's being "*good*" can hardly be supposed to furnish a reason for action only to those with a connoisseur's interest in goodness. Any account of *good* that is to be adequate must connect it intimately with action, and explain why to call something good is always to provide a reason for acting in respect of it in one way rather than another.

That it does connect *good* with action is the chief virtue of the other seminal moral philosophy of the twentieth century, that of John Dewey. For Dewey the chief trap in all epistemology is the tendency to abstract our knowledge both from the methods by which we acquired it and from the uses to which we may put it. We only acquired whatever knowledge we have now because we had certain purposes, and the point of that knowledge is for us inseparable from our future purposes. All reason is practical reason. Moral knowledge is not a separate branch of knowledge; it is simply the knowledge we have—in physics, biology, history, or what you will—considered in relation to those purposes. To characterize something as good is to say that it will provide us with satisfaction in our purposes. As means or as end? As both, and Dewey is concerned to emphasize what he takes to be the interrelated character of good-as-a-means and good-as-an-end. We are as far as it is possible to be from Moore's concept of the "intrinsically good" with its sharp separation of means and ends. Dewey concentrates on the agent, while Moore concentrates on the spectator. Dewey almost obliterates the distinction between fact and value, between *is* and *ought*, while Moore emphasizes it. Dewey thinks that in making choices we are guided by considerations which we express in statements of an ordinary empirical kind, statements which presuppose the direction of the agent's purposes and interests, but which do not differ from, which in fact *are* the statements of our empirical studies. That Dewey has not been more influential, particularly in England, is perhaps explicable by the fact that he so seldom attends explicitly to the problem which has been at the center of Anglo-Saxon moral philosophy in this century, that of the meaning of moral predicates. And where Dewey did exert a major influence it was indirectly, in a discussion that stemmed from Moore.

Moore's immediate heirs were of two kinds. There were those who carried on moral philosophy of the same type as Moore's, the so-called intuitionists, such as Prichard, Ross, and Carritt. It ought to be emphasized both that these writers did not in fact acquire their views from Moore, but independently, and that the value of their writings is not only a matter of how cogently they presented their own views. Carritt, for example, will be remembered for his power as a critic of utilitarianism (as well as for his writings on aesthetics). This particular succession of writers was ushered in by a text as dramatic in its way as *Principia Ethica*: a paper by H. A. Prichard in 1912, entitled "Does Moral Philosophy Rest upon a Mistake?" Prichard takes the task which moral philosophy has set itself to be that of providing a reason or justification for holding that something which we take to be our duty is indeed our duty. But he argues that the demand for such a reason or justification is utterly misconceived. In defense of this position he offers in effect two sorts of reason. I may try to justify the view that something is my duty by showing that it is to my interest or would lead to my happiness. But if this is what provides me with a reason, then I am not treating whatever I take my duty to be as a *duty* at all. For what I do because it is to my interest, I thereby do not do as a duty. Or I may try to justify the view that something is my duty by showing that to perform it would be to produce some good. But—so Prichard says—that something is good does not entail that it is obligatory on me to bring it about. This first kind of argument starts from a list of what Prichard presumably takes to be the only possible types of alleged justification. His second consists in appeals to that of which we are all alleged to be conscious. The apprehension of duty is said to be immediate and unquestionable, and therefore not to be supported by reasons.

Prichard's outstanding characteristic, and one which he shares with Moore as well as with other intuitionists, is the treatment of *good, right, duty, obligatory*, and the rest of the moral vocabulary as though it was a coinage of permanently fixed values and simple scrutiny. It is doubtless because of this that the proportion of assertion to argument is so high in Prichard. In other intuitionist writers, such as Sir David Ross, who holds that we have independent intuitions of "rightness" and "goodness," the standards of argument are much higher. But all intuitionist writers suffer from one difficulty: they are, on their own view, telling us only about what we all know already. That they sometimes disagree about what it is that we all know already only makes them less boring at the cost of making them even less convincing.

The two most powerful critics of intuitionism were R. G. Collingwood and A. J. Ayer. Collingwood, whose attack extended to many other recent writers in ethics, attacked them for their lack of historical sense, for their tendency to treat Plato, Kant, and themselves as contributors to a single discussion with a single subject matter and a permanent and unchanging vocabulary. They are, he says in his *Autobiography*, like men who translate the Greek word τριήρης by steamship, and when it is pointed out to them that the characteristics which Greek writers assign to the τριήρης are not at all the characteristics of a steamship, they reply that this just shows what odd and mistaken ideas about steamships Greek writers held. We ought rather, according to Collingwood in the *Autobiography*, to understand moral and other concepts in terms of a developing historical sequence. What this might entail I shall consider later in this chapter.

Ayer's critique of intuitionism has quite different roots. In *Language, Truth, and Logic* he revived some of Hume's positions, but did so in the context of a logical-positivist theory of knowledge. So moral judgments are understood in terms of a threefold classification of judgments: logical, factual, and emotive. In the first class come the truths of logic and mathematics, which are held to be analytic; in the second come the empirically verifiable or falsifiable truths of the sciences and of common-sense knowledge of fact. The third class necessarily appears as a residual category, a rag-bag to which whatever is not logic or science is consigned. Both ethics and theology find themselves in this category, a fact in itself sufficient to make us suspicious of the classification. For on the face of it, statements about the intentions and deeds of an omnipotent being and judgments about duty or about what is good do not obviously belong together. We can, however, easily detach the emotive theory of moral judgment from this dubious classification; all that we need retain from it is the contrast between the factual and the emotive. In this form the most powerful exponent of emotivism has been C. L. Stevenson. Stevenson's writing exhibits many influences, above all, those of both Moore and Dewey, and his position can perhaps be most easily expounded by returning to Moore.

I said earlier that Moore had two kinds of heirs, the first of whom were the intuitionists. What the intuitionists continue is the philosophical appeal to what we all are alleged to recognize in moral matters. But Moore himself was, above all, anxious to clear up the *philosophical* confusions over the concept of goodness so that he could proceed to a second task, that of saying which things are, in fact, good. In his chapter on conduct he makes it clear that right action is valuable only as a means to what is good. In his chapter on The Ideal, Moore tells us what is good. "Once the meaning of the question is clearly understood the answer to it, in its main outlines, appears to be so obvious, that it runs the risk of seeming to be a platitude. By far the most valuable things which we know or can imagine, are certain states of consciousness which may be roughly described as the pleasures of human intercourse and the enjoyment of beautiful objects." J. M. Keynes has described for us how this view of the supremacy of personal relationships and of the beautiful broke upon the generation immediately younger than Moore with all the force of a revelation. Almost half a century later Keynes could write: "I see no reason to shift from the fundamental intuitions of *Principia Ethica*; though they are much too few and too narrow to fit actual experience. That they furnish a justification of experience wholly independent of outside events has become an added comfort, even though one cannot live today secure in the undisturbed individualism which was the extraordinary achievement of the early Edwardian days." It all depended, of course, on who "one" was and to which social class one belonged. The values which Moore exalts belong to the realm of private rather than public life; and, supremely important as they are, they exclude all the values connected with intellectual inquiry and with work. Moore's values are those of a protected leisure, though it is in what he excludes rather than in what he does value that the parochial and classbound character of his attitudes appears. It is worth commenting on this feature of Moore's views simply to emphasize the fact that they are not, as he apparently supposed, beyond controversy. For Moore combines highly controversial moral views with an appeal to the evidence of simple recognition in order to establish them. Keynes, in the memoir quoted earlier, *My Early Beliefs*, gives us a penetrating account of the consequent behavior of Moore's disciples. They would compare alternative possible situations and solemnly inquire in which there was most good, inspecting each in turn and comparing them. They would then announce what they "saw."

In an extremely homogeneous group, like that of Moore's immediate disciples, the congruence between what different people "see" is likely to be fairly high. But the arrival of D. H. Lawrence on the scene, who reacted against the attitudes of this group with all the passion at his disposal, might have made them aware that if challenged on their valuations, their own position allowed them no use for argument, but only for reinspection and reassertion. Since there is in fact no simple, nonnatural property which *good* names, the whole process is merely an elaborate game of bluff. And it would not be unfair to remark that what this group did was to invoke Moore's philosophical theory in order to endow their own expressions of attitude with an authority which those expressions would not otherwise have possessed.

"But if there is no such property as Moore supposes, then all they can be doing is to express their own feelings." Perhaps in some such reaction to Moore lies one of the seeds of emotivism. Moore himself staked everything on the appeal to objectivity. In an argument which he used in an essay written after *Principia Ethica* he contended that moral judgments cannot be reports of our feelings, for if they were, two men who uttered apparently contradictory judgments upon a moral issue would not in fact be disagreeing. A man who said, "You ought to do X" would no more be disagreeing with a man who said, "You ought not to do X" than would someone who said, "I stacked my hay yesterday" be disagreeing with someone else who said, "I didn't stack my hay yesterday." To which argument Stevenson's reply was that two men who disagree on a moral question need not be involved in any factual disagreement; they need only be involved in disagreement on the facts of the case; the issue between them at this level can be settled by an empirical inquiry. But they may further disagree in their attitudes; and this disagreement can only be resolved by one party changing his attitude. The primary function of moral words, according to Stevenson, is to redirect the attitudes of others so that they accord more fully with our own. In concentrating on the dynamic function of moral words, Stevenson shows the influence of Dewey, and it is through Stevenson mainly that Dewey influenced later moral philosophers.

Moral words are able to have this dynamic function of which Stevenson speaks because they are emotive. "The emotive meaning of a word is the tendency of a word, arising through the history of its usage to produce (result from) affective responses in people." Ayer, in his version of the emotive theory, concentrated upon my expression of my own feelings and attitudes; Stevenson, in his, concentrates upon my attempt to influence your feelings and attitudes. As to what the key moral words mean, Stevenson offers two models, stressing in each case that the nature of emotive meaning is such that we cannot hope to arrive at more than a rough approximation. His first model is one in which "This is good" is elucidated as roughly equivalent to "I like this. Do so as well." In his second model he attends to those expressions which embody what he names "persuasive definitions." Such expressions have a descriptive meaning, and they associate with that meaning an emotive one; we can thus always analyze them into two component elements. Two men in controversy may, for example, use *just* in such a way that each associates different descriptive meanings with the emotive element in the meaning of that word.

Stevenson's view of moral expressions leads to a number of other positions. It follows from his view, for example, that for *good* and for other evaluative expressions no complete definition in descriptive terms can ever be given. Thus Stevenson agrees with Moore that *good* cannot function as the name of a natural (empirically descriptive) property. The facts are logically divorced from the evaluations for Stevenson as much as for Moore. Secondly, Stevenson commits himself to the view that philosophical ethics is a morally neutral activity. The doctrines that we hold about the meaning of moral expressions cannot commit us to any particular moral view. Clearly the emotive theory itself, if true, does appear, at least on the surface, to be morally neutral. For presumably we can use emotive words to commend any class of actions whatsoever. Moreover, if Stevenson is right, evaluative disagreement may always be interminable. There is no limit to the possibilities of disagreement, and there is and can be no set of procedures for the resolution of disagreements. It is not surprising that this should be a consequence of Stevenson's position, since he himself initially laid it down as one of the prerequisites for a successful theory that it should provide for disagreement to be interminable. Finally, on Stevenson's view, the reasons which we cite to support our evaluative, and more specifically, our moral judgments cannot stand in any logical relationship to the conclusions which we derive from them. They can only be psychological reinforcements. It follows that words like *because* and *therefore* do not function as they do in other parts of discourse.

The difficulties which can be raised about emotivism are of several different kinds. The notion of "emotive meaning" is itself not clear. What makes certain statements guides to, or directives of, action is not that they have any *meaning* over and above a factual or descriptive one. It is that their utterance on a specific occasion has import for, or relevance to, the speaker or hearer's interests, desires, or needs. "The White House is on fire" does not have any more or less meaning when uttered in a news broadcast in London than it does when uttered as a warning to the President in bed, but its function as a guide to action is quite different. Emotivism, that is, does not attend sufficiently to the distinction between the meaning of a statement which remains constant between different uses, and the variety of uses to which one and the same statement can be put. (Of course, meaning and possible range of use are intimately related; but they are not the same.)

Moreover, not only does Stevenson tend to conflate meaning and use, but, the primary use which he assigns to moral expressions is not, and cannot be, their primary use. For the use to which he attends is the second-person use in which we try to move other people to adopt our own views. Stevenson's examples all picture a thoroughly unpleasant world in which everyone is always trying to get at everyone else. But in fact one is only in a position to try to convert others to one's own moral views when one has formed views of one's own; yet none of those uses of moral language which are necessary to the formation and expression of one's views with an eye to one's own actions figure in Stevenson's initial account.

Finally, one can justifiably complain of the emotive theory not only that it is mistaken, but also that it is opaque. For its proponents seek to elucidate moral expressions in terms of the notions of attitudes and feelings, and it is relevant to ask for further characterization of the attitudes and feelings in question. How, for example, are we to identify these attitudes and feelings so that we may distinguish them from other attitudes and feelings? Emotivist writers are, in fact, largely silent on this point; but the suspicion is strong that they would be compelled to characterize the attitudes and feelings under discussion as just those attitudes and feelings which are given their definitive expression in acts of moral judgment. Yet if this is so, the whole theory is imprisoned in uninformative circularity.

Nonetheless, some of its central features are preserved by its immediate successors. The moral neutrality of philosophical analysis, the logical gap between fact and value, the interminality of disagreement all remain upon the scene. What is altered in later writers is the attention paid to two intimately related topics, the question of the criteria which are employed in calling things, acts, or people good or bad, and the question in the nature of moral reasoning. If I call something good or commend it in some other way, I can always be asked upon what criterion I am relying. If I say that I ought to do something, I can always be asked, And what if you do not? and, On account of what ought you to do it? What is the relation between my answers to these questions and my beliefs as to what is good and as to what I ought to do?

One systematic answer to these questions is to be found in R. M. Hare's *The Language of Morals*, and his views are added to and further elucidated in *Freedom and Reason*. Hare specifies the nature of moral language by means of an initial distinction between prescriptive and descriptive language. Prescriptive language is imperatival, in that it tells us to do this or that. It is itself subdivided into two classes, that comprising imperatives in the ordinary sense, and that comprising properly evaluative expressions. All value judgments are practical, but in different ways. *Ought* sentences, for example, if they are genuinely evaluative, entail imperatives addressed to anyone in the relevant situation, and *anyone* here includes the person who utters the sentence. The criterion of uttering the *ought* sentence sincerely is that, on the relevant occasion and if the speaker can, he does in fact act in obedience to the imperative entailed by the *ought* which he utters to himself. *Good*, by contrast, is used to commend; to call X good is to say that it is the kind of X we should choose if we wanted an X. The criteria which I employ in calling something good are criteria which, if I am engaged in genuine evaluations, I have chosen, and which I endorse by my very use of them. Evaluative expressions and moral rules are thus both expressions of the agent's fundamental choices. But the role of choice in Hare's prescriptivism is far clearer and far less objectionable than the role of attitudes or feelings was in emotivism. Unlike the latter, it does not preclude the use of argument in morals.

Hare was, in fact, a pioneer in the logical investigation of imperatives. He pointed out that in imperatival discourse, conclusions can follow from premises in a perfectly straightforward way, violating none of the ordinary rules of entailment. *Because* and *therefore* carry their usual meanings, and genuine moral argument is possible. But, so Hare further holds, the meaning of evaluative prescriptive expressions is such that no evaluative or prescriptive conclusion can follow from premises which do not include at least one evaluative or prescriptive premise. In other words, Hare reiterates the thesis that no *ought* follows merely from *is*. So far as the doctrine of *The Language of Morals* goes, it seemed to follow that the pattern of moral argument is a transition from a moral major premise and a factual minor premise to a moral conclusion. Wherever I appear to pass from fact to value ("I ought to help this man because he is starving"), there is a gap in the argument, a concealed major premise ("I ought to help the starving"). This major premise itself may figure as the conclusion of some other syllogism, but at some point the chain of reasoning must terminate in a principle which I cannot justify by further argument, but to which I must simply commit myself by choice. Once more it seems to follow, as it did with emotivism, that on matters of ultimate principle, assertion cannot be met by argument but only by counterassertion.

In *Freedom and Reason*, Hare argued that this was not entailed by his view; that the universalizability of moral judgments provides an argumentative weapon against those who hold unacceptable moral principles. For of a man who holds, for example, that other men ought to be treated in certain unpleasant ways merely because their skins are black, we can always ask, Are you then prepared to allow that you should be treated in the same way if your skin were black? And Hare believes that only a minority, whom he denominates fanatics, would be prepared to accept the consequences of replying Yes to this. This last contention is a question of fact on which I believe that recent social history does not bear Hare out. But I do not want to quarrel with this part of Hare's view so much as to emphasize that it still remains true on Hare's view that, as a matter of logic and of the concepts involved, what I call good and what I hold I ought to do depend upon my choice of fundamental evaluations, and that there is no logical limit to what evaluations I may choose. In other words, Hare's prescriptivism is, in the end, a reissue of the view that behind my moral evaluations there is not and cannot be any greater authority than that of my own choices. To understand evaluative concepts is to understand that our use of these concepts does not of itself commit us to any particular set of moral beliefs. The criteria for true belief in matters of fact are independent of our choices; but our evaluations are governed by no criteria but those which we ourselves choose to impose upon them. This is a repetition of Kant's view of the moral subject as lawgiver; but it makes him an arbitrary sovereign who is the author of the law that he utters, and who constitutes it law by uttering it in the form of a universal prescription.

An ambiguity in Hare's whole enterprise, an ambiguity pointed out by Mary Warnock,[63] becomes important here. When Hare characterizes evaluation and prescription, is he in fact defining these terms in such a way as to protect his thesis against possible counterexamples? If we produce an example of *ought* which does not entail a first-person imperative, or an example of good in which the criteria are not a matter of choice, will Hare be able to reply that these are simply nonprescriptive and nonevaluative uses of *ought* and *good*? Hare certainly recognizes that there are some nonprescriptive and nonevaluative uses. But if he has simply legislated so that evaluation and prescription shall be what he says they are, why should we assent to his legislation? If he is not legislating, then we must have the class of evaluative and prescriptive expressions delimited for us independently of Hare's characterization, in a way that Hare himself never delimits it. He seems indeed to rely on an almost intuitive understanding of what is to be included or left out of the class of evaluative expressions.

Why is this important? It is important partly because Philippa Foot[64] and Peter Geach[65] have challenged Hare with prima facie convincing counterexamples. Philippa Foot's attention has been concentrated on evaluative expressions connected with the virtues and vices, such as *rude* and *courageous*; Geach's on *good* and *evil*. The criteria for the correct application of *rude* and *courageous* are, so Mrs. Foot argues, factual. If certain factual conditions are fulfilled, this is sufficient to show that these epithets apply and their application could only be withheld by someone who failed to understand their meaning. So if a man at a concert spits in the face of an acquaintance whom he knows slightly and who has done nothing hostile to him, then he is certainly rude. Equally, if a man with a reasonable prospect of saving the lives of others by

sacrificing his own does sacrifice his own life, he is certainly courageous. But in each of these cases, when we show that the necessary
and sufficient conditions apply to justify the epithet, we could rewrite
what we say so that the necessary and sufficient conditions appear as
premises which in virtue of the meaning of *rude* or *courageous* entail the
conclusion "So he was rude" or "So he was courageous." But if any
conclusions are evaluative, these are. Thus some factual premises do
appear to entail evaluative conclusions.

Equally, it is clear that in many cases at least where I call something
or someone good, the appropriate criteria are determined by the kind
of case it is and are not open to choice. The criteria for calling something "a good X" depend, as Geach has pointed out, on the nature of X.
"A good watch," "a good farmer," "a good horse," are cases in point.
But what about "a good man?" Here surely, it might be argued, we do
use a variety of criteria and we have to choose between them. Here
surely, an argument like Hare's is the convincing one. I do not want to
pursue this as yet unfinished argument further; I want rather to inquire
what sort of argument it is, and why it arises.

It is important to see that a whole range of interconnected differences of view are involved here. On the one side, it is held that facts can
never entail evaluations, that philosophical inquiry is neutral between
evaluations, that the only authority which moral views possess is that
which we as individual agents give to them. This view is the final
conceptualization of the individualism which has had recurrent mention in this history: the individual becomes his own final authority in
the most extreme possible sense. On the alternative view, to understand
our central evaluative and moral concepts is to recognize that there are
certain criteria we cannot but acknowledge. The authority of those
standards is one that we have to recognize, but of which we are in no
way the originators. Philosophical inquiry, which reveals this, is therefore not morally neutral. And factual premises do on occasion entail
evaluative conclusions.

Each view systematically insulates itself from the other by its choice
of examples. And neither will allow that the issue between them could
be settled by an empirical inquiry into the way in which evaluative
concepts are actually used. For each is quite prepared to allow that the
ordinary usage in morals may on occasion be confused, or indeed

perverted, through the influence of misleading philosophical theory. Perhaps, however, this controversy is one that cannot be settled, and perhaps the reason why it cannot be settled can be seen if we try to place in historical perspective the concepts which generate it. But before we can do that we must consider certain very unsophisticated points which locate this controversy as one not merely for philosophers, but for all contemporary moral agents.

Emotivism and prescriptivism initially alienate us because their explanations of evaluative language in terms of the notions of feelings, liking, choice, and imperatives leave us asking why there should exist any specifically evaluative language over and above the ordinary language of feelings, liking, choice, and imperatives. When I say, "You ought to do this," or when I say, "This is good," I want to protest that I say more and other than, "You or anyone else—do this!" or, "I like this. Do so as well." For if that is what I mean, that is what I could and would say. If that is what I *do* say, then certainly what I say will have no authority but that which I confer upon it by uttering it. My attitudes and my imperatives have authority for me just because they are mine. But when I invoke words such as *ought* and *good* I at least seek to appeal to a standard which has other and more authority. If I use these words to you, I seek to appeal to you in the name of those standards and not in my own name. Yet even though this may be what I seek to do, it does not necessarily follow that I succeed. Under what conditions might I succeed? Under what conditions must I fail?

Suppose a society of the kind which I tried to characterize when I discussed Greek society, in which the form of life presupposes agreement on ends. Here there are agreed criteria for the use of *good*, not only when we speak of "good horse" and "good farmer" but also when we speak of "good man." In this society there is a recognized list of virtues, and established set of moral rules, an institutionalized connection between obedience to rules, the practice of virtues, and the attainment of ends. In such a society the contrast between evaluative language and the language of liking or of choice will be quite clear. I may tell you what I like or choose, and I may tell you what you ought to do; but the second makes a claim upon you which the first does not. You may disregard what you ought to do through annoyance or negligence; but you cannot use the moral vocabulary and consistently deny the force of *ought*, and you cannot remain within the social commerce of the community, and abandon the moral vocabulary.

Is moral criticism in such a society impossible? By no means; but it must proceed by an extension of, and not by a total break with, the established moral vocabulary. Does this mean that the authority of the morality does not extend beyond the community whose social practices are in question? One is tempted to reply, Does the authority of arithmetical rules extend beyond the community in which the practice of counting is established? This is intended as a genuine, and not as a rhetorical question, which deserves a fuller answer; but at the least, to connect rules and social practice in this way is not obviously to give moral rules less of a hold on us than mathematical, except that no society could advance far without the same type of simple counting, whereas there can be wide variations in the social practice to which moral rules are relevant.

In discussing Greek society, I suggested what might happen when such a well-integrated form of moral life broke down. In our society the acids of individualism have for four centuries eaten into our moral structures, for both good and ill. But not only this: we live with the inheritance of not only one, but of a number of well-integrated moralities. Aristotelianism, primitive Christian simplicity, the puritan ethic, the aristocratic ethic of consumption, and the traditions of democracy and socialism have all left their mark upon our moral vocabulary. Within each of these moralities there is a proposed end or ends, a set of rules, a list of virtues. But the ends, the rules, the virtues, differ. For Aristotelianism, to sell all you have and give to the poor would be absurd and meanspirited; for primitive Christianity, the great-souled man is unlikely to pass through that eye of the needle which is the gateway to heaven. A conservative Catholicism would treat obedience to established authority as a virtue; a democratic socialism such as Marx's labels the same attitude servility and sees it as the worst of vices. For puritanism, thrift is a major virtue, laziness a major vice; for the traditional aristocrat, thrift is a vice; and so on.

It follows that we are liable to find two kinds of people in our society: those who speak from within one of these surviving moralities, and those who stand outside all of them. Between the adherents of rival moralities and between the adherents of one morality and the adherents of none there exists no court of appeal, no impersonal neutral standard. For those who speak from within a given morality, the connection between fact and valuation is established in virtue of the meanings of the words they use. To those who speak from without, those who speak from within appear merely to be uttering imperatives which express their own liking and their private choices. The controversy between emotivism and prescriptivism on the one hand and their critics on the other thus expresses the fundamental moral situation of our own society.

We can in the history of moral philosophy situate certain writers usefully in terms of this account. Kant, for example, stands at the point at which the loss of moral unity means that morality can be specified only in terms of the form of its rules, and not of any end which the rules may serve. Hence his attempt to derive the content of moral rules from their form.

Kant also stands at the point at which moral rules and the goals of human life have become divorced to such a degree that it appears *both* that the connection between abiding by the rules and achieving the goals is merely a contingent one *and* that, if this is so, it is intolerable. It is Kant's grasp of the former point, as well as of the vagueness about goals which had led to the notion of happiness becoming vague and indefinite, that leads him to enjoin us to seek not to be happy, but to be deserving of happiness. It is his grasp of the latter point that leads him to invoke God as a power that will crown virtue with happiness after all. Kant seeks to hold together an earlier and a later view of morals; the tension between them is apparent.

Eighteenth-century English moralists and nineteenth-century utilitarians write from within a society in which individualism has conquered. Hence they present the social order not as a framework within which the individual has to live out his moral life, but as the mere sum of individual wills and interests. A crude moral psychology makes of moral rules instructions as to effective means for gaining the ends of private satisfaction. Hegel, Green, and to a lesser extent, Bradley are not only critics of this view of morals, they try to specify the type of community within which the moral vocabulary can have a specific and distinctive set of uses. But the philosophical analysis of the necessary form of such community is no substitute for the deed of re-creating it;

and their natural successors are the emotivists and the prescriptivists, who give us a false account of what authentic moral discourse was, but a true account of the impoverished meanings which evaluative expressions have come to have in a society where a moral vocabulary is increasingly emptied of content. Marx resembles Hegel and the English idealists in seeing a communal framework as presupposed by morality; unlike them, he sees that it no longer exists; and he proceeds to characterize the whole situation as one in which moralizing can no longer play a genuine role in settling social differences. It can only be an attempt to invoke an authority which no longer exists and to mask the sanctions of social coercion.

All this of course does not entail that the traditional moral vocabulary cannot still be used. It does entail that we cannot expect to find in our society a single set of moral concepts, a shared interpretation of the vocabulary. Conceptual conflict is endemic in our situation, because of the depth of our moral conflicts. Each of us therefore has to choose both with whom we wish to be morally bound and by what ends, rules, and virtues we wish to be guided. These two choices are inextricably linked. In choosing to regard this end or that virtue highly, I make certain moral relationships with some other people, and other moral relationships with others impossible. Speaking from within my own moral vocabulary, I shall find myself bound by the criteria embodied in it. These criteria will be shared with those who speak the same moral language. And I must adopt some moral vocabulary if I am to have any social relationships. For without rules, without the cultivation of virtues, I cannot share ends with anyone else. I am doomed to social solipsism. Yet I must choose for myself with whom I am to be morally bound. I must choose between alternative forms of social and moral practice. Not that I stand morally naked until I have chosen. For our social past determines that each of us has some vocabulary with which to frame and to make his choice. Nor can I look to human nature as a neutral standard, asking which form of social and moral life will give to it the most adequate expression. For each form of life carries with it its own picture of human nature. The choice of a form of life and the choice of a view of human nature go together.

To this view, each side in the contemporary philosophical controversy will reply in its own terms. The emotivists and prescriptivists will stress the role of choice in my account. Their critics with an already existing evaluative vocabulary. Each will try by their choice of examples to redefine their opponent's case away. And the same attempt is already being made in other controversies elsewhere. Indeed, it is a reinforcement for the view that this philosophical controversy is an expression of our social and moral situation that it should have occurred in quite a different context in the arguments that have proceeded in France between Catholic moralists, Stalinists, Marxists, and Sartrian existentialists.

For both Catholics and Stalinists the moral vocabulary is defined in terms of certain alleged facts. Each has their own characteristic list of virtues. For Sartre, by contrast, at least for the Sartre of the immediate postwar period, to live within a readymade moral vocabulary is necessarily an abdication of responsibility, an act of bad faith. Authentic existence is to be found only in a self-conscious awareness of an absolute freedom of choice. Kierkegaard's view of the act of choice is detached from its theological context, and made by Sartre the basis for political as well as for moral decision. Sartre does not locate the source of the necessity of the act of choice in the moral history of our society, any more than Kierkegaard did. He locates it in the nature of man: a conscious being, *être-pour-soi*, differs from a thing, *être-en-soi*, in his freedom and his consciousness of freedom. Hence men's characteristic experiences of anxiety before the gulf of the unmade future, and their characteristic attempts to pretend that they are not responsible. Thus Sartre locates the basis of his moral view in a metaphysics of human nature, just as much as the Catholic or the Marxist does.

Like Sartre, the prescriptivist and emotivist do not trace the source of the necessity of choice, or of taking up one's own attitudes, to the moral history of our society. They ascribe it to the nature of moral concepts as such. And in so doing, like Sartre, they try to absolutize their own individualist morality, and that of the age, by means of an appeal to concepts, just as much as their critics try to absolutize their own moralities by means of an appeal to conceptual considerations. But these attempts could only succeed if moral concepts were indeed timeless and unhistorical, and if there were only one available set of moral concepts. One virtue of the history of moral philosophy is that it shows us that this is not true and that moral concepts themselves have a history. To understand this is to be liberated from any false absolutist claims.

# NOTES

1. "On the Analysis of Moral Judgments," in *Philosophical Essays*, pp. 245–246.
2. *Merit and Responsibility in Greek Ethics*, pp. 32–33.
3. For later discussions, see Chap. XII, pp. 157, and Chap. XVIII, pp. 249.
4. *Odyssey*, Book XXII.
5. *Iliad*, Book I.
6. See H. Frisch, *Might and Right in Antiquity*.
7. Thucydides, *Peloponnesian War*, Book V, 105.
8. Thucydides, *Peloponnesian War*, Book III, 82.
9. Introduction to *Ethics* by P. H. Nowell-Smith.
10. *Theatetus*, 167c.
11. *Metaphysics*, 1078b.
12. For an alternative view, see R. Robinson, *Plato's Earlier Dialectic*, pp. 15–17.
13. *Eudemian Ethics*, 1216b.
14. *Through the Looking-Glass and What Alice Found There*, Chap. VI.
15. *The Open Society*, Vol. I, Chap. 6, p. 78.
16. *Republic*, Book V, 475e–476a.
17. *Nichomachean Ethics*, Book I, 1094a.
18. "An Outline of Intellectual Rubbish," in *Unpopular Essays*.
19. *Nichomachean Ethics*, 1130b; *Politics*, 1277b.
20. "Does Moral Philosophy Rest on a Mistake?", in *Mind* (1912), reprinted in *Moral Obligation*.
21. H. J. Kelsen, *The Philosophy of Aristotle and the Hellenic-Macedonian Policy*, International Journal of Ethics, XLVIII, 1.
22. Diogenes Laërtius, *Lives of the Philosophers*, 7, 89.

23. *History*, VI, 36, 2.
24. *Cur Deus Homo.*
25. The discussion of this theme by J. N. Figgis in *From Gerson to Grotius* is still unsurpassed.
26. *Lives*, p. 150.
27. *The English Works of Thomas Hobbes*, ed. W. Molesworth, VII, 73.
28. *Ibid.*, IV, 53.
29. *Ibid.*, III, 130.
30. *Ibid.*, III, 154.
31. *Ibid.*, III, 158.
32. *Serious Reflections of Robinson Crusoe.* p. 325. This view of Defoe I owe of course to the analysis of Professor Ian Watts in *The Rise of the Novel*, a book whose interest for the student of morality can scarcely be overrated.
33. *Enquiry Concerning the Principles of Morals*, Sec. III, Part II.
34. Putney Debates, in *Puritanism and Liberty: Being the Army Debates (1647–8) from the Clarke Manuscripts*, selected and edited by A. S. P. Woodhouse.
35. *An Arrow Against All Tyrants*, p. 3.
36. *Second Treatise of Civil Government*, Sec. 5.
37. *Ibid.*, Sec. 119.
38. *Characteristics of Men, Manners, Opinions, Times* (1773 edition), II, 415.
39. *An Enquiry into the Original of our Ideas of Beauty and Virtue*, II, 3.
40. *Fifteen Sermons*, 2, 8.
41. *Ibid.*, 2, 14.
42. *Treatise of Human Nature*, II, 3, 3.
43. *Ibid.*, III, 1, 2.
44. *Ibid.*, III, 1, 1.
45. *Ibid.*, III, 1, 2.
46. *Whole Duty of Man*, Sunday, XIII, Sec. 30.
47. *Treatise*, III, 1, 1.
48. *Ibid.*, III, 2, 1.
49. *Enquiry Concerning the Principles of Morals*, V, 2.
50. *De L'Esprit des Lois*, XXIV, 24.
51. *Du Contrat Social*, II, 3.
52. *On the Saying: That may be all right in Theory but it is no good in Practice*, in *Kant*, edited and translated by G. Rabel.
53. *Hegel: A Re-examination*, p. 111.
54. *Discussion of Press Debates*, in *Marx-Engels Gesamtausgabe*, I, 1, i.
55. *History of Philosophy and Religion in Germany*, translated by J. Snodgrass, p. 158.
56. *Ibid.*, pp. 159–160.
57. *The Antichrist*, 39.
58. *The Twilight of the Idols*, 1, 2.
59. "We are afraid to put men to live and trade each on his own stock of reason; because we suspect that this stock in each man is small, and that the individuals would do better to avail themselves of the general bank and capital of

natures and of ages."—*Reflections on the Revolution in France*, Everyman edition, p. 84.

60. *Loc. cit.*
61. *Works*, ed. Bowring, II, 253.
62. See the *Science of Ethics*.
63. *Ethics Since 1900*, pp. 128–129.
64. "Moral Arguments," in *Mind* (1958).
65. "Good and Evil," in *Analysis*, Vol. 17.

# INDEX

# Routledge Classics
## Get inside a great mind

### Writing and Difference
Jacques Derrida

'Almost from the moment deconstruction emerged as a glittering force on the academic scene, its many detractors have been saying that it is "dead". And yet the term deconstruction has penetrated almost every aspect of culture.'
*New York Times*

In the 1960s a radical concept emerged from the great French thinker Jacques Derrida. He called the new process 'deconstruction'. The academic community was rocked on a scale hitherto unknown, with *Writing and Difference* attracting both accolades and derision. Read the book that changed the way we think; read *Writing and Difference*, the classic introduction.

Hb: 0–415–25537–6     Pb: 0–415–25383–7

### Archaeology of Knowledge
Michel Foucault

'Foucault's work is the most noteworthy effort at a theory of history in the last 50 years.'
*Library Journal*

In France, a country that awards its intellectuals the status other countries give their rock stars, Michel Foucault was part of a glittering generation of thinkers, one which also included Sartre, de Beauvoir and Deleuze. One of the great intellectual heroes of the twentieth century, Foucault was a man whose passion and reason were at the service of nearly every progressive cause of his time. Arguably his finest work, *Archaeology of Knowledge* is a challenging but fantastically rewarding introduction to his ideas.

Hb: 0–415–28752–9     Pb: 0–415–28753–7

For these and other classic titles from Routledge, visit
**www.routledgeclassics.com**

# Routledge Classics
## Get inside a great mind

### The Phenomenology of Perception
Maurice Merleau-Ponty

'The work of Merleau-Ponty has never been more timely, or had more to teach us ... Essential reading for anyone who cares about the embodied mind.'
*Andy Clark, author of Being There*

Challenging and rewarding in equal measure, *The Phenomenology of Perception* is Merleau-Ponty's most famous work. Impressive in both scope and imagination, it uses the example of perception to return the *body* to the forefront of philosophy for the first time since Plato. Drawing on case studies such as brain-damaged patients from the First World War, Merleau-Ponty brilliantly shows how the body plays a crucial role not only in perception but in speech, sexuality and our relation to others.

Hb: 0–415–27840–6     Pb: 0–415–27841–4

### Evolution as a Religion
#### Strange hopes and stranger fears
Mary Midgley

'A graceful, refreshing and enlightening book, applied philosophy that is relevant, timely and metaphysical in the best sense.'
*New York Times Book Review*

Considered one of Britain's finest philosophers, Midgley exposes the illogical logic of poor doctrines that shelter themselves behind the prestige of science. In *Evolution as a Religion* she examines how science comes to be used as a substitute for religion and points out how badly that role distorts it. As ever, her argument is flawlessly insightful: a punchy, compelling, lively indictment of these misuses of science. Both the book and its author are true classics of our time.

Hb: 0–415–27832–5     Pb: 0–415–27833–3

For these and other classic titles from Routledge, visit
## www.routledgeclassics.com

# Routledge Classics
Get inside a great mind

### Wickedness
**A philosophical essay**
Mary Midgley

'Mary Midgley is a philosopher with what many have come to admire, and some to fear, as one of the sharpest critical pens in the West.'
*Stephen Rose, author of The Conscious Brain*

In *Wickedness*, Midgley sets out to delineate not so much the nature of wickedness as its actual sources. Midgley's analysis proves that the capacity for real wickedness is an inevitable part of human nature. She provides us with a framework that accepts the existence of evil yet offers humankind the possibility of rejecting this part of our nature. *Wickedness* offers an understanding of human nature that enhances our very humanity.

Hb: 0–415–25551–1     Pb: 0–415–25398–5

### The Sovereignty of Good
Iris Murdoch

'Iris never minded being unfashionable. That's what makes *The Sovereignty of Good* so good – what makes it, still, one of the very few modern books of philosophy which people outside academic philosophy find really helpful.'
*Mary Midgley*

Throughout her distinguished and prolific writing career, Murdoch explored questions of good and bad, myth and morality. The framework for her questions – and her own conclusions – can be found in *The Sovereignty of Good*. The *Boston Review* hailed these essays as 'her most influential pieces of philosophy'.

Hb: 0–415–25552–X     Pb: 0–415–25399–3

For these and other classic titles from Routledge, visit
## www.routledgeclassics.com

# Routledge Classics
## Get inside a great mind

### The Logic of Scientific Discovery
#### Karl Popper

'One of the most important documents of the twentieth century.'
*Peter Medawar, New Scientist*

First published in English in 1959, Karl Popper's *The Logic of Scientific Discovery* revolutionized contemporary thinking about science and knowledge and is one of the most widely read books about science written last century. In presenting his now-legendary doctrine of 'falsification', it electrified the scientific community and it now ranks alongside *The Open Society and its Enemies* as one of Popper's most enduring and famous books and contains insights and arguments that demand to be read to this day.

Hb: 0–415–27843–0     Pb: 0–415–27844–9

### The Poverty of Historicism
#### Karl Popper

'Karl Popper was a philosopher of uncommon originality, clarity and depth, and his range was exceptional.'
*The Times*

On its publication in 1957, *The Poverty of Historicism* was hailed by Arthur Koestler as 'probably the only book published this year which will outlive the century.' A devastating criticism of fixed and predictable laws in history, Popper dedicated the book to all those 'who fell victim to the fascist and communist belief in Inexorable Laws of Historical Destiny.' Short and beautifully written, it has inspired generations of readers, intellectuals and policy makers and stands as a searing insight into the ideas of this great thinker.

Hb: 0–415–27845–7     Pb: 0–415–27846–5

For these and other classic titles from Routledge, visit
## www.routledgeclassics.com

# Routledge Classics
Get inside a great mind

## Sketch for a Theory of the Emotions
Jean-Paul Sartre

'The best source for Sartre's theoretical views on the nature of psychology.'
*Mary Warnock*

Anticipating his great work, *Being and Nothingness*, this book is considered to be one of Jean-Paul Sartre's most important pieces of writing. By arguing that we choose how to utilize our emotions, and identifying their evanescent nature, Sartre places *us* firmly in control. A witty and dazzling journey into one of the most intriguing theories of our time.

Hb: 0–415–26751–X     Pb: 0–415–26752–8

## A Short History of Modern Philosophy
### From Descartes to Wittgenstein
Roger Scruton

'Anyone seeking a short and intelligible introduction to the ideas and intentions of Spinoza, Hume, Kant, Hegel and Marx, among others, need look no further.'
*Good Book Guide*

In this guide, Scruton takes us on a fascinating tour of modern philosophy, from founding father René Descartes to Ludwig Wittgenstein. He clearly summarizes the thought of each major figure and outlines the major preoccupations of Western philosophy. This book paints a vivid, animated and engaging picture of modern philosophy and is already established as the classic introduction. Read it and find out why.

Hb: 0–415–26762–5     Pb: 0–415–26763–3

For these and other classic titles from Routledge, visit
### www.routledgeclassics.com

# Routledge Classics
## Get inside a great mind

### Tractatus Logico-Philosophicus
Ludwig Wittgenstein

'The *Tractatus* is one of the fundamental texts of twentieth-century philosophy – short, bold, cryptic, and remarkable in its power to stir the imagination of philosophers and non-philosophers alike.'
*Michael Frayn*

Perhaps the most important work of philosophy written in the twentieth century, *Tractatus Logico-Philosophicus* was the only philosophical work that Ludwig Wittgenstein published in his lifetime. He famously summarized the book in the following words: 'What can be said at all can be said clearly; and what we cannot talk about we must pass over in silence.'

Hb: 0–415–25562–7     Pb: 0–415–25408–6

### Relativity
#### The special and the general theory
Albert Einstein

'He was unfathomably profound – the genius among geniuses who discovered, merely by thinking about it, that the universe was not as it seemed.'
*Time*

*Time*'s 'Man of the Century', Albert Einstein is the unquestioned founder of modern physics. His theory of relativity is the most important scientific idea of the modern era. In this short book Einstein explains, using the minimum of mathematical terms, the basic ideas and principles of the theory which has shaped the world we live in today. This remains the most popular and useful exposition of Einstein's immense contribution to human knowledge.

Hb: 0–415–25538–4     Pb: 0–415–25384–5

For these and other classic titles from Routledge, visit
## www.routledgeclassics.com